BAHAMAS
GUIDE

YOUR PASSPORT TO GREAT TRAVEL!

CRITICAL ACCLAIM FOR
OPEN ROAD TRAVEL GUIDES!

*Whether you're going abroad or planning a trip in the United States, take Open Road along on your journey. Our books have been praised by **Travel & Leisure, The Los Angeles Times, Newsday, Booklist, US News & World Report, Endless Vacation, American Bookseller, Coast to Coast**, and many other magazines and newspapers!*

Don't just see the world – experience it with Open Road!

ABOUT THE AUTHOR

Ron Charles is the author of five Open Road publications: Bahamas Guide, Bermuda Guide, Holland Guide, Portugal Guide and Spain Guide. He has been a specialty tour operator, a freelance writer, and a photographer. Originally from New York, Ron now lives in Montreal, Canada.

HIT THE OPEN ROAD – WITH OPEN ROAD PUBLISHING!

Open Road Publishing now has guide books to exciting, fun destinations on four continents. As veteran travelers, our goal is to bring you the best travel guides available anywhere!

No small task, but here's what we offer:

• All Open Road travel guides are written by authors with a distinct, opinionated point of view – not some sterile committee or team of writers. Our authors are experts in the areas covered and are polished writers.

• Our guides are geared to people who want great vacations, great value, and great tips for both standard tourist sights *and* fun, unique alternatives.

• We're strong on the basics, but we also provide terrific choices for those looking to get off the beaten path and *experience* the country or city – not just *see* it or pass through it.

• We give you the best, but we also tell you about the worst and what to avoid. Nobody should waste their time and money on their hard-earned vacation because of bad or inadequate travel advice.

• Our guides assume nothing. We tell you everything you need to know to have the trip of a lifetime – presented in a fun, literate, no-nonsense style.

• And, above all, we welcome your input, ideas, and suggestions to help us put out the best travel guides possible.

BAHAMAS GUIDE

YOUR PASSPORT TO GREAT TRAVEL!

RON CHARLES

OPEN ROAD PUBLISHING

OPEN ROAD PUBLISHING

We offer travel guides to American and foreign locales. Our books tell it like it is, often with an opinionated edge, and our experienced authors always give you all the information you need to have the trip of a lifetime. Write for your free catalog of all our titles, including our golf and restaurant guides.

Catalog Department, Open Road Publishing
P.O. Box 20226, Columbus Circle Station, New York, NY 10023

Or you contact us by e-mail at:
Jopenroad@aol.com

This book is respectfully dedicated to Helen Fillmore, Ona Bullard, Pam Armbrister, Sam Gray, Hilton Johnson, Danielle Knowles, and all the hundreds of Bahamians that went well out of their way to help me find the heart & soul of their beautiful nation.

Front cover photo and back cover photo of woman on beach courtesy of EarthWater, Virginia Beach, Virginia. Back cover photo of little boy and dog courtesy of Bahamas Tourist Board, New York. Inside photos by Ron Charles. Maps by Rob Perry.

The author has made every effort to be as accurate as possible, but neither the author nor the publisher assume responsibility for the services provided by any business listed in this guide; for any errors or omissions; or any loss, damage, or disruptions in your travels for any reason.

TABLE OF CONTENTS

Contents

Contents

Contents

Contents

Contents

MAPS

SIDEBARS

1. INTRODUCTION

The Bahamas offers some of the most spectacular resorts, beaches, reef diving, snorkeling, and serious relaxing anywhere in the world! There are more than 750 islands and cays in The Bahamas, but since the vast majority of these land masses are uninhabited, there are just a few dozen that offer a combination of historic villages, crescent-shaped sandy beaches, traditional fishing towns, former slave hamlets, and unique seaside resorts that are well worth the effort to explore. Each island described in this publication unveils yet another mysterious and enchanting sight.

It's relatively easy to cover many parts of the country in comfort by plane, boat, and in some cases rental car. In these islands it is entirely possible to spend your hard-earned dollars staying in a combination of stunning full service seaside resort hotels, romantic bed and breakfast inns, and charming villa colonies for less money than you might imagine.

This book has been designed to give you all of the information necessary to create your own itinerary. You will find many recommendations included in each chapter to point you in the right direction. In the space of just one or two weeks, depending on your specific interests, you can sunbathe and swim on some of world's best beaches, walk around beautifully planted sub-tropical gardens, take day trips to old Loyalist-era villages filled with antique colonial mansions, ride horses along the coast, scuba dive and snorkel in reefs inhabited by countless species of colorful marine life, and play golf on exceptional championship courses.

Or you can sail to deserted islands for romantic picnic lunches, stroll through historic city neighborhoods, compete in amateur tennis tournaments, take every type of excursion imaginable, shop in fine designer boutiques and duty free shops, challenge your luck in one of four world-class casinos, wine and dine in enchanting gourmet restaurants, and party all night with the friendly locals. Whatever kind of vacation you have in mind, you can do it all in The Bahamas!

2. EXCITING BAHAMAS! - OVERVIEW

The following are brief descriptions of the major islands that are covered in-depth in this book. Each destination chapter in this guide contains comprehensive walking tours, beach and water sports facilities, restaurant and hotel reviews, nightlife listings, excursion possibilities, and other specific details to ensure that you have the trip of a lifetime!

NEW PROVIDENCE

This densely populated island is home to The Bahamas' capital of **Nassau**, the nation's largest city. Surrounded by a series of picturesque beaches lined by resort hotels, the island has plenty of interesting museums, countless monumental buildings, awesome churches, peaceful gardens, public squares, world-class designer and duty free boutiques, a world-famous straw market, dozens of ethnic restaurants, two major casinos, and a thriving nightlife scene that lasts until sunrise. New Providence's heavily developed beach-side tourist zones, such as **Cable Beach** and nearby **Paradise Island**, have over 8,000 hotel rooms that continue to attract more vacationers than any other destination in The Bahamas. It is fairly easy to visit a vast amount of the island in a limited time, since there is a vast network of inexpensive jitney busses, ferries, and taxis that frequently service all major points of interest.

While in Nassau, make sure to stop off at **Rawson Square** and its Ministry of Tourism information kiosk, **Parliament Square** where many of the most important 18th and 19th-century Government Buildings are found, the limestone **Queen's Staircase** carved by slaves over 160 years ago, the **Nassau Public Library & Museum** that formerly served as the city jail, the bustling **Bay Street** shopping district known for duty free shopping and a massive indoor **Straw Market**, the **Bahamas Historical Society Museum**, the superb **Graycliff** and **Buena Vista** restaurants, the unusually shaped **Fort Fincastle** and sea-front **Fort Montagu**, the nearby

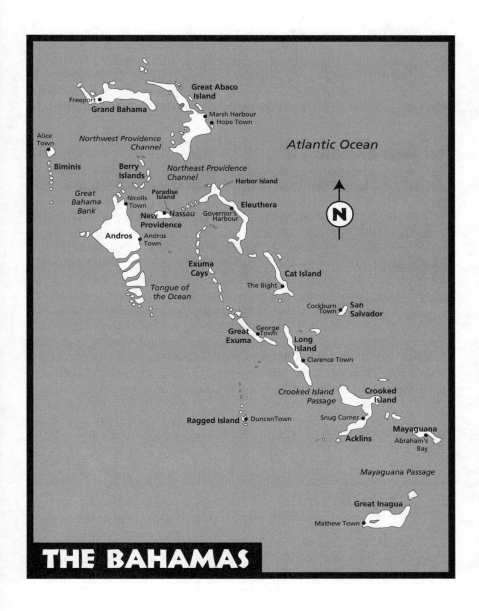

THE BAHAMAS

18 acre **Nassau Botanical Gardens**, the **Ardastra Gardens** zoo where marching pink flamingos perform several times each day, and the sandy shores of world-famous **Cable Beach**, where there are many fine hotels including the incomparable **Sandals Royal Bahamian** resort and spa.

Other great diversions await you over towards Paradise Island, where you should make it a point to pop inside the awesome **Atlantis** resort and casino with its imaginative **Waterscape** (the world's largest open air aquarium), the 14th-century Augustinian **Cloisters**, and beautiful long sandy coastal areas such as **Pirate Beach** and **Cabbage Beach** that line much of this exclusive area.

GRAND BAHAMA

Now in the process of rebuilding after the economic devastation of its tourism establishments during the American recession, Grand Bahama Island is the second most popular vacation destination in the country. A huge chunk of the island, including the large city of **Freeport** and beach-side resort development of **Lucaya**, is privately owned and operated as a tax exempt port and tourism sector by the powerful Port Authority. While easy transportation between these two main districts is available via inexpensive jitney busses and taxis, most tourists find relatively little of historic or cultural interest on Grand Bahama.

Most of what is known as "downtown" Freeport looks like a Florida boulevard with shops housed in low rise malls on both sides of the road. The most famous attractions here are a small outdoor **Fruit & Vegetable Market**, the **International Bazaar** shopping center, the rather successful **Bahamas Princes Hotels and Casino** complex, the massive **Harbour** filled with government buildings surrounding a variety of cruise ships, and nearby **Xanadu Beach**.

The Lucaya area is known for the **Port Lucaya Marketplace** shopping center & marina with its **Count Basie Square** restaurant and nightlife venues, the **Unexso** dolphin encounter facility, a nice **Straw Market**, a good beach area, plenty of hotels and timeshare apartments, several golf courses, a less than impressive casino, and the nearby 12 acre **Garden of the Groves** botanical gardens.

Those a bit more adventurous may wish to rent a car or go on a jeep safari to reach the east end of Grand Bahama where you can explore much nicer beaches at **Lucayan National Park**, a variety of wildlife over at the **Rand Memorial Nature Centre**, or even take a motorboat ride to **Sweeting's Cay**. Over on the west end of Grand Bahama, there are plenty of small former rum-running villages still laced with local charm.

ABACO

Known primarily as a premier deep sea fishing resort, the Abaco islands are a delightful place for those interested in any water-based sporting activity. While the largest city here is **Marsh Harbour**, for me it's the small islands of **Green Turtle Cay** and **Hope Town** that make Abaco so special. Among the many facilities for sea and sun on Great Abaco are the fantastic **Great Abaco Beach Resort & Marina**, where sport fishing tournaments and charter boats provide year round excitement, as well as many nice local restaurants and bars where locals and tourists can be found puffing on fine Cuban cigars.

Over on the historic Loyalist-era settlement of Hope Town, there are plenty of antique Virginian-inspired colonial mansions and a growing colony of artisans, while on pristine Green Turtle Cay there is the charming village called **New Plymouth** filled with extremely friendly natives and two fantastic little resort hotels (with private marinas), called the **Bluff House** and the **Green Turtle Club**.

ELEUTHERA & HARBOUR ISLAND

First settled in the 17th-century by Puritans exiled from Bermuda, the beautiful island of Eleuthera is an amazingly peaceful 110 mile-long narrow land mass with dozens of secluded beaches. Known for superb bonefishing, great little restaurants, and plantations that grow the best pineapples on earth, Eleuthera has finally begun to recover from the destruction caused by Hurricane Andrew a handful of years ago. Among my favorite spots here are the Old World villages of **Gregory Town**, **Rock Sound**, and **The Current**, the bustling little port city of **Governor's Harbour**, and small affordable seaside inns. Also worthy of attention is the hilltop castle (home to the bizarre **Macmillan-Hughes Art Gallery**) and the **Rock Sound Ocean Hole**. While a couple of huge all-inclusive resorts have sprung up on the central part of the island, I would strongly advise you to rent a car to explore the area, and stay at one of the smaller and more intimate establishments here such as **The Cove Eleuthera** or the **Rainbow Inn**.

Just offshore from Eleuthera is a superb little getaway called **Harbour Island** that has been attracting more affluent vacationers from England and North America for several decades. Thousands of people come here year after year to experience the world-renowned **Pink Sand Beach**, which is the best in all of The Bahamas, and stay in expensive luxury hotels such as the wonderful **Pink Sands** and **Runaway Hill**. The village has dozens of very photogenic pastel colored Cape Cod style colonial homes. Golf carts can be rented for those who wish to hit the off-the-beaten-path locations on the outer edges of the island.

CAT ISLAND

If getting away from it all is the reason you have picked The Bahamas, Cat Island is the best place to head. This long thin island (now thought to be the sight of Christopher Columbus's first landfall in the New World) in the heart of the Bahama Islands is among the most relaxing and tranquil places in the universe! While there are no casinos, duty free shops, or major resorts on the island, what you'll find here are some of the friendliest locals you will ever meet, incredible deserted cove beaches, serious fishing and scuba diving spots, and several small inns and restaurants that will make you feel like staying forever.

The highlights here include a dozen or so settlements populated by the descendants of former slaves including **Port Howe**, **Old & New Bight**, **Athur's Town**, and **Orange Creek**. Make sure to check out the charming open air night clubs and bars where locals can be found playing dominos or billiards between cold beers, the stunning **Mt. Alvernia Hermitage** built by a hermit priest atop the highest peak in the country, and a few **Straw Markets**. Although there is a weird (and rather hostile) nudist colony here, I suggest that you instead choose to stay over at the fabulous **Fernandez Bay Village** or **Hawks Nest** resorts.

THE EXUMAS

The Exumas are a chain of some 365 or so islands and cays that stretch for over 92 miles in the south-central section of The Bahamas. Known as a quiet shipbuilding and fishing center, this is a fantastic place to boat or drive around in search of some of The Bahamas' most dramatic beaches and best bonefishing. The largest two islands here are **Great Exuma Island** and **Little Exuma Island**. While the main city of the Exumas is **George Town**, other important villages (mainly founded by freed slaves) include **Williams Town** and **Rolletown**.

The most spectacular sights and attractions around these towns are **Beacon Hill**, the large crescent shaped **Palm Bay Beach**, a truly remarkable stretch of sand and turquoise water called **Tropic of Cancer Beach**, the **St. Christopher's Anglican Church** (the nation's smallest house of worship), a white cottage that is home to Gloria Patience (a.k.a. **The Shark Lady**), a powder blue 19th-century **Anglican Church**, a small daily open air **Straw Market**, a private getaway for European royalty called **Goat Cay,** and the offshore **Stocking Island**. Those looking to spend a few nights here in complete comfort can choose between the expensive **Peace & Plenty Beach**, the quaint sea-front **Coconut Cove Hotel**, and more affordable selections such as the **La Shanté Beach Guest House**, **Mount Pleasant Suites**, and the rustic **Two Turtles Inn**.

ANDROS

Thinly populated by just over eight thousand permanent residents that mostly live in the northern communities of **Andros Town** and **Nicholl's Town**, and the southern hamlet of **Congo Town**, as well as by several hundred U.S. Naval forces, this is the place to visit for serious scuba diving and bonefishing adventures. The main attraction of these islands is the amazing 120 mile-long **Andros Reef**, which is the third largest barrier reef in the world and has an average depth of 13 feet. The reef is just off the islands' eastern coast and is a fantastic place to scuba dive through caves, shipwrecks, blue holes, coral gardens full of marine life, and a sharp drop off on its edge called the Tongue of the Ocean that descends for well over 1,000 feet. It is this same beach-lined eastern coast that attracts most visitors to Andros, and has been the sight of a few interesting small-scale hotel and resort developments. The only community that beckons day trips by foot and bicycle is **Andros Town**.

BIMINI

Bimini is considered the sport fishing capital of The Bahamas and has just one main town. Located on the south tip of North Bimini, **Alice Town** was the home of American writer Ernest Hemingway in the 1930's. Alice Town is still bordered by a beach and small main road called **King's Highway** on its western side, and the bustling harbor-side **Queen's Highway** on its eastern flank, where almost all the hotels, marinas, fishing charter operations, restaurants, shops, and docks are located.

Sights in town include the **Compleat Angler Hotel & Bar**, where several hundred pieces of Ernest Hemingway memorabilia are displayed, a small **Straw Market**, and the **Fisherman's Hall of Fame**. Pretty much everything else here is geared to providing services to the fishing vessels and their passengers, so there are plenty of action-packed night spots and good restaurants around. The town is most busy during the March through May tournament season, when rooms and marina slips must be reserved as much as a year in advance!

3. SUGGESTED ITINERARIES

For The Perfect Bahamas Vacation!

A QUICK WEEKEND AROUND NASSAU

(3 days/2 nights)

This tour is designed especially for those who have limited time in The Bahamas (perhaps those on cruise ships or weekend packages) and wish to focus on the area in and around Nassau.

DAY 1

Arrive in Nassau.

Take a 1 1/2 hour guided walking tour of Nassau from the Ministry of Tourism offices on Rawson Square.

Have lunch.

Take jitney bus #10 or #38 to Cable Beach for an afternoon swim.

Enjoy a Bahamian dinner.

Party with the locals at one of several night clubs.

Return to your hotel or cruise ship.

Overnight in **Nassau**.

DAY 2

Take a taxi over the bridge to Paradise Island.

Visit the 14th-century Cloisters.

Visit Cabbage Beach for a great swim and sun tanning session.

Enjoy a fresh seafood lunch.

Visit the Waterscape park and casino at the Atlantis resort.

Enjoy an exotic dinner.

Return to your hotel or cruise ship.

Overnight in **Nassau**.

DAY 3

Last minute duty free shopping.

Depart The Bahamas via cruise ship or airplane for home.

A QUICK WEEKEND ON GRAND BAHAMA

(3 days/2 nights)

This tour is designed especially for those who have limited time in The Bahamas (perhaps those on cruise ships or weekend packages) and wish to focus on the areas around Freeport and Lucaya.

DAY 1

Arrive in Freeport.
Take a jitney bus or taxi to the Port Lucaya Marketplace.
Visit the Count Basie Square dining and entertainment venues.
Have a quick dip in the sea at nearby Lucaya Beach.
Have a simple al fresco lunch.
Book a late afternoon Dolphin Encounter at Unexso.
Enjoy a Bahamian dinner.
Party with the locals at one of several night clubs.
Return to your hotel or cruise ship.
Overnight in **Freeport** or **Lucaya**.

DAY 2

Take a jitney bus or taxi to the International Bazaar and shop till you drop.
Visit the adjacent Bahamas Princess Casino.
Enjoy a fresh seafood lunch.
Take a taxi to either Xanadu or Tiano Beach for a nice late swim.
Enjoy an exotic dinner.
Return to your hotel or cruise ship.
Overnight in **Freeport** or **Lucaya**.

DAY 3

Visit any number of duty free shops.
Return to your hotel or cruise ship.
Depart The Bahamas via cruise ship or airplane for home.

THE LAID-BACK - YET DELUXE -
ALL-INCLUSIVE VACATION ON NEW PROVIDENCE

(7 days/6 nights)

This is the way to go for those who want to stay in one full service all-inclusive hotel and decide each morning whether to enjoy one of many activities or just relax all day.

This is a great way to spend a week of well-deserved vacation at one of the better full service seaside luxury resorts, such as Sandals Royal Bahamian or Breezes Bahamas.

EACH DAY
Have a wonderful buffet breakfast.
Relax by the pool and the beach most of the day and get a great tan.
Partake in one of many water or land-based activities and adventures, such
as scuba, snorkeling, water skiing, bicycle tours, golf, tennis, or
volleyball.
Enjoy late afternoon top shelf frozen drinks like mud slides and piña
coladas.
Have a fine gourmet dinner at your resort.
Socialize with several like-minded guests at a piano bar or dance the night
away.
Overnight on **Cable Beach**.

THE BASIC TOUR OF THE BAHAMAS

(7 days/6 nights)
This is a good choice for those who want to see Nassau, and would like
to also visit a nearby major island.

DAY 1
Arrive in Nassau.
Check into your hotel.
Have lunch.
Take a walk, taxi ride, or jitney bus to Cable Beach for a good swim.
Enjoy a simple international dinner.
Return to your hotel.
Overnight in **Nassau** or **Cable Beach**.

DAY 2
Take a taxi or jitney bus to Downtown Nassau's Bay Street.
Hit the Straw Market and duty free shops.
Have a simple light lunch.
Take a 1 1/2 hour guided walking tour of Nassau from the Ministry of
Tourism offices on Rawson Square.
Return to your hotel to change clothes.
Enjoy an superb gourmet meal at either Graycliff or Buena Vista.
Visit some of Nassau's great bars and clubs.
Take a taxi back to your hotel.
Overnight in **Nassau** or **Cable Beach**.

DAY 3
Check out of your hotel.
Take a taxi to the airport.

Board a 40 minute flight to nearby North Eleuthera Island.
Take a taxi from North Eleuthera Airport to nearby Three Islands Dock.
Take a 15 minute ferry ride to Harbour Island.
Take a taxi from Government Dock on Harbour Island to your hotel.
Check into your hotel.
Walk over to Pink Sands for a great exotic lunch.
Take a short walk to the Pink Sands Beach for a long swim.
Walk over to any restaurant in Dumore Town for a casual dinner.
Return to your hotel.
Overnight on **Harbour Island**.

DAY 4
Take a walk into Dunmore Town.
Rent a golf cart to explore the island's sights.
Enjoy a simple lunch at Ma-Ruby's restaurant.
Ride over to Pink Sand Beach for a relaxing swim.
Enjoy a casual dinner at a waterside restaurant.
Party at one of several local bars and clubs.
Return to your hotel.
Overnight on **Harbour Island**.

DAY 5
Return your golf cart.
Check out of your hotel.
Take a taxi back to Government Dock.
Take a ferry back to Three Islands Dock.
Take a taxi to the North Eleuthera airport.
Board a 40 minute flight back to Nassau's or Paradise Island's airport.
Take a taxi over to your hotel on Paradise Island.
Check into your hotel.
Have a nice big seafood lunch.
Walk or take a taxi to Pirate's Beach.
Relax for the rest of the day on Paradise Island.
Enjoy a good dinner in a local restaurant.
Overnight on **Paradise Island**.

DAY 6
Follow the Paradise Island walking tours as listed in this book.
Have lunch.
Visit the Atlantis Casino.
Have a gourmet dinner over at the Courtyard Terrace or Villa D'Este.
Walk back to your hotel.
Overnight on **Paradise Island**.

DAY 7
Last minute duty free and gift shopping.
Check out of your hotel.
Take a taxi back to Nassau airport.
Depart The Bahamas for home.

THE ACTION-PACKED VACATION ON NEW PROVIDENCE
(7 days/6 nights)
For those getting a good deal on a 7 night package in a good hotel on New Providence, this sample trip will help you plan activities while keeping costs down.

DAY 1
Arrive in Nassau.
Check into your hotel.
Have lunch.
Walk or take a jitney bus to Cable Beach for a good swim all afternoon.
Enjoy a casual homemade Italian dinner at the Capriccio Ristorante.
Return to your hotel.
Overnight in **Nassau**, **Cable Beach**, or **Paradise Island**.

DAY 2
Take a taxi or jitney bus to Downtown Nassau's Bay Street.
Hit the Straw Market and duty free shops.
Have a simple light lunch at the Caripelago Café.
Take an inexpensive 1 1/2 hour guided walking tour of Nassau with
    optional museum visits from the Ministry of Tourism offices on
    Rawson Square.
Take a jitney bus over to the Cable Beach area.
Enjoy a good hearty dinner at the Rock & Roll Café.
Visit some of Nassau's bars and clubs like the Zoo or the Silk Cotton Jazz
    Club.
Take a taxi back to your hotel.
Overnight in **Nassau**, **Cable Beach**, or **Paradise Island**.

DAY 3
Pack a simple picnic lunch with provisions from an area deli or market.
Take a jitney bus to Prince George's Dock in Nassau.
Take an 8 minute water taxi ride to the far side of the Paradise Island
    Bridge.
Visit the 14th-century Cloisters.
Visit Cabbage Beach for a great swim and sun tanning session.

Enjoy a fresh seafood lunch.
Visit the Waterscape park and casino at the Atlantis resort.
Have a good inexpensive dinner.
Return to your hotel.
Overnight in **Nassau**, **Cable Beach**, or **Paradise Island**.

DAY 4
Take a jitney bus to Chippingham Road.
Walk a few minutes to reach the Botanical Gardens.
Walk 5 more minutes to reach the Ardastra Gardens & Zoo.
Take a jitney bus to Downtown Nassau.
Enjoy a healthy fast food meal at Subway.
Finish your duty free shopping and window browsing.
Enjoy dinner at Conch Fritters.
Take a jitney bus to Fort Montagu.
Explore the Fort and its adjacent park.
Walk to the Waterloo Club for a fun evening of drinking and dancing.
Take a taxi back to your hotel.
Overnight in **Nassau**, **Cable Beach**, or **Paradise Island**.

DAY 5
Take an excursion that offers free hotel pick up and drop off service. Take either Hartley's Undersea Walk, Powerboat Adventure, a Swim with the Dolphins, an Atlantis Submarine ride, or a scuba/snorkeling trip.
Return to your hotel.
Walk to a nearby restaurant for dinner.
Overnight in **Nassau**, **Cable Beach**, or **Paradise Island**.

DAY 6
Pack a simple picnic lunch with provisions from an area deli or market.
Take a jitney bus to the beach of your choice for a full day in the sun.
Enjoy a fine beachfront picnic lunch.
Return to your hotel and change clothes.
Walk to a nearby restaurant for dinner.
Take a taxi to Club Enigma for a fun night out.
Take a taxi back to your hotel.
Overnight in **Nassau**, **Cable Beach**, or **Paradise Island**.

DAY 7
Last minute shopping and sun tanning.
Check out of your hotel.
Take a taxi to Nassau's or Paradise Island's airport.
Depart for home.

THE MULTIPLE ISLAND TOUR OF THE BAHAMAS
(12 days/11 nights)

This sample trip has been created for people who want to visit a few different unforgettable islands in a fairly short amount of time.

DAY 1
Arrive in Nassau.
Check into your hotel.
Have lunch.
Take a walk, taxi ride, or jitney bus to Cable Beach for a good swim.
Enjoy a simple international dinner at Dicky Moe's.
Return to your hotel.
Overnight in **Nassau**, **Cable Beach**, or **Paradise Island**.

DAY 2
Take a taxi or jitney bus to Downtown Nassau's Bay Street.
Hit the Straw Market and duty free shops.
Have a simple light lunch.
Take a 1 1/2 hour guided walking tour of Nassau from the Ministry of
   Tourism offices on Rawson Square.
Return to your hotel to change clothes.
Enjoy a superb gourmet meal at either Graycliff or Buena Vista.
Visit some of Nassau's great bars and clubs.
Take a taxi back to your hotel.
Overnight in **Nassau**, **Cable Beach**, or **Paradise Island**.

DAY 3
Check out of your hotel.
Take a taxi to the airport.
Board a 40 minute flight to nearby North Eleuthera Island.
Take a taxi from North Eleuthera Airport to nearby Three Islands Dock.
Take a 15 minute ferry ride to Harbour Island.
Take a taxi from Government Dock on Harbour Island to your hotel.
Check into your hotel.
Walk over to Pink Sands for a great exotic lunch.
Take a short walk to the Pink Sands Beach for a long swim.
Walk over to The Landing for a casual dinner.
Return to your hotel.
Overnight on **Harbour Island**.

DAY 4
Take a walk into Dunmore Town.
Rent a golf cart to explore the island's sights.

Enjoy a simple lunch at Ma-Ruby's restaurant.
Ride over to Pink Sand Beach for a relaxing swim.
Enjoy a fine gourmet meal at the seaside patio of Runaway Hill.
Party at one of several local bars and clubs.
Return to your hotel.
Overnight on **Harbour Island**.

DAY 5

Return your golf cart.
Check out of your hotel.
Take a taxi back to Government Dock.
Take a ferry back to Three Islands Dock.
Rent a car (call in advance) or arrange for free airport pick-up at North
    Eleuthera.
Check into your hotel.
Spend the day exploring Eleuthera's fine secluded beaches.
Enjoy a simple casual dinner at either The Cove Eleuthera or Elvina's.
Return to your hotel.
Overnight on **Eleuthera**.

DAY 6

Follow Eleuthera tour as listed in this book.
Stop off for lunch in Rock Sound at either Sammy's or the Harbourside
    Lounge.
Continue your car tour of the island.
Have a great casual fish dinner at Rainbow Inn.
Return to your hotel.
Overnight in **Eleuthera**.

DAY 7

Check out of your hotel.
Drive back to the most convenient airport.
Return your rental car at the pre-arranged time.
Take a 40 minute flight back to Nassau.
Take a 35 minute connecting flight (if possible) to Treasure Cay airport
    on Abaco.
Take a 5 minute taxi ride to the nearby Treasure Cay ferry dock.
Take a 15 minute water taxi to Green Turtle Cay ferry landing.
Either take a taxi or the same water taxi to your hotel.
Check into your hotel.
Spend the rest of the day fishing, swimming, sailing, or relaxing in a
    hammock.
Take a taxi or boat transfer to Bluff House for a delicious dinner.

Return to your hotel
Overnight on **Green Turtle Cay**.

DAY 8
Take a boat transfer or hike over to New Plymouth village.
Follow the New Plymouth walking tour as listed in this book.
Enjoy lunch at the Wrecking Tree.
Take a taxi or hike to Ocean Beach.
Return to your hotel to change clothes.
Enjoy a peaceful semi-formal dinner at the Green Turtle Club.
Take a taxi or boat transfer into New Plymouth.
Party all night at the Roosters Rest Club or Burt's Sea Garden Club.
Return to your hotel.
Overnight on **Green Turtle Cay**.

DAY 9
Take an excursion that offers free hotel pick up and drop-off service. I
    suggest either a deserted island tour with fresh seafood barbecue, a
    fishing adventure, a self chartered sailboat or whaler ride, or a scuba/
    snorkeling trip.
Enjoy a dinner at the restaurant of your choice.
Return to your hotel
Overnight on **Green Turtle Cay**.

DAY 10
Check out of your hotel.
Either take a taxi or water taxi to the Green Turtle Cay Dock.
Take the same water taxi across the way to Treasure Cay ferry dock.
Take a 5 minute taxi ride to Treasure Cay airport.
Take a 35 minute flight to Nassau's or Paradise Island's airport.
Take a taxi to your hotel on Paradise Island.
Enjoy a fine dinner at the Courtyard Terrace.
Hit the Atlantis Casino.
Return to your hotel.
Overnight on **Paradise Island**.

DAY 11
Follow the Paradise Island walking tours as listed in this book.
Have lunch.
Walk over to Cabbage Beach for a good swim and sun tan session.
Return to your hotel to change clothes.
Have a gourmet dinner over at the Bahamian Club or Villa D'Este.
Overnight on **Paradise Island**.

DAY 12
Last minute shopping.
Take a taxi back to Nassau's or Paradise Island's airport.
Depart The Bahamas for home.

THE HIGHLIGHTS OF THE OUT ISLANDS TOUR
(13 days/12 nights)

    If you are looking to find the prettiest islands in the country that have not become heavily developed, this is for you. Regularly scheduled flights are sometimes difficult to arrange for this tour, so check with each selected hotel for possible time-saving charter flight alternatives.

DAY 1
Arrive in Exuma.
Take a taxi to George Town.
Check into your hotel.
Enjoy a great lunch at Sam's Place.
Take an afternoon ferry ride to Stocking Island's fine beach.
Walk or take a taxi to George Town.
Have dinner at Eddie's Edgewater restaurant.
Return to your hotel.
Overnight in **Exuma**.

DAY 2
Rent a car from Sam Gray's enterprises or 2 Turtles Inn.
Follow the Exuma tour as listed in this book.
Make sure to stop off at the Shark Lady's cottage.
Take a nice ride over to the Tropic of Cancer beach.
Have lunch at the La Shanté restaurant.
Continue following the Exuma tour by car.
Enjoy dinner at the Fisherman's Inn.
Drive back to George Town.
Have drinks at the 2 Turtles Inn outdoor bar.
Return to your hotel.
Overnight in **Exuma**.

DAY 3
Check out of your hotel.
Take a 25 minute charter flight to Cat Island.
Check into your hotel.
Relax all day at the beach.
Enjoy a fine lunch at your hotel.

Go swimming, sailing, snorkeling, fishing, or scuba diving in the afternoon.

Enjoy a fine dinner at your hotel.

Overnight on **Cat Island**.

DAY 4

Rent a car.

Follow the Cat Island Tour as listed in this book.

Have a wonderful fresh conch lunch over at Bachelor's Rest restaurant.

Make sure to hike up to the Hermitage.

Have a fantastic beachfront dinner at Fernandez Bay Village.

Hang out at the Sailing Club or Lover's Boulevard for evening drinks and dancing.

Return to your hotel.

Overnight on **Cat Island**.

DAY 5

Check out of your hotel.

Return your rental car at the pre-arranged time.

Take a 25 minute charter flight to Eleuthera.

Rent a car (call in advance) or arrange for free airport pick-up at North Eleuthera.

Check into your hotel.

Spend the day driving exploring Eleuthera's fine secluded beaches.

Enjoy a fun-filled dinner at Mate & Jenny's Pizza Shack.

Return to your hotel.

Overnight on **Eleuthera**.

DAY 6

Follow Eleuthera tour as listed in this book.

Stop off for lunch in Rock Sound at either Sammy's or the Harbourside Lounge.

Continue your car tour of the island.

Have a great casual fish dinner at Rainbow Inn.

Return to your hotel.

Overnight in **Eleuthera**.

DAY 7

Check out of your hotel.

Take a taxi to the Three Islands Dock.

Take a 15 minute ferry ride to Harbour Island.

Take a taxi from Government Dock on Harbour Island to your hotel.

Check into your hotel.

Walk over to the Harbour Lounge for lunch.
Take a short walk to the Pink Sands Beach for a long swim.
Walk over to The Landing for a casual dinner.
Return to your hotel.
Overnight on **Harbour Island**.

DAY 8
Take a walk into Dunmore Town.
Rent a golf cart to explore the island's sights.
Enjoy lunch at the Dunmore Deli restaurant.
Ride over to Pink Sand Beach for a relaxing swim.
Enjoy a fine gourmet meal at Pink Sands.
Party at one of several local bars and clubs.
Return to your hotel.
Overnight on **Harbour Island**.

DAY 9
Check out of your hotel.
Take a taxi back to Government Dock.
Take a ferry back to Three Islands Dock.
Take a taxi to North Eleuthera airport.
Take a 25 minute charter flight to Marsh Harbour airport.
Take a taxi to your hotel.
Take a taxi to the Great Abaco Resort's nice beach for a day in the sun.
Enjoy a fine lunch at the Sand Bar.
Walk over to Sapodilly's restaurant for a nice casual dinner.
Return to your hotel.
Overnight on **Abaco**.

DAY 10
Take a 5 minute taxi ride to the Marsh Harbour ferry dock.
Take a 15 minute water taxi to Elbow Cay.
Follow the Elbow Cay (Hope Town) tour as listed in this book.
Enjoy an al fresco lunch at the Harbour's Edge restaurant.
Walk to the Hope Town ferry dock.
Take a 15 minute water taxi ride back to Marsh Harbour.
Return to your hotel and change clothes.
Enjoy a lavish dinner at Mangoes.
Return to your hotel.
Overnight on **Abaco**.

DAY 11

Take a 45 minute taxi ride to the Treasure Cay ferry dock.

Take a 15 minute water taxi to Green Turtle Cay ferry landing.

Either take a taxi or the same water taxi to your hotel.

Check into your hotel.

Spend the rest of the day fishing, swimming, sailing, or relaxing in a hammock.

Take a taxi or boat transfer to the Bluff House for a delicious dinner.

Return to your hotel.

Overnight on **Green Turtle Cay**.

DAY 12

Take a boat transfer or hike over to New Plymouth village.

Follow the New Plymouth walking tour as listed in this book.

Enjoy lunch at the Wrecking Tree.

Take a taxi or hike to Ocean Beach.

Return to your hotel to change clothes.

Enjoy a peaceful semi-formal dinner at the Green Turtle Club.

Take a taxi or boat transfer into New Plymouth.

Party all night at the Roosters Rest Club or Burt's Sea Garden Club.

Return to your hotel.

Overnight on **Green Turtle Cay**.

DAY 13

Check out of your hotel.

Take a water taxi all the way back to Treasure Cay ferry dock.

Take a 5 minute taxi ride to Treasure Cay airport.

Depart The Bahamas to return home by plane.

4. LAND & PEOPLE

LAND

The beautiful nation of **The Commonwealth of The Bahamas** is made up of more than 750 limestone-based islands and cays, spread out over 5,400 square miles in the North Atlantic Ocean. Starting from a point just 50 miles east of lower Florida, there are less than three dozen inhabited islands that are home to about 255,000 residents. The Bahamas also boasts over 5% of the earth's total reef mass, which has made it one of the premier destinations for those who love scuba diving, snorkeling, fishing, and viewing a variety of unusual marine life in its natural habitat.

The Bahamas is blessed with a fantastic year round semi-tropical marine climate, with an average daily high temperature of 81° F (27° C). There are nearly 2,200 miles of dramatic coasline to enjoy the Gulf Stream-cooled sea waters while being caressed by the sun's bronzing rays. Other than a few months when hurricanes blow this way (between June and October), rainfall is usually light and the evening air is infused by gentle breezes.

The more famous islands of **Grand Bahama** and **New Providence** have historically attracted the largest number of vacationers, with their awesome array of large resorts and world-class casinos, but the tranquil and less developed **Out Islands** tend to have much nicer beaches, more intimate inns in all price ranges, and some of the friendliest inhabitants in the nation. The latest available figures show that more than 3.2 million visitors came to stay for a vacation or day trip in The Bahamas, bringing with them some $1.2 billion in revenues. Their average length of stay was one week; 75% were American, 8% Canadian, and 7% European.

BAHAMAS' FACTS & FIGURES

	Area (Sq. Miles)	Highest Point	Population
The Bahamas	**5,443**	**206'**	**254,685**
New Providence	80	123'	171,542
Grand Bahama	530	68'	41,035
Abaco	649	120'	10,061
Acklins	192	142'	428
Andros	2,300	118'	8,155
Berry Islands	12	80'	634
Bimini Islands	9	20'	1,638
Cat Island	150	206'	1,678
Cay Sal Bank	2	10'	0
Conception I.	4	66'	0
Crooked I. & Long Cay	93	155'	423
Eleuthera	200	190'	10,584
Exuma & Cays	112	130'	3,539
Great Inagua	599	109'	985
Little Inagua	49	99'	0
Long Island	230	178'	3,107
Mayaguana	110	131'	308
Ragged Island	14	103'	89
Rum Cay	30	97'	53
San Salvador	63	123'	486
Samana Cay	15	80'	0

PEOPLE

While not geographically part of the Caribbean, The Bahamas does in fact border on the Caribbean Sea and has many social and historical ties to the rest of that region. The people of The Bahamas are a mixed lot, with a majority population of about 83% black, who in many cases are direct descendants of former slaves from colonial-era American plantations. The remainder is about 14% white and 3% other assorted races.

English is the official language here, but you may still find many locals that speak a strange dialect which may sometimes be hard to understand. There are literally hundreds of churches throughout the islands, but the major religious groups are Baptists (32%), Anglican (20%), Roman Catholic (19%), Protestant (12%), Methodist (6%), and Church of God (5%). In many towns and villages there are an equally impressive number of churches and bars which often are found just down the block from one another.

The people here are extremely friendly and polite to all who reach their shores. Over 90% of all Bahamians are fully literate, and over 45% of the local workforce is employed in some segment of the tourism related industries which in turn contributes about half the gross domestic product. Additional major aspects to the country's economy include off-shore banking, insurance, regional oil refining, construction, pharmaceutical manufacturing, fishing, rum exportation, and to some degree the illegal transshipment of cocaine and marijuana to the US.

Very few consumer goods are produced here, and agricultural production is rather limited on these islands. Since The Bahamas imposes no income taxes on its residents, most of the tax revenue comes from 35% to 270% duties imposed on most imported products.

The nation's capital city is the large, congested metropolis of **Nassau** on New Providence Island. This medium-sized island is home to over 60% of the nation's population, many in and around Nassau, and is the destination of choice for most vacationers to The Bahamas.

JUNKANOO

Among the most prevalent Bahamian traditions are the world-famous *Junkanoo* celebrations held each year. The term Junkanoo relates to a special event with rituals and superstitions that were brought here by slaves whose routes can be traced back to West Africa. Somewhat similar in look and feel to Carnival festivities throughout the globe, Junkanoo celebrates the specific times when slaves were given a day off from working for their masters and were allowed to drink and party in colorful costumes through the islands' streets.

At the strike of 3:00am on both December 26 and New Years Eve, bands of highly costumed locals dance through the streets (mainly in downtown Nassau) and either bang drums and cowbells, blow into conch shells, or whistle to the sounds of this hypnotic Goombay symphony in motion. Thousands of these costumed Junkanoo dancers wear long strings of beads, cover their faces in glitter or hand-crafted masks fitted with colorful paper and feathers, suit up in unusual shoulder pieces, and in some cases disguise themselves as gigantic stilted figures representing wild animals or the likeness of famous people from around the world.

While reproductions of Junkanoo style dances may be seen at some resorts and nightclubs throughout the year, the real event is not to be missed if you happen to be in The Bahamas during the last week of December. If you are here any other time of the year, be sure to stop in at the new *Junkanoo Museum* just off the Prince George Dock behind Bay Street in downtown Nassau. Inside you will find some of the most elaborate costumes worn in recent years, as well as a series of fine photos and video clips of this uniquely Bahamian cultural event that has people lining both sides of the street late at night in anticipation of an awesome sight.

5. A SHORT HISTORY

THE EARLY YEARS

The first inhabitants of The Bahamas were mystical hunters and gatherers called the **Lucayan Indians** (also known as Arawaks), who most likely arrived here by the 10th century AD from South America in dug-out trees fashioned into canoes. It was these peaceful Indians that anxiously greeted Christopher Columbus when he first anchored in the New World and came ashore on the island of San Salvador (or perhaps at Cat Island, as some historians now believe) in October 1492. Although he did not find the intended route from Europe across the Atlantic Ocean to Asia (unfortunately the Americas ended up being in the way!), Columbus claimed the island in the name of King Ferdinand and Queen Isabella of Spain.

After departing San Salvador without the riches he had hoped to find in the Orient, he returned a year or so later and began the process of enslaving the Lucayans and taking them with him. By 1520, all of the Lucayans had been forcibly removed from The Bahama Islands and eventually died of exhaustion and disease as slaves in the Spanish gold mines of the New World. Additional Spanish discoverers, such as Juan Ponce de Leon, soon also came this way, but well over a century passed until the next wave of settlers would inhabit these islands.

THE EUROPEAN PURITANS ARRIVE

Although an attempt was made by French settlers to colonize in what is now Abaco in 1625, it was not until 1629 that King Charles I of England gave all the land rights for the Carolinas and The Bahamas to Sir Robert Heath, his Attorney General. The next group of European inhabitants came here in 1648, when a ship full of about 70 Puritans referred to as the **Eleutheran Adventurers** led by Captain **William Sayle** went into exile here from the British colony of Bermuda, where religious freedoms were not easy to come by. Captain Sayle (actually a former governor of Bermuda) soon found his ship wrecked upon the reefs off the coast of what is now Eleuthera (named after the Greek word meaning "Freedom") and created a settlement in the Preachers Cave area. Soon a republican government was set up under the terms of the *Articles & Orders of the Eleutheran Adventurers.*

After finding themselves in a place where the land was unsuitable for mass cultivation, and running drastically low on provisions, Sayle journeyed to the British-colony of Virginia to ask for their assistance to sustain his new colonies. After returning with plenty of foodstuffs and supplies for the Adventurers, a ship was sent back to Virginia laden with precious Brazilletto wood to repay the Virginians' generosity. A large quantity of this wood was also donated to raise funds for the newly founded Harvard College in the Massachusetts Bay Colony (the largest single donation ever granted to the now famous university in those days).

Some of these settlers, including Captain Sayle himself, found life in The Bahamas too difficult and soon departed. A small group remained here, though, and after vigorous infighting split up into additional hamlets on Harbour Island and Spanish Wells. The Adventurers quickly learned the art of "wrecking" ships by setting false safety beacons along dangerous reef areas. The precious cargo of many a wrecked ship was salvaged by these inventive locals. In 1666, a group of Bermuda-based sailors landed on New Providence Island and started settling near what is now Nassau.

By the 1670s, English King Charles II granted The Bahamas as crown lands to six different **Lord Proprietors** from the South Carolina colony, who basically didn't care a whole lot for their new possessions. Since little funds were given to defend these new lands, pirate ships took control over the nearby seas and plundered many gold-laden Spanish Galleons and merchant vessels. Infamous **pirates** such as Henry Morgan, Edward "**Blackbeard**" Teach, and Anne Bonney were a rich and happy lot for quite some time during this period. The Spanish retaliated for these pirate attacks by burning Nassau to the ground on four separate occasions during this time.

After losing many valuable shipments here, the British government finally retook official control of these islands and established the **Colony of The Bahamas** in 1718. The king appointed former privateer **Woodes Rogers** as the new Royal Governor of The Bahamas and he soon started the process of staving off the pirate raiders and the Spanish, pardoning some pirates, hanging a few criminals, and building a series of massive fortresses. Lacking the proper funding and arms to finish the job, Governor Rogers actually ended up in the poor house back in England for a while after spending all his own money to buy cannons. When Rogers returned to The Bahamas, he was finally able to form the **Bahamian House of Assembly** in 1729. Political stability was short lived, however, and in 1783 the Spanish once again invaded and then occupied Nassau. The next year ships under the command of **Colonel Andrew Deveaux** (a Loyalist from America) fooled the Spanish into thinking they were about to be attacked by a massive navy, and as the Galleons retreated he retook The Bahamas for the English crown.

THE LOYALISTS MOVE IN

During the American Revolution, many wealthy English colonialists and plantation owners from Georgia and the Carolinas did not agree with George Washington's attempts to create an independent country. These so-called **Loyalists** remained true to King George during the revolution and found themselves persecuted (and occasionally murdered) for their political convictions. Many fled penniless to the Spanish-held territories of Florida, once Florida was captured by Spain in 1783. These same Loyalists started sailing for The Bahamas and thus almost tripled the islands' population to around 11,250.

With their vast experience in growing cotton, and a strong work force of African slaves, these new inhabitants started creating cotton plantations on many of the Out Islands. Unfortunately, the soil was not the best for cotton cultivation, and an epidemic of **Chenille infestation** killed off most of the crops. Many of the Loyalists soon packed up and left; in some cases (such as on Exuma), they just sailed away leaving their former slaves stranded on the island to fend for themselves. After The **Bahamas Emancipation Act of 1833** abolished slavery, new towns were established for use by these now freed slaves.

TOURISM & RUM RUNNING

By 1861, The Bahamian economy really took off. Not only was the colony's first tourist hotel (The Royal Victoria Hotel) built in Nassau, but steamships from cruise lines like Cunard brought in adventurous travelers from places such as New York. At around the same time, The Bahamas also profited greatly from illicit trade to the blockaded southern states of the **Confederacy**. In exchange for vast quantities of cotton need by the English textile mills, the Confederate states were supplied with huge amounts of British arms shipped in under cover of night by entrepreneurial Bahamians.

Once the Civil War ended with the reunification of America, the islands had little choice but to support themselves by various methods including wrecking, minimal agriculture, and the harvesting and export of sea sponges. It was not until America established Prohibition of alcoholic beverages between 1920 and 1932 that these islands again prospered, this time as bootleggers and **Rum Runners** distilled and then smuggled rum to supply the Mafia-controlled speakeasys in major cities all over the American northeast. Pan-American Airways started its first flights in 1929 between Miami and Nassau, and within the next several decades many resorts began to spring up all over the islands' beaches, and Nassau's harbor was enlarged to accommodate the giant cruise ships that still visit The Bahamas on a weekly basis.

During World War II, The Bahamas was the sight of a flight training school for England's Royal Air Force, but never had to defend itself against attack. Once the war had finished, the Duke of Windsor was appointed the Royal Governor (he was the king who, just before World War II, had given up the throne to marry the woman he loved, an American named Wallace Simpson). The jet set begin to arrive and made Nassau and several chic little Out Island hideaways their favored vacation spots.

RECENT EVENTS

The Bahamas drew up its first Constitution in 1964, and a multiparty British style parliamentary system was established. In 1969, the nation's name was altered to the **Commonwealth of The Bahamas**. The country was granted its **independence** on July, 10, 1973, and is currently run by elected officials belonging mainly to the PLP (Progressive Liberal Party) and the FNM (Free National Movement). The country was then divided into 21 districts that are broken up into chains of adjacent islands.

In the 1992 elections, FNM candidate **Hubert A. Ingraham** became the new Prime Minister, although **Queen Elizabeth** of England remains the figurative Head of State. Although the local economy was terribly hurt by the American recession of the late 1980s, the country's fragile tourism industry is finally making a remarkable come-back. Recently a series of **district elections** has brought local communities the power to fund their own projects without having to wait years for ministers in Nassau to approve them.

There are relatively few major divisive issues in this country, but there are constant debates about local elections and other political topics. Although the days when Bahamian men would have children (known as out-children) with several different women in the same community are ending, there is still a high teenage pregnancy rate that is currently being addressed by both the church and the state.

Crime is only a real problem in the shanty towns behind Nassau and on the fringes of Freeport, and the large-scale drug transshipment problems of the 1970's and 1980's have been greatly reduced due to US Drug Enforcement Agency operations and bases throughout the nation. All of the evidence seems to show that recent government efforts have paid off in fighting crime and unemployment.

The Bahamas still needs to reduce its trade imbalance and internal operating budget, and has unfortunately started to reduce many of the social benefits that their citizens have counted on for years. As it becomes increasingly difficult for the current generation to find gainful employment after graduating from high school or a foreign university, the educated youth are among the first to feel the pinch.

6. PLANNING YOUR TRIP

BEFORE YOU GO

WHEN TO VISIT

HIGH SEASON

While The Bahamas is a great place to visit anytime of the year, most vacationers tend to arrive during the **high season** of late November through mid-March (winter). This is certainly the best time to enjoy great weather on every island of the country, but high season is also the time of year when the sights, attractions, and cities are at their busiest, so the hotels all tend to charge their highest rates. Although I have enjoyed the winters in The Bahamas, they are typically crowded and not much of a bargain.

LOW SEASON

The **low season** runs from late March through early June, and offers the visitor pleasant but often rather hot weather. If you don't mind wearing lighter clothing and plenty of sun screen, you can still comfortably run around the country and have an excellent time. This is a good time to arrive if you don't want to see huge amounts of fellow travelers.

If you are interested in swimming in warm ocean waters and basking under the heat of the sun, this is a great time to arrive. Since most Europeans receive a full month of vacation with pay usually during the summer, the airlines and resorts have no difficulty attracting Europeans during this period – although many get their vacations in August, so that month brings the most Europeans. Another benefit to these months is the abundance of available accommodations and airfare at discounted off-season rates.

HURRICANE SEASON

The **hurricane season** can start as early as June and extend into late November, and is often filled with short spells of rainy and windy days. If you have to visit during these months, it's best to stick to visiting the major islands, since many small resorts on the quieter Out Islands close at this time. As many as 25% of the hotels and attractions on the Out Islands may close down during this off-off-season. Rain and overcast skies are not uncommon, but you may still find several bright clear days to enjoy.

In the event of a hurricane passing through The Bahamas, the entire country may come to a complete standstill, and all airline services may cease operation for a few days, so make sure your airplane tickets back home are changeable. This is usually the quietest time of year to tour the country, however, and there are few tourists found anywhere outside of Grand Bahamas and New Providence islands.

OFFICIAL HOLIDAYS

New Year's Day, January 1
Good Friday, late March or early April
Easter Monday, late March or early April
Whitmonday, May
Labour Day, early June
Independence Day, June 10
Emancipation Day, early August
Discovery Day, October 12
Christmas, December 25
Boxing Day, December 26

*Note: The government of The Bahamas occasionally moves holidays around to form long weekends for its citizens. Many additional regional holidays exist (such as **Regattas**) which are not included in this list as they vary with each island. During these days, expect many museums, banks, government offices, and several private companies to be closed.*

For more details on these and local holidays throughout the islands, see Chapter 7, Basic Information, "Festivals & Local Events."

CLIMATE

The Bahamas is a sub-tropical destination with minor temperature fluctuations from one island to another. While locals may complain about a 75°F winter day as cold, most North Americans will certainly disagree. With summer high temperatures reaching over 100°F and winter low temperatures rarely falling below as 66°F, this is a pleasant place to visit any time of the year. Even on the hottest days there seems to be a constant breeze coming up from the passing Gulf Stream.

Summer is considered June through September, and winter is considered October through May. As mentioned above, hurricane season is officially between June through November.

AVERAGE DAILY TEMPERATURE & RAINFALL

	Average High Temp.	Inches of Rain
January	70°F 21°C	1.85"
February	70°F 21°C	1.7"
March	72°F 22°C	1.5"
April	76°F 24°C	1.9"
May	77°F 25°C	4.6"
June	80°F 27°C	8.9"
July	82°F 28°C	5.9"
August	82°F 28°C	6.2"
September	81°F 27°C	7.5"
October	78°F 26°C	8.1"
November	75°F 24°C	2.4"
December	70°F 21°C	1.3"

WHAT TO PACK

There are several items you ought to pack that will come in handy. The main concern about what to bring should be based on the season, and its typical climatic conditions. In the winters there may be a few chilly nights, so make sure to take a lightweight waterproof jacket and some jeans in your luggage. Since summers can be quite hot, I suggest lots of thin cotton, silk, and linen clothing as well as several good bathing suits.

In all seasons, I suggest that you pack sun tan lotion (SPF 15 or better), sun glasses, a money belt or sac, an umbrella, bathing suits, a sweater, comfortable walking shoes, sneakers, a waterproof wind breaker, extra glasses or contact lenses, all necessary medications with copies of the prescriptions, personal hygiene items, an empty nylon bag for gifts and shopping, a hair dryer, a good camera, a disposable waterproof camera, lots of film and batteries, a waterproof key holder for swimming, photocopies of your passport, travel insurance documents, plenty of travelers checks and a valid ATM cash card, a list of travelers check numbers and the phone numbers of your travel provider and credit card companies in case of emergencies, a flashlight, and of course this book.

Most visitors will have little need for suits, ties, expensive dresses, and formal clothing. Only a handful of expensive gourmet restaurants and equally snobby nightclubs will enforce a strict dress code. Any hotel will be pleased to welcome guests that are comfortably attired.

PASSPORT & VISA REGULATIONS

To enter The Bahamas as a tourist for up to 8 months, all US and Canadian citizens must have proof of citizenship such as a birth certificate with raised official seal, or a voter's registration card plus a government issued photo ID, or a valid passport, and a valid return cruise ship or airline ticket. At the present time, no special vaccines or visas are required to gain entry for North Americans.

Visitors who intend to spend over 8 months or wish to work in The Bahamas may need to register in advance with the government's Immigration Department in Nassau to receive official permission. Call the Bahamian consulate in your own country before departure for exact details (see phone numbers and addresses below).

CUSTOMS REGULATIONS

Upon Arrival in The Bahamas

Customs and immigration officials are usually easy for tourists to deal with in The Bahamas. I have rarely seen anyone be subjected to a luggage search upon arrival at an airport or cruise ship terminal here. The following are excerpted from the official Bahamian customs regulations at press time. Check with The Bahamas consulates if you need further details.

North Americans arriving in The Bahamas are allowed to bring up to $10,000 in cash for means of payment for tourist, gift, casino, and travel expenses. If more cash is brought it must be reported upon arrival to the Bahamian Customs authorities.

Adults are each allowed to import into The Bahamas the following amounts of these products:

- Cigarettes – 200
    - or
- Cigarillos – 100
    - or
- Cigars – 50
    - or
- Tobacco – 454 grams

• Perfumes	50 grams
• Eau de Cologne	1/2 liter

- Liquor (over 44 proof)   1 liter
    - or
- Liquor (under 44 proof)   2 liters

• Wine	2 liters
• Coffee	500 grams
• Tea	100 grams

All North American visitors are allowed, for temporary importation, objects for personal use which must leave with them upon departure, including: Personal clothing, jewelry, cameras and video cameras, a reasonable quantity of film and accessories, binoculars, sports equipment such as golf clubs and tennis racquets, fishing gear, non-motorized bicycles, wind surfing boards, delta wings, musical instruments, non-professional sound recording equipment, radios and televisions, video recorders, typewriters, calculators, and personal computers.

If you have any additional questions, contact one of The Bahamas Embassies, Consulates, or High Commissioner's offices on this side of the ocean before you depart!

Upon Return to the US

All US citizens can return to America with up to $600 without paying duty if you have left the US for over 48 hours and haven't made another international trip within the last 30 days. Each family member is eligible for the same limits, and these amounts may be pooled together. Normally a 10% duty will be assessed on goods that have exceeded the $600 value, but are below $1600 in total value. Above this point the duty will vary with the specific merchandise being imported but starts at an additional 10%.

Each adult may also bring in up to 2 liters of wine or alcohol and either 100 cigars (except from Cuba) or 200 cigarettes. There is no duty on antiquities or works of art over 100 years old, or on General System of Preference (G.S.P.) items that have been manufactured in The Bahamas. Bring all receipts with the merchandise to customs to avoid additional problems.

Upon Return to Canada
All Canadian citizens can return to Canada with up to $500 CD once each year if you have left Canada for over 7 days, up to $200 CD several times each year if you have left Canada for over 48 hours, or up to $50 several times each year if you have left Canada for over 24 hours. Each family member is eligible for the same limits per person. Normally a combination of federal and provincial taxes will be assessed on goods that have exceeded the duty free values depending on the specific items involved and your length of stay.

Each adult can also bring in 1.14 liters of alcohol, or 8.5 liters (24 cans or bottles each with 12 ounces) of beer. Also allowed for those at least 16 years old are up to 50 cigars, 200 cigarettes, and 400 grams of tobacco. Bring all receipts with the merchandise to customs to avoid additional problems.

BAHAMIAN GOVERNMENT REPRESENTATIVES IN NORTH AMERICA
- **Bahamas Embassy**, *2220 Massachusetts Ave., N.W., Washington, D.C. 20008. Tel. (202) 319-2660*
- **Bahamas Consulate in Miami**, *25 S.E. 2nd Ave., Suite 818, Miami, Florida 33131. Tel. (305) 373-6295*
- **Bahamas Consulate in New York**, *231 East 46th Street, New York, N.Y. 10017. Tel. (212) 421-6420*
- **Bahamas High Commissioner in Canada**, *360 Albert Street, Suite 1020, Ottawa, Ontario K1R-7X7. Tel. (613) 232-1724*

STUDENT TRAVEL & YOUTH ID CARDS
For full time students under the age of 26 who can provide documentation of their current status, there is a great card called the **International Student Identity Card** (I.S.I.C.), valid for one year. It can be obtained in North America before you depart for about $15. It allows its holder to get discounts on some international flights, museums, public transportation, and other services.

Included in the US with the cost of these cards is special emergency medical insurance, which can cover around $3,000 in medical bills as well as perhaps $100 a day in hospital bills for up to around two months. Another card known as the **International Youth Card** is also available with similar features for young adults under 26 who are no longer in school.

To obtain one of these cards, contact one of the following student travel companies:
• **Council Travel**, *New York, Tel. (212) 661-1450*
• **Travel Cuts**, *Toronto, Tel. (416) 979-2406*

ACCESS FOR THE PHYSICALLY CHALLENGED

For physically challenged people, The Bahamas is not the most accessible country in the world, but it can be enjoyed with a fair amount of advance planing. Getting here is generally hassle free, as most international airlines offer special seating assignments, wheelchair storage, and boarding assistance to anyone who requests so in advance. Upon arrival in Nassau International Airport, additional special airport assistance services are also offered free of charge by the airlines.

Now that you have arrived in The Bahamas, things can still get a little difficult. Although well marked, reserved "handicapped" parking spaces can be found in most cities and public parking lots, almost none of the major rental car companies offer specially adapted vehicles. A heightened sense of public responsibility is starting to have a positive effect on the availability of special services and facilities, especially in the larger cities of Nassau and Freeport.

The **Bahamas Tourism Offices** in New York and Toronto can mail you listings of hotels with specially adapted rooms, taxi companies that offer special mini-van shuttles, and companies that book vacations for those with specific challenges. Wheelchair accessible bathrooms, entrance ramps, and well designed elevators with Braille and chime features are starting to become more common in the larger 4 and 5 star hotels in resort areas and business centers. Whenever possible I have included a special notation in the hotel listings where special facilities are offered. Each regional tourist information centre may be able to direct visitors to additional transportation services, adapted accommodations, and restaurants which are properly equipped.

The offices of **Bahamas Association for the Physically Disabled** in Nassau can also provide you with much more detailed information on this subject. Their address is: *Dolphin Drive, P. O. Box N 4252, Nassau, N.P., The Bahamas, Tel. (242) 322-2393.*

Helpful Organizations
• **Society for The Advancement of Travel for the Handicapped**, New York, New York, Tel. (212) 447-7284. A members-only service with

basic information about travel needs for the physically challenged. Yearly membership is $45 US for adults and $25 for students.

- **Information Center for Individuals with Disabilities**, *Boston, Massachusetts, Tel. (800) 462-5015*
- **MossRehab Travel Information Services**, *Philadelphia, Pennsylvania. Tel. (215) 456-9600*. A free information and referral service with valuable hints and suggestions on companies that offer travel services for the physically challenged.
- **Flying Wheels Travel**, *Owatonna, Minnesota. Tel. (800) 535-6790*. A great full service travel agency and group tour operator that can provide helpful information and reservations for the physically challenged. Services include all forms of special transportation and accommodation reservations, and guided group tours.

BAHAMAS TOURISM OFFICES - BTO

Before you begin to plan your vacation in The Bahamas, it would be a good idea to contact one of your country's branches of the **Bahamas Tourism Office** (known as the BTO). If you ask a few questions relating to your specific interests, these offices will send you a manila envelope full of maps, assorted magazines filled with basic tourist information, sports listings, hotel directories, restaurant indexes, and maybe even a few glossy brochures from major tour operators.

The staff at these offices are usually very informative Bahamians who are trying their best to keep up with the tidal wave of daily inquiries. If their line seems constantly busy, or if they don't seem to have the time to answer many questions, it's only because they don't have a large staff to keep up with such a large volume of calls. These are nice people who have a huge amount of work to do, so you must consider the fact that they just can't spend lots of time with calls. On the other hand, a personal visit to one of the BTO offices can result in a somewhat more intensive discussion and the chance to receive much more specific printed material.

The BTO either prints or distributes dozens of useful documents in several languages which are then eventually sent along to the tourist offices which they control throughout the world. Call them toll-free in the US at *(800) 422-4262* and in Canada at *(800) 667-3777*.

BTO Offices in North America
- *150 East 52nd Street, 28th Floor North, New York City, N.Y. 10022. Tel. (212) 758-2777, Fax (212) 753-6531*
- *8600 West Bryn Mawr Ave., Suite 820, Chicago, Illinois 60631. Tel. (312) 693-1500, Fax (312) 693-1114*
- *3450 Wilshire Boulevard, Suite 208, Los Angeles, California 90010. Tel.*

(213) 385-0033, Fax (213) 383-3966
- *19495 Biscayne Boulevard, Suite 809, Aventura, Florida 33180. Tel. (305) 932-0051, Fax (305) 682-8758*
- *121 Bloor Street East, Suite 1101, Toronto, Ontario, Canada M4W-3M5. Tel. (416) 968-2999, Fax (416) 968-6711*

THE BAHAMA OUT ISLANDS PROMOTION BOARD

*If you want to get away from the major resorts and want accurate, honest, and well researched information on the wonderful **Out Islands** (formerly known as the Family Islands), there is a great organization you should call immediately. The amazing **Bahama Out Islands Promotion Board** is a special office funded by most of the better quality hotels on Abaco, Andros, Berry Islands, Bimini, Cat Island, Deep Water Cay, Eleuthera, Exuma, Harbour Island and Long Island, and is staffed by Helen Fillmore and Maura Brassil, two of the most insightful travel industry personnel I have ever spoken with during my 15 years in the business.*

They can send you free copies of their superb "Getaway" magazine, a giant Out Island Travel Map & Guide, and dozens of color brochures on some of the country's most memorable hotels in all price ranges. They also have a special telephone transfer system to allow you to reach many of their member properties toll-free via their offices. This is one of the first places to call when considering a vacation in The Bahamas, and is highly recommended.

*You can contact them at: **Bahama Out Island Promotion Board**, 1100 Lee Wagener Boulevard, Suite 204, Ft. Lauderdale, Florida 33315. Tel. (800) 688-4752, Fax (305) 359-8098. Their internet address is: http://www.bahama-out-islands.com.*

BOOKING YOUR VACATION

With the help of this guidebook, you will have the information and suggestions necessary to begin planning your trip. The next step is to begin to book and pay for the elements that will create a perfect vacation. I strongly advise that you consider prepaying the airfare, rental car, and some (if not all) of your accommodations.

If you are traveling to The Bahamas between November and March, do not expect to find availability in many hotels and inns by just showing up. It is best advised to book your most desired high season accommodations well in advance. In the low season, I suggest that you book at least the first and last few nights in advance, and if you are adventurous you can find a few places along the way as you go.

I would like to point out the many advantages of using a travel professional to help with reservations. A good travel agent or specialty tour operator can provide detailed information on hotels, airfare, and car rentals without the need for travelers to spend hundreds of dollars calling around The Bahamas. They also have access to special prices that are not available to the general public. If anything goes wrong and you need a refund or to change your schedule, a good travel professional with advance notification can often avoid certain penalties that would normally apply.

TRAVEL AGENTS

Travel agents are hard working consultants who usually get paid on a commission basis. If you desires to book a package vacation or cruise, no additional fee should be charged, as the agent's commission of between 8% and 12% is deducted from the trip's list (retail) price. For special fully customized vacations (known in the industry as an F.I.T.) or unusual boat charters, travel agents may charge as much as $100 additional in advance to cover the extra hours and long distance calls that will be required. Each revision or cancellation to your vacation package can carry significant penalties, or may even be completely non-refundable (unless you have purchased special insurance).

Travel agencies have access to computer databases which can search out the least expensive regularly scheduled airfares offered by international airlines, and also can look up information on over 8,500 hotels throughout the world. Travel professionals (and a few savvy frequent travelers) also have access to large hotel information books like the *Hotel and Travel Index* and the *Official Hotel Guide*, published by the Reed Travel Group, which gives great basic listings on tens of thousands of major hotels. Other more detailed travel industry and hotel review publications include the *Star* and *Caribbean Gold Book* series.

Unfortunately, the best deals on airfare, cruises, and the most remarkable accommodations in The Bahamas are not necessarily going to appear in all travel agents' computers. If you are looking for a great deal on a cruise vacation, you may find yourself contacting one of many "Cruise Only" agencies that have been known to find great deals on assorted sailings and last minute vacancies. What distinguishes a great agent from a good agent is quite clear. A good travel agent will either know first-hand about the country you are visiting, or will offer to make a few calls and find out more. A great agent (and they are out there if you look a bit!) will spend lots of time and energy researching your destination, and will work with you to book exactly what you want. No matter who you pick to assist with your travel plans, make sure you are at least as equally well informed. The more specific that you can be about what type of trip and price range you want, the closer you'll get to matching your dreams with reality.

TOUR OPERATORS

These are the wholesale sources for well over 90% of the packages and 15% of the F.I.T. custom Bahamas vacations sold in North America. A good tour operator will specialize in just one or a few different countries, and have a staff of experts who have been to almost every hotel, inn, and cruise located in the countries that they represent.

Unfortunately most tour operators do not sell directly to the public and prefer to deal with agencies to avoid lengthy phone calls and having to act like government tourist offices. I strongly suggest asking your travel agent to contact various tour operators with whom they have dealt successfully to get you competitive quotes on a series of different pre-packaged vacations at the hotel(s) of your choice. In the event that you want to book small inns and Out Island destinations (the tour operators and travel agents usually will know little if anything about these places), you will have to do plenty of your own research!

HANG OUT WITH A BAHAMIAN FAMILY!

*A popular government sponsored program called **People to People** gives international vacationers to New Providence, Grand Bahama, Bimini, Eleuthera, or Exuma the unusual opportunity of spending a few days hosted by a gracious Bahamian family. With a month or so advance notice, a special office at the Bahamas Ministry of Tourism will match you to an available host family that will take you around on their daily chores and adventures, and perhaps invite you to either church or dinner with them. The service is completely free and is a really good way to learn about life in this part of the world. You'll certainly end up realizing that people are basically the same no matter where they live, and they all like to meet strangers from strange lands. Although you will still spend your evenings in the hotel of your choice, this will give an extra dimension to your vacation that most visitors will never come close to experiencing.*

*For more details, contact the **BTO** office in your country or **The Bahamas Ministry of Tourism**, "People to People" Department, P. O. Box N-3701, Nassau, N.P., The Bahamas, Tel. (242) 326-9781, Fax (242) 328-0945.*

TRAVEL EMERGENCY & MEDICAL INSURANCE

One of the most important issues of any trip abroad is what to do in an emergency. Since the possibility of a medical problem is always a factor of risk, it is strongly advised that you take out an insurance policy. The best types of travel insurance are in the **Primary Coverage** category. In an emergency, most of these policies will provide 24 hour toll-free help desks, lists of approved specialists, the ability to airlift you to a hospital with the proper facilities for your condition, and additional kinds of assistance, including refunds on additional expenses and unused hotel nights.

Trip Cancellation & Interruption Insurance

Many special policies also cover vacation refunds if a family member gets ill and you must cancel your trip, if the airline you were supposed to be flying on goes out of business, if you must depart early from your trip due to sickness or death in the family, if the airline fails to deliver your baggage on time (a common occurrence in The Bahamas), if your luggage is stolen from your car, if your stay is extended do to injury, etc.

One element normally not covered are airplane schedule changes, missed connections, and flight cancellations that are rather common in The Bahamas. Please check with your travel agent, tour operator, or the Canadian and American Automobile Association for further details.

Travel Insurance Companies in North America
- **Mutual of Omaha (Tele-Trip)**, *Tel. (800) 228-9792 in the US; Tel. (402) 351-8000 in Canada*
- **Travel Guard**, *Tel. (715) 345-0505 in the US and Canada*
- **Crown Life Travel Insurance**, *Tel. (800) 265-0261 in Canada*
- **Access America**, *Tel. (800) 284-8300 in the US and Canada*

ACCOMMODATIONS

There are well over 150 different government-licensed accommodation providers in The Bahamas. I have included extensive descriptions in this publication's regional chapters of nearly 80 of the properties throughout The Bahamas that I have personally inspected at least twice, and can appropriately suggest to my readers. I have listed each destination's properties in up to four separate price categories that are relevant to the average room rate of that specific city. Within each of the price categories, I have listed the hotels from top to bottom in the order of my personal preference.

While the quality and facilities of accommodations may change from season to season, I have given you the most up to date information currently available to help you select the best places to fit your requirements. The price guidelines for all types of accommodations that I have used in my reviews are based on the lowest price room rate for two people staying in a double room, not necessarily including either taxes or service charges. In some cases, I have listed either a year round or weekend price. Keep in mind that many hotels have up to 50% surcharges during special festivals, regattas, the high season, and holidays. If you are traveling around The Bahamas without all your nights already pre-reserved, any local tourist information office can book a hotel room for you.

HOTEL INDUSTRY TERMS USED IN THIS BOOK

Low Season - *Usually from about April through October, excluding holidays*

High Season - *Usually from about November through March*

Rack Rate - *The full retail price of a room; special rates may also be available*

Corporate Rate - *Available to almost anyone who presents a business card*

Weekend Rate - *A limited number of discounted rooms Friday through Sunday*

Special Packages - *Discounts given during quiet times of the year*

Double Room - *A room designed and priced for two people staying together*

Apartment - *A unit with cooking facilities built in*

EP - *European Plan, no meals included in the price*

CP - *Continental Plan, a small breakfast included in the price*

BP - *Breakfast Plan, a full breakfast (typically a buffet) included in the price*

MAP - *Modified American Plan, full breakfast and dinner included in the price*

AI - *All Inclusive Plan, all meals (and drinks in most cases) included in the price*

Hotels in The Bahamas run the full gamut of quality and accommodations. **Hotels** throughout the country may be housed in everything from converted mansions to brand new towering resort complexes on the sea. Low priced hotel properties will often be loaded with additional facilities including a restaurant, parking, cable TV, private bathrooms, an outdoor pool, in-room phones, elevators, and perhaps even mini-bars.

Most better quality hotels and resorts have multiple restaurants, semi-private beach areas, water sports facilities, snack bars, lounges, air conditioning, a daily selection of activities, health clubs, evening entertainment, deluxe marble or tile bathrooms, late night or 24-hour room service, business meeting rooms, garage parking, tour desks, luxury suites, a concierge desk, and bell boys.

Guest houses are usually bed and breakfast style accommodations that have either private or shared bathrooms, nice simple furnishings, air conditioning or ceiling fans, complimentary continental breakfast, and in many cases plenty of charm.

Keep in mind that upon check-in you will almost always be asked to leave a credit card imprint as a deposit against incidentals and non-prepaid charges. The room tax in The Bahamas is currently 4%, although some hotels that are members of industry organizations and promotion boards can charge an additional 4% fee. Other hotels add up to $3.50 per person per day for maid gratuities, and unfortunately also include so-called resort levies or energy surcharges, which are nothing more than unfair ways to nickel and dime you to death!

GETTING TO THE BAHAMAS

SCHEDULED NON-STOP FLIGHTS TO THE BAHAMAS FROM NORTH AMERICA

Air Canada
• *in the US and Canada, Tel. (800) 361-6340*
   Air Canada offers non-stop service between Toronto and Nassau once a week or so during the high season only.

American Airlines
• *in the US and Canada, Tel. (800) 433-7300*
   American Eagle has small prop planes that fly from Miami to Nassau and Freeport daily, as well as to Marsh Harbour, George Town, and Governor's Harbour several times a week. The service is very good, the prices are low, and you can easily connect to other American Airlines flights via major North American airports and receive frequent flyer points for the whole trip.

Bahamasair
• *in the US and Canada, Tel. (800) 422-4262*
   Bahamasair schedules multiple jet and prop planes between Miami and Nassau or Freeport at competitive rates. They also offer special add-on fares, like the unique "Miami-Nassau Plus 3 Out Island" fares that can save you some serious money while island hopping.

Carnival Airlines
• *in the US and Canada, Tel. (800) 824-7286*
   Carnival has swift non-stop 727 and 737 jet service between Newark, JFK-New York, and Ft. Lauderdale airports almost every day of the week

at really low prices. The in-flight service is limited, but for the rates they charge it's a bargain!

Delta Airlines
• *in the US and Canada, Tel. (800) 221-1212*
   Delta has daily non-stop service between their hub in Ft. Lauderdale and Nassau via jet, as well as daily prop plane service between Ft. Lauderdale and Freeport. Their subsidiary, known as **Comair**, also has daily prop plane flights between Orlando and Nassau.

Gulfstream International Airlines
• *in the US and Canada, Tel. (800) 992-8532*
   Gulfstream International can fly you daily on non-stop prop planes between Miami and Nassau or Freeport. Several times a week they also offer flights from other Florida cities such as Daytona Beach, Jacksonville, Gainsville, Key West, Naples, Orlando, Tallahassee, Tampa, and West Palm Beach to destinations such as Nassau, Freeport, Treasure Cay, Marsh Harbour, Rock Sound, Andros Town, George Town, and North Eleuthera.

   This is my favorite airline for Bahamas travel, and is linked with United Airlines flights and frequent flyer programs. Their in-flight service is outstanding, and the prices are among the lowest for this region.

Island Express
• *in the US and Canada, Tel. (305) 359-0380*
   The ever-expanding array of flights on **Island Express** includes non-stop small prop plane service between Ft. Lauderdale and Chub Cay, Marsh Harbour, Stella Marris, and Treasure Cay. They also will charter other flights for unusual schedules.

Laker Airways
• *in the US and Canada, Tel. (800) 545-1300*
   So you thought you heard the last of Freddy Laker some years ago, but I told you he would be back! Laker now offers super cheap scheduled charter flights several times a week on new 727 jets to Freeport via major American cities such as Hartford, Baltimore, Richmond, Cleveland, Cincinnati, Chicago, and Ft. Lauderdale

Pan Am Air-Bridge
• *in the US and Canada, Tel. (800) 424-2557*
   Formerly known as Chalk's, this small personable airline offers a unique chance to fly between downtown Miami and Ft. Lauderdale to either Paradise Island or Alice Town on North Bimini on vintage

Grumman amphibious sea-planes several times a day. For a once in a lifetime flight experience, consider reserving a fun-filled flight with this fine aviation company.

USAir

• *in the US and Canada, Tel. (800) 622-1015*

USAir has a series of commuter prop planes that can get you from either Miami, Ft. Lauderdale, or West Palm Beach to Paradise Island. They also offer prop planes from Ft. Lauderdale to Marsh Harbour, Treasure Cay, and North Eleuthera. Non-stop flights are also available from Charlotte to Nassau.

AVERAGE NON-STOP JET FLIGHT TIMES TO THE BAHAMAS	
Ft. Lauderdale to Nassau	*45 minutes*
Ft. Lauderdale to Freeport	*25 minutes*
Miami to Nassau	*50 minutes*
Miami to Freeport	*35 minutes*
New York to Nassau	*2 hours & 30 minutes*
Charlotte to Nassau	*2 hours & 15 minutes*
Toronto to Nassau	*3 hours & 5 minutes*

FLIGHTS WITH CONNECTIONS TO THE BAHAMAS

Several international airlines offer connecting service to The Bahamas from dozens of North American cities. These flights take longer than the above-mentioned airlines because they require a change of planes (most commonly in Miami or Ft. Lauderdale) before continuing on to Nassau, Paradise Island, Freeport, or the Out Islands. Call your favorite airline or travel agent for exact pricing and scheduling details from your home city.

CHARTER FLIGHTS

Several charter operators offer flights during the high season to The Bahamas from cities such as Atlanta, Boston, Chicago, Cleveland, Cincinnati, Miami, Nashville, New York, Newark, Raleigh, Toronto, Nashville, Vancouver, and other North American gateways. Be extra careful whenever booking a charter flight, as they are not bound by the same regulations as normal scheduled carriers.

It is not uncommon for these flights to be delayed for hours (or even days!) waiting for replacement equipment, while you are stuck sleeping in the airport lobby. Charter flight tickets are normally non-changeable/non-refundable and are often not covered by travel insurance. For more details, call your travel agent.

DISCOUNT TICKET CONSOLIDATORS

There are many discount ticket brokers who offer last minute and special advance purchase round-trip fares for airlines who have not sold enough seats on specific flights. I only suggest this method when you have not been able to find a reasonable deal for tickets directly with major airlines for the desired dates. While some of these companies are in the habit of ripping off clients, several large companies have been doing a fairly good job of supplying the traveling public with good deals on highly restrictive tickets. It is advised that you first ask your travel agent for their recommendations, or call the local consumer protection agency or Better Business Bureau about any complaints on file about the consolidator you are considering.

I strongly recommend that you either purchase your consolidated tickets from a travel agent or specialty tour operator, and be sure to use a major credit card to purchase this type of ticket. This way you will be better protected in case of any problems.

These are some consolidators with a good reputation:
• **Travac**, *(212) 563 3303*
• **Air Travel Discounts**, *(212) 922-1326*
• **Unitravel**, *(800) 325-2222*
• **World Travel**, *(800) 886-4988*
• **Travel Cuts**, *(416) 979-2406*
• **TFI Tours**, *(800) 745-8000*

7. BASIC INFORMATION

BUSINESS HOURS

Most **retail stores** are open from 9:00am until about 6:00pm from Monday through Friday, and from 10:00am and 5:00pm on Saturdays. Sunday retail hours do exist, but only in Nassau and Freeport port areas when major cruise ships are in town, and in selected shopping centers, some convenient stores, and a few boutiques in the most touristy areas. On every day of the week you can, however, find open restaurants, bars, corner grocers, pharmacies, airports, taxi stands, and cafes.

Banks are generally open from about 9:30am until 3:00pm from Monday through Thursdays, and from 9:30am until 5:00pm on Fridays with several on Grand Bahama Island and New Providence Island offering 24-hour NYCE, Plus, Visa, and Cirrus ATM cash machines.

Post Offices are usually open Monday through Friday from 8:30am until 5:30pm and Saturday from 8:30am until 12:30pm.

Government offices tend to be open from Monday through Friday between 9:00am and 5:00pm with some Ministry of Tourism information kiosks also keeping limited Saturday morning hours.

Many **museums** are open Monday through Friday between 10:00am and at least 4:00pm, but these hours differ greatly from one museum to another.

CASINOS

There are currently four full service 20,000 to 35,000 square foot casinos operated by private companies. About 25% of their profits go to the government. They differ in style from one another, but the selection of games, odds, special services, and house rules are pretty much the same. To enter a Bahamas casino establishment, you must be a foreigner (absolutely no Bahamians are allowed to gamble), have proof that you are over 18 years old (I have never seen anyone get proofed), wear suitable attire (no wet bathing suits), and leave your cameras and cellular phones shut off. There is no cover charge for entering any casino in this country.

Games of chance offered include Blackjack, American Roulette, Craps, Poker, Video Poker, Baccarat, The Big Wheel, and in some cases a Sports Book section. While there are a full assortment of 5 cent to $5 slot machines, other games have differing minimum bet levels ranging from $2 and way up. For exact details about any of their facilities, just pop into any of the establishments listed below to learn more. These same casinos also offer Vegas-style revues, restaurants, lounges, free drinks and junkets to top players, credit card cash advances, and in some cases even a line of credit.

Casinos are open from 10:00am until 4:00am daily, with the slot machines open 24 hours a day 7 days a week. The four casinos are:
• **Atlantis Casino**, *Paradise Island (New Providence), Tel. (242) 363-3000*
• **Crystal Palace Casino**, *Cable Beach (New Providence), Tel. (242) 327-6200*
• **Bahamas Princess Casino**, *Freeport (Grand Bahama), Tel. (242) 352-6721*
• **Lucayan Casino**, *Lucaya (Grand Bahama), Tel. (242) 373-7777*

ELECTRICITY

Bahamian outlets are designed for 110 Volts AC and 60 Hertz appliances, just like American and Canadian outlets, and all electrical plugs are tipped by two standard flat pins. If you are bringing electrical appliances or components from North America, you do not need to bring any special transformers or adapters.

EMBASSIES & CONSULATES
• **American Embassy in Nassau**, *Queen Street, Tel. (242) 322-1181*
• **Canadian Consulate in Nassau**, *Shirley Street, Tel. (242) 393-2123*

FESTIVALS & LOCAL EVENTS

Every island in The Bahamas hosts several festivals, fairs, concerts, religious processions, and special celebrations each year. The following list contains some of the most important religious, cultural, historical, gastronomic, sporting, and agricultural festivities. To receive information on the exacts dates of each specific event, please contact the **BTO** offices in your country or a local tourist information office in The Bahamas.

JANUARY
Junkanoo Night - A special Bahamian street parade and festival starting at 3:00am on New Year's Day on most islands (especially interesting in Nassau). Costumed and masked dancers and musicians celebrate the days when slaves where given a day off to party.
New Year's Day Regattas - Exciting sail boat races on Montagu Bay in

Nassau as well as off Staniel Cay in the Exumas.

Supreme Court Opening - Each year in early January the Supreme Court's first yearly quarter is opened in Rawson Square, Nassau, by the Chief Justice in a ceremony that includes inspections of the guards of honor and a performance by the Bahamas Police Force Band. The event starts at 10:00am on differing dates each January.

FEBRUARY

Annual Archives Exhibitions - A month of special free exhibitions of Bahamian relics and historical items including documents, paintings, and photographs held during normal business hours at the lobby of the Post Office Building on East Hill Street in Nassau.

MARCH

Snipe Winter Sailing Championships - Held in late March off of Montagu Bay in Nassau.

Out Islands International Gamefish Tournament - Held at Stella Marris resort on Long Island.

APRIL

Bahamas Family Island Regatta - A late April sailing event for four days in George Town, Exuma, when the harbor gets packed with hundreds of hand-made sailing boats and sloops from each Out Island competing for prizes. Landlocked spectators may also watch beauty pageants, fashion shows, native cooking exhibitions, and much more. A real treat!

MAY

Long Island Sailing Regatta - A four day sailing race held in late May of each year off Long Island.

What's Out There Fishing Tournament - This gamefishing tournament is held each year in May off of Great Harbour Cay in the Berry Islands.

Bimini Festival & Fishing Tournament - This yearly event held at the Bimini Big Game Fishing Club in Alice Town on North Bimini is among the most famous fishing tournaments in The Bahamas.

JUNE

Caribbean Muzik Festival - Nassau becomes filled with Calypso, Soca, Reggae, Soul, Gospel, and Junkanoo bands from around the globe in various indoor and outdoor venues.

Eleuthera Festival of Pineapples - The folks of Gregorytown show off their recipes and prize winning pineapples (the world's best!).

JULY

Independence Day Festivities - For a week staring on or about July 10th, most islands have special parades, pyrotechnics displays, and amusing regattas in honor of Bahamian independence.

The Abaco Regatta - All of Abaco gets filled up with participants and spectators of this world-class race starting around July 4th for a full week.

AUGUST

Emancipation Day Festivities - A series of public commemorations of the abolishment of slavery on August 7, 1834. Events are usually scheduled at the Fox Hill parade grounds in Nassau.

OCTOBER

Discovery Day - Celebrations on the October 12th anniversary of Christopher Columbus landing on San Salvador (or Cat Island, depending on who you believe).

NOVEMBER

Guy Fawkes Day - The city of Nassau burns a figure of Englishman Guy Fawkes on November 5th, followed by parades and street parties.

North Bimini Wahoo Challenge - Fishermen come to North Bimini from around the globe to catch their own Wahoo.

DECEMBER

Plymouth Historical Weekend - Residents of Green Turtle Cay in Abaco hold art exhibits, live concerts, and large parties celebrating their history and unique culture in early December.

Junkanoo Parade - A special Bahamian street parade and festival starting at 3:00am on Boxing Day (December 26th) on most islands (especially interesting in Nassau). Costumed and masked dancers and musicians celebrate the days when slaves where given a day off to party.

HEALTH & MEDICAL CONCERNS

The Bahamas currently requires no inoculations or special immunizations for visitors from America and Canada. In fact, there haven't been any outbreaks of major infectious diseases here in many years. The best thing to do in case you worry about these things is to contact the US State Department Information Center and ask if there are any current travel advisories on this destination. I am pretty sure you will find none.

If you are currently under medication, you should bring a copy of your prescription (with the generic name for the drug) along with your medicine. If necessary, a local pharmacy may be able to either refill it or refer you to a doctor who can write a new prescription. **Hospitals** are available in most major population areas, and can be found by calling directory assistance *(916)* or in case of an emergency calling *(322-2221)* for an ambulance.

Every major city has at least one major medical center that is open 24 hours a day, 7 days a week. Out Island towns may have one or two Government Clinics that are open during limited hours and cannot handle major medical emergencies. While there are some good hospitals in The Bahamas, such as **Doctors Hospital** and **Princess Margaret Hospital** in the Nassau area, many Bahamians and tourists alike find themselves opting for a flight to Miami for more complicated conditions and surgery.

INSURANCE COVERAGE

Since you are not a Bahamian citizen, health care may not be provided to you for free while visiting here. North Americans with private insurance may be covered for reimbursement under their current policy, but that may only help you after months of detailed paperwork. Canadians may find that their provincial health insurance may cover or reimburse certain procedures, but don't count on it. Check Travel Emergency and Trip Cancellation Insurance sections of the Chapter 6, *Planning Your Trip*, for important advice on this subject.

For exact laws regarding the use of The Bahamas health care system as a foreigner, please contact the Bahamian Consulate, Embassy, or High Commission in your home country before departure.

LOST OR STOLEN PASSPORTS

Just in case you happen to somehow misplace your passport, or need the help and advice of your own government, contact your embassy at the numbers given above in this chapter. They can also provide other services that your tax dollars are paying for, including travel advisories on other nations which you may wish to visit while overseas, lists of local medical specialists, and other valuable details.

MONEY & BANKING

The units of Bahamian currency are called the **Bahamian Dollar** and are exactly equal to $1 US if used in these islands. The Bahamian Dollar can be divided into smaller units of 100 cents. This money comes in denominations of coins at 5 cents, 10 cents, 15 cents, 25 cents, 50 cents, and colorful bills embossed with the Queen's portrait that are worth $1, $3, $5, $10, $20, $50, $100, and $500.

Since US dollars are accepted as legal tender everywhere in the Bahamas, and Bahamian bills are almost impossible to exchange at North American banks, I strongly suggest you avoid having too much local currency at any one time. Only the Central Bank of The Bahamas on Market Street in Nassau is allowed to exchange more than $70 Bahamian for US or foreign currencies, so either spend all your Bahamian currency while on vacation, or keep a good quantity of small denomination US dollar travelers checks with you.

EXCHANGE RATES

At press time the value of $1 US is equal to $1 Bahamian, while the value of $1 Canadian is equal to about 72 cents Bahamian. In this book, all dollar prices given are US dollar prices unless otherwise noted.

Most banks in The Bahamas are open from Monday through Thursdays from about 9:30am until around 3:00pm, and Friday from 9:30am until 5:00pm. All banks and business establishments impose a very small **tax stamp fee** of between 25 cents and $1 per cashed travelers check instead of a commission. If you want to exchange your travelers checks, you must present the bank teller, hotel cashier, or boutique sales clerk with a valid passport (despite what your travelers check company tells you). When entering a bank, look for the exchange sign and wait in line.

There is no black market in The Bahamas, so don't even try to look for it. Computerized 24-hour ATM machines (Cirrus, NYCE, Plus, Visa, Amex) filled with either US or Bahamian currency are available in many downtown locations, casinos, and banks with offices in popular tourist zones. Currently, there are no ATM machines for non-Bahamian accounts on the Out Islands.

Credit Cards

Credit cards have become a necessary part of most vacations. These days it is often necessary in many cases to present a credit card at hotel front desks for an imprint to cover any unpaid phone calls, mini-bar usage, or room service fees charged to your hotel bill. Also, many rental car companies will not let you rent from them without a credit card deposit. Most Bahamian hotels will accept Visa, Mastercard, and occasionally American Express and Discover Card.

Because of the high usage fees and commissions they are billed, many smaller tourist related establishments have been known to charge an additional 3% to 5% surcharge for using these credit cards instead of cash. The fact is that these surcharges are definitely not permitted by the credit card companies, and can be successfully disputed upon your return from

The Bahamas if the documentation and receipts clearly show a lower cash price for the same products or services. It is a good idea to have a combination of cash, travelers checks, and credit cards to use during your travels.

Another advantage to bringing your credit cards is that if you need a cash advance, this may be possible (depending on your specific credit card company's policies about using special pre-arranged PIN number access).

Travelers Checks

In most places travelers checks are easily accepted. One suggestion is that you should try to keep the denominations fairly small so the cashier will have enough cash on hand to give you proper change, and so you won't get stuck with too much Bahamian currency. While Thomas Cook and Visa travelers checks are usually not a problem, American Express Travelers Checks are much more widely accepted.

Also, with American Express, if you have lost or stolen checks, their refund centers in Nassau and Freeport can be reached from anywhere in The Bahamas for prompt replacements. You might also try to call American Express collect at *(919) 333-3211* for a U.S. travelers check refund and replacement office.

- **American Express in Nassau**, *Shirley Street, Tel. (242) 322-2931*
- **American Express in Freeport**, *Regent Centre 4, Tel. (242) 352-6641*

Electronic Cash Transfers

If you have a major problem and need to receive some cash quickly while on vacation, the easiest way is via **Western Union**, which has an international money transfer service. For a fee of around 6% to 12%, a friend or relative back home can call Western Union with their credit card and arrange a cash transfer to be processed to you in either Nassau or Freeport.

You must present an official ID such as a passport and wait on line at the British-American Bank branch to get these funds during normal banking hours only. The process takes about an hour after the call has been made.

- **British-American Bank in Nassau**, *Frederick Street, Tel. (242) 325-3273*
- **British-American Bank in Freeport**, *East Mall Drive, Tel. (242) 352-6676*

INTERNET USE & INFORMATION

This is one area that Bahamians have to be dragged kicking and screaming into the 20th-century. At press time I still could not find one service provider or "electronic café" where I could easily plug in my laptop and pay by the hour for brief Internet service from The Bahamas to anywhere else. There are in fact a few Nassau-based Internet access providers, but they are for yearly subscription only and are not geared for traveling business people and computer freaks that are here for brief time periods. My best suggestion is to call a local computer shop and ask if you can do a quick E-Mail upload or download using their own Internet line and address (perhaps offer them a few dollars for the favor!).

In terms of getting accurate details about The Bahamas from the Internet while still at home, there has been some progress. A recent search on my regular net service provider via the Netscape browser led me to well over 200 pages of text and images of tourism-related topics and establishments. I was able to pre-plan several aspects of my last trip using the available maps, weather charts, hotel and restaurant descriptions, history, and general island information found via links at some of the web sights listed below.

Try some of these Internet addresses for further information. Happy surfing!

http://www.interknowledge.com/bahamas
http://www.bahama-out-islands.com
http://www.microstate.com/pub/micros/bahamas
http://www.odci.gov/cia/publications/95fact/bf.html
http://www.opendoor.com/Bahamas-bahamas/Hotels
http://www.bahamasnet.com
http://www.caribbean-on-line.com
http://flamingo.bahamas.net

NEWSPAPERS & MAGAZINES

There is a vast assortment of local and imported English language dailies and weeklies that can easily be purchased at any newsstand, hotel lobby, or local tobacco shop. Major local dailies include the Nassau-based *Tribune* and *Guardian* papers. If you search around the major city and resort area newsstands, you may also find current copies of the *European Wall Street Journal, The New York Times, The London Times, International Herald Tribune, Miami Times, The European,* and *USA Today.*

Current editions of magazines such as *Time, Newsweek, Playboy, Rolling Stone, Cosmopolitan, GQ, The National Inquirer, The Economist,* and *Penthouse* are also available at newsstands and at the gift shops in leading hotels.

NIGHTLIFE

Each city and town in The Bahamas has a vast assortment of evening entertainment. There are several venues where you can enjoy Reggae concerts, jazz bands, casual conversation, heavy disco action, and even casino gaming (see *Casinos* above). Among the more typical places to hang out for Bahamian people are each town's little **bars** (on small islands these places may have domino games or pool tables), where a beer like locally brewed *Kalik* costs around $3.75 and a mixed drink can go for about $4.50. At hotel bars, big discos, beach-side bars, and tourist infested areas the beers can cost upwards of $5 each and drinks can go up to $7.50 a piece.

Most younger Bahamian residents tend to hit the bars and clubs by around 10:00pm on Friday and Saturday nights, and stay at just one or two different places until closing time (somewhere between 2:00am and 5:00am depending on local requirements). The club scene in Nassau is becoming rather exciting, and one-night stands are still a frequent occurrence here. If you are going to spend the night with someone while here, make sure you are smart and safe about it.

I have included lists of local nightlife in each island's chapter, but you should always try to ask a few like-minded local residents or night shift taxi drivers to fill you in on the most happening spots.

POST OFFICES & MAIL

Throughout the country there is a good network of post offices that are open from around 8:30am until about 5:30pm from Monday through Friday, some with limited Saturday morning hours from 8:30am until 12:30pm. Letters sent via air mail from The Bahamas to North America normally cost around 55 cents per 14 grams (1/2 once) and can still take up to two weeks to arrive. Letters sent via mail boat from The Bahamas to North America cost about 45 cents per once and usually find their way to the addressee in about 3-4 weeks.

Postcards sent from The Bahamas to North America via airmail cost 40 cents each and may arrive in about 9 days. Letters between one Bahamian address and another via airmail cost 25 cents per ounce and can take between 4 and 11 days to arrive. For details about these and other postage-related topics, contact the state-run post office headquarters at: *East Hill Street, downtown Nassau, Tel. (242) 322-3344.*

You can also receive mail and telegrams via the **American Express Travel Services** offices in Nassau and Freeport if you contact Amex before you depart North America at *(800) 221-7282* and arrange for this special service. These client letter services are free to American Express cardholders, vacation clients, and traveler's check holders, but can sometimes be obtained by others for a small fee. Both DHL and Federal Express can deliver packages between North America and The Bahamas, and visa versa, within three business days.

Here are a few mail service addresses and phone numbers:
- **Bahamian Post Office Headquarters**, *Shirley Street, Nassau, Tel. (242) 322-3344*
- **DHL Worldwide Express**, *Nassau Street South, Nassau, Tel. (242) 325-8266*
- **Federal Express**, *Hillside Plaza 3, Nassau, Tel. (242) 325-2650*

RADIO

There are a growing number of Bahamian am and fm radio stations broadcasting every type of music and political talk show imaginable. The government's ZNS-1 radio station signal is beamed across The Bahamas 24 hours a day with a concentration of local news and current events programming. Most of the other commercialized stations have either religious talk shows or play lots of great soul, Reggae, Calypso, soft rock, or international music.

SAFETY ISSUES

After being in The Bahamas over a dozen times, I have never run into any problems. The only people that I personally know of that have been victims of street crime are those tourists stupid enough to be out late at night in bad neighborhoods looking to score drugs! To help avoid any chance of theft, make sure to remove or at least cover any visible items in the luggage or hatch area of rental cars. Do not leave luggage, cameras, or any type of valuable item within eyesight. If you have any special jewelry or other items you are traveling with, leave them in the safety deposit box or an in-room mini-safe at your hotel.

Always carry a wallet with less than $50 cash inside, and keep the rest of your cash, credit cards, and important papers in a separate money belt. Be careful about walking around dark and deserted city streets at night (especially in the back end of Nassau and Freeport). If you take these simple precautions, you are almost sure to all but avoid the possibility of a major problem. In case you run into a thief, just give up your wallet, let them run away, and then visit the nearest police station.

To make an insurance claim, assuming you have coverage on either your homeowner's or a special policy, you must have a copy of a detailed police report to report the incident. For **emergency assistance** anywhere in The Bahamas, just call *919* from any phone, and an emergency response team will usually be dispatched within a few minutes.

SHOPPING

Shopping in The Bahamas is a great pleasure. Both New Providence and Grand Bahama have literally hundreds of boutiques offering fine imported jewelry, Swiss and Japanese timepieces, Cuban cigars, fine European leather goods, lace, porcelain, bone china, perfume, linens, ceramics, embroidery, crystal, swim wear, imported liqueurs, and all sorts of additional items that can be found at about 25% below their typical North American price.

The majority of the jewelry sold here is made in Europe, with 10 though 18 karat gold, or better quality sterling silver. Remember that most retail stores are open from 9:00am until about 6:00pm from Monday through Friday, and from 10:00am and 5:00pm on Saturdays. Sunday retail hours do exist, but only in selected shopping centers and a few boutiques in the most touristy areas and larger cities. Several islands in The Bahamas also produce unique regional crafts such as straw products and wood carvings, which can easily be found in the shops, straw markets, crafts fairs, and artisan's kiosks.

The Bahamas has allowed so-called **Duty Free Shops** to sell such luxury items as china, crystal, watches, jewelry, cameras, sweaters, perfumes, wines, liquor, leather goods, and linen at prices that can range from 15% to 40% lower than at most North American retailers. There are no special forms to fill out or bonding procedures to worry about here; just carry your purchase and receipts with you and inform customs when you return back home. A number of local merchants display the **pink flamingo logo** that indicates they are accredited by the Bahamas Duty Free Association, which requires that they meet specific product quality levels and also sell only authentic brand name merchandise.

TAXES & SERVICE CHARGES

There are absolutely no additional sales taxes on items bought, or meals purchased, in The Bahamas. The way the government makes its money is by hitting almost every available retail item with **import duties** that are included in the price already and can range between 35% to 270%. This means that the $5.50 pack of American cigarettes or the $3.50 disposable pen that you would find in the stores are this expensive due to the duties alreadyincluded in the price tag. Duty free shops can sell you alcohol, tobacco, and luxury products free of these duties for use once you have left the islands. The only other important tax that you will need to be aware of is a $15 per person **departure tax** at the airport or cruise ship terminal upon your departure.

Most, but not all, restaurants will add a 15% **service charge** to all food and beverage orders instead of asking you to leave a tip. The only additional taxes and service charges that you will end up paying here are on the hotel rates. Hotel room tax is only 4%, but several hotels are also allowed to charge an additional 4% more if they are a member of a major official hotel association or promotion board. All inns and hotels are also allowed add a $5 per room per night service charge to cover tips for maid service.

If you are charged for a so-called "energy surcharge," dispute this as a ridiculous fee that is not legitimate. A surcharge for energy was first imposed during the short-lived Arab oil embargo of the 1970s and at the present time should not be added to your bill. If you have any debatable fees or surcharges added to your bill that you want to dispute, pay by credit card, keep an itemized bill showing the disputed charges, and send a carefully worded letter of complaint directly to your credit card company as soon as you get home.

TELEPHONES, TELEGRAMS, & FAXES

The phone system in The Bahamas is getting more modern and convenient to use, thanks to imported Canadian technology. To begin with, most pay phones provide detailed written instructions for local and international calling procedures. Of course, you could always place a local or long distance call from your hotel, but you can expect to get hit with a surcharge of up to 500% above pay phone rates. About the only time I suggest using a hotel's equipment is when I need to send or receive a call immediately. Another possibility is to place calls (or even faxes and telegrams) from just about any **Batelco** (Bahamas Telephone Company) business branch office. There you will be shown to a small cabin and after making a call you pay a reasonable rate.

The standard street corner digital screen pay phone accepts **Phonecards**, plastic cards that can be purchased in quantities of $5, $10, and $20 denominations that are available from Batelco offices, and a small assortment of shops that act as authorized Phonecard dealers. These cards keep track of every completed call, and show the balance, as well as the price of your current call, on a digital display on the phone.

Only about 25% of the pay phones in The Bahamas still accept coins, and most of these are found only in public establishments, hotel lobbies, and city street corners. Instead of taking a plastic Phonecard, these older devices accept only multiple coins of 25 cents and in most cases will not allow for long distance calls (off the island you are dialing from) unless they are made collect or third party. These pay phones need a minimum of 25 cents before processing a 5 minute local call.

I should also mention that many North American 800 and 888 numbers do not work in the normal way from The Bahamas. In many cases, you must instead dial 1-880 plus the last seven digits of the toll-free number and pay a surcharge of around $1 per minute. Many hotels will also charge a minimum of $5 per attempt for dialing functioning toll-free numbers, using your own telephone company charge card, third party or collect billing, or even letting an unanswered international call ring more than five times from the phone in your hotel room.

Batelco's headquarters in Nassau and a few large branch offices can also send **faxes** and **telexes** for those who need to send documents and messages around the globe. These selected phone company offices provide telex service at about $3 per minute to North America, and fax service for about $2.75 per page to North America. A new Batelco **video conferencing** service has been set up in Nassau and Freeport, but the rates are complicated, so call them directly for details. **Telegrams** are still the domain of the Bahamas Post Office and tend to cost 24 cents a word to North America if transmitted from their main offices in Nassau or Freeport.

Contact:
- **Batelco Centralized Telephone Office**, *East Street, Nassau, Tel. (242) 323-6414*
- **Bahamian Post Office Headquarters**, *Shirley Street, Nassau, Tel. (242) 322-3344*
- **Batelco Telex information**, *Tel. (242) 325-3790*
- **Batelco Video Conferencing**, *Tel. (242) 394-5000*

TELEPHONE BASICS

To Call the US and Canada from The Bahamas
Dial 1 followed by the desired North American area code and phone number.

To Call The Bahamas from the US and Canada
Dial 1-242 and then the 7 digit Bahamian phone number.

To Call Between Two Bahamian Islands
Dial 1-242 and then the 7 digit Bahamian phone number.

A typical call within one island should cost around 25 cents per 5 minutes. Calling from one Bahamian island to another region can bring the cost up to as much as 75 cents per minute. Calling internationally can cost $1.75 or more per minute. In general, calling long distance or internationally from The Bahamas is cheapest after 11pm on weekdays. If you need to call internationally, you can use MCI, Sprint, AT&T, Bell, and a variety of private phone company's access codes from within The

Bahamas to reach English speaking operators for collect, credit card, and third party calls. It is even possible to use these cards in the hotel's lobby pay phone.

When you use your North American calling card, or call collect from a hotel room, you may still end up paying at least a $5 surcharge on your hotel room bill. So use your hotel room phone sparingly or not at all if you can avoid it.

NEW AREA CODE & IMPORTANT PHONE NUMBERS

*The **area code** for The Bahamas recently changed from 809 to **242**. All phone and fax numbers listed in this book reflect this new area code, but many hotel and attraction brochures have not yet been reprinted with the new info!*

Here are some important phone numbers for your trip:

Bahamas Directory Assistance, *916*
International Operator Assistance, *0*
USA Country Code, *1*
Canada Country Code, *1*
USA Direct, *1-800-872-2881*
Canada Direct, *1-800-389-0004*
MCI Call USA, *1-800-964-8218*
Sprint Express, *1-800-389-2111*
Police & Fire Emergencies, *919*
Bahamas Air/Sea Rescue, *(242) 322-3877*
Weather Hotline, *915*
Exact Time of Day, *917*

Cellular Telephones

Cellular telephones are becoming quite popular in The Bahamas, but your North American cell phone will not function properly on Batelco's cellular operating system unless you pre-arrange **roaming privileges** down here. If you're like me, and like to have some means of communicating while on the road, you best option is to contact your cellular service provider to see if they have an agreement with Batelco. The normal fee is $3 per day and 99 cents per minute of use above your normal cellular rates. Those trying to reach you via cell phone while you are in The Bahamas may have to dial a special Batelco roaming access number (such as the one listed below), wait for a second dial tone, and then dial in your normal area code and phone number.

If you need to dial out of The Bahamas to a number in North America, use the normal long distance calling procedures listed above. The per minute incoming and outgoing charges vary depending on the hours and the locations the service will be used, but a quick call or fax to your cellular service provider should get you all the information you need.

• **Batelco Cellular Roaming Access Number**, *Tel. (242) 359-7626*

TELEVISION

Take advantage of the wide selection of local and satellite media that is easily available. To begin with, the country runs its own Broadcasting Corp. of The Bahamas television network called **ZNS** on Channel 13 of most normal, cable, and satellite televisions. They offer a 6+ hour a day schedule on weekdays, and a 10+ hour schedule on weekends of local news, English-language soap opera, international documentary, and North American sports programming. The signal reaches most of the Out Islands to some degree.

Many of the better hotels also offer a selection of other North American and European satellite TV programs (in some cases you will find CNN) on their satellite or cable televisions.

TIME

The Bahamas is located in the **Eastern Standard Time Zone** (GMT minus 5 hours). This means that the hour is the same as any North American Eastern Time Zone City such as New York, Boston, Washington, Philadelphia, Montreal, and Toronto.

They are 1 hour ahead of the North American Central Time Zone, 2 hours ahead of the North American Mountain Time Zone, and 3 hours ahead of the North American Pacific Time Zone. The Bahamas follows the same **daylight savings time** system plan as most of North America does from April through October.

TIPPING

There are many situations in which a gratuity may be appropriate. In most cases, just use your judgment based on the quality of services rendered. Below I've listed the most common services and amounts to tip. All-inclusive resorts may request that you do not tip their staff. If someone refuses a tip, do not take it as an insult.

- • Taxi Driver   8% of the agreed or metered rate.
- • Hotel Porter $1.50 bag
- • Airport Porter $1 per bag
- • Hotel Concierge $3 per small favor, $10 per big favor
- • Room Service $2 per person per meal
- • Hotel Doorman $1 per taxi
- • Bartender $1 per round
- • Waiter   10% to 15% of the bill if no service charge

- Private Guides $15 per person per day
- Private Drivers $15 per person per day
- Tour Guides $10 per person per day
- Tour Bus Drivers $7.50 per person per day

8. CRUISING TO THE BAHAMAS

All year long a number of small to massive cruise ships and luxury liners depart South Florida for 1, 3, and 4 day trips to the Bahamian ports of Nassau, Freeport, Lucaya, and several small private cays nearby. While the vessels, scheduling, ports of call, pricing, and typical passengers vary greatly from one cruise line to another, they all offers some of the same basic features.

Once at sea, you can enjoy exciting casino action, live music and entertainment, kids programs, plenty of duty-free shopping, onboard movie theaters, lounges, optional baby sitting services, and plenty of fun-filled scheduled activities. As many as seven meals a day are included in the cruise price (even when you are docked at port) and for a small surcharge a number of optional day trips and excursions (such as swim with the dolphin programs) may be booked while onboard.

Cabins come in all sizes and categories depending on how much you are willing to spend. Keep in mind that a port charge and departure tax of between $50 and $85 per person (including children) may not be included in the price, so ask for details when you reserve your space. Additional suggested tips totaling about $10 per passenger per day should also be anticipated.

The following is a listing of the major cruise lines operating in The Bahamas. Make sure to call around and compare prices between travel agencies, cruise-only discount agencies, and different cruise companies.

THE BIG RED BOAT
• *(800) 327-7113 in the US and Canada*
Known for creating exciting 3 and 4 day Bahamas cruises on medium-sized boats geared for families traveling with children, **The Big Red Boat** cruise lines has a 35,000 ton ship called the *Starship Atlantic* with 1,500 passengers, and a 39,000 ton vessel called the *Starship Oceanic* with 1,800

passengers. Each departs twice a week from Florida's Port Canaveral area (50 miles east of Orlando) for a night at sea, a full day docked in downtown Nassau, another evening at sea, a full day at Port Lucaya in Grand Bahama, and either one or two more nights at sea before returning to Port Canaveral.

When docked offshore from Port Lucaya, the passengers will board small tenders to transfer them to the adjacent Marina at the Port Lucaya Marketplace. The cruise's emphasis is mainly family-style vacations, including supervised kids programs, a kids activity center in the Port Lucaya Marketplace, optional baby-sitting service, available family-oriented day trips to the beach barbecue at Salt Cay, and much more.

Rates start at about $250 per adult double occupancy per cruise, and from $99 per child, plus $85 in port charges and departure taxes, for a 3 day cruise-only vacation. Add-on airfare and special pre- and post-cruise Walt Disney World packages are available from most major North American cities for a good price.

CARNIVAL CRUISE LINES
• *(800) 327-9501 in the US and Canada*

Carnival has several impressive mid-size to large modern luxury liners filled with active singles and couples of all ages that want to have some serious fun while visiting The Bahamas. Their giant new *Ecstasy* and *Fantasy* 70,000 ton vessels each hold upwards of 2,040 passengers each. The *Ecstasy* departs Miami on Fridays for an evening at sea, stays in Nassau all day and night on Saturday, and leaves Sunday morning to reach Miami by Monday morning. The *Fantasy* leaves Port Canaveral (about 50 miles east of Orlando) on Thursdays for a similar schedule as the *Ecstasy*, but also departs on Sundays for a 4 day cruise, including one full day in Nassau and a day plus evening in Freeport.

The rates begin at around $249.50 per adult double occupancy per cruise, plus about $99 per child, plus $85 in port charges and departure taxes per person. Known for great evening entertainment and large casinos, Carnival is a good way to go. Add-on airfare is available from most major North American cities.

DISCOVERY CRUISES
• *(800) 866-8687 in the US and Canada*

For a quick cruise to Freeport you can also choose to take **Discovery**. Their 11,000 ton *Discovery Sun* brings just under 1,000 passengers on Mondays, Wednesdays, and Sundays at 7:45am on a four hour cruise from Ft. Lauderdale to Freeport, and returns the same day at 5:00pm. They leave Ft. Lauderdale at 6:45am and return at 5:00pm on Fridays only.

Passengers can travel round-trip on the same day, or return after staying some time in The Bahamas.

The price is $148.99 per adult per cruise, and $88.99 per child under 12 years old, including meals, taxes, and port charges. Cabins may be rented for between $75 and $135 each way per couple or family. They also have fly/drive and resort packages available in Freeport.

DOLPHIN (MAJESTY) CRUISE LINES

• *(800) 222-1003 in the US and Canada*

The folks over at **Dolphin** schedule a nice relaxing 3 day cruise to The Bahamas aboard the 21,486 ton *Ocean Breeze* with some 776 passengers every Friday afternoon. The ship arrives in Nassau on Saturday morning, then on Sunday the occupants take a small tender to nearby Blue Lagoon Island, famous for its optional swim-with-the-dolphin excursions and fine sandy beaches, before returning to the main vessel to sail back to Miami by Monday morning.

The price is about $175 per person, plus $89.50 in port fees and taxes; for the third or fourth passenger in the same cabin (adults or children) the price is just $75 each plus the normal port fees and taxes.

NORWEGIAN CRUISE LINES

• *(800) 327-7030 in the US and Canada*

NCL offers great 3 day Bahamas cruises from Miami aboard their intimate 25,000 ton *Leeward* ship once a week all year. You and another 949 passengers will spend Friday evening at sea, most of Saturday docked offshore downtown Nassau, Saturday evening at sea, most of Sunday at their private island getaway at Great Stirrup Cay, Sunday evening at sea, and an early Monday morning disembarkation in Miami.

Cruise-only prices start at just $250 per adult double occupancy (discounted additional children's' rates available) per cruise, plus $78.50 per person in port charges and departure taxes. The crowd is a good mix of first time and repeat cruisers of all ages, and is heavily favored by couples and families looking for a quick break away from big city life. Add-on airfare is available from most major North American cities for a reasonable surcharge.

ROYAL CARIBBEAN CRUISE LINES

• *(800) 327-6700 in the US and Canada*

RCCL has, in my experience, continued to run the most comfortable and luxurious cruise line vacations available to The Bahamas. Known for its fine gourmet cuisine, personal service, world-class entertainment, and superb spacious cabins, their medium-sized 45,000 ton *Nordic Empress* vessel carries 1,598 discriminating passengers and departs each Friday night from Miami on superb 3 day cruises that include a full day in Nassau and a full day on their Coco Cay private island and beach area. The same ship also departs on Mondays from Miami for a 4 day trip similar to the above that also includes a full day in Freeport.

Cruise-only prices for this wonderful adventure at sea start at about $279 per adult per cruise, free for children under 12 in most cases, plus $79 in port charges and departure taxes per person. They also have great Walt Disney World add-on vacation packages in top rated hotels and resorts, as well as add-on airfares from most big American and Canadian cities.

SEAESCAPE CRUISES

• *(800) 327-7400 in the US and Canada*

For those interested in good affordable same-day cruise transportation between South Florida and Freeport, SeaEscape is a really good way to travel. The 39,000 ton *Scandinavian Dawn* departs Ft. Lauderdale at 8:00am laden with up to 1,070 passengers embarking on a four hour long voyage to The Bahamas on Sundays, Mondays, and Wednesdays, and returns the same days at 4:45pm. Each Friday the schedule shifts to a 7:00am Ft. Lauderdale departure and a 2:15pm return voyage from Freeport. You can either sail round-trip on the same day, or better yet arrange to cruise back on a later date after vacationing a while in The Bahamas.

Prices start at $118 per cruise including meals, all taxes, and port charges, $88 for children under 11 years old; optional cabins cost just $60 extra each direction per couple or family. They also offer optional gourmet dining upgrades to the fabulous "Windows on the Ocean" dining room, optional transfers from major Ft. Lauderdale hotels, kids programs, and a full range of inexpensive hotel and rent a car packages on Freeport.

9. GETTING AROUND THE BAHAMAS

BY AIR

Getting from one Bahamian island to another is usually a rather simple task if you make the arrangements well in advance. In terms of regularly scheduled service, **Bahamasair** (the government-owned national airline of The Bahamas) has a monopoly on many of the inter-island routes. They offer a series of flights on a variety of mid-size *Shorts* and *Dash* commuter prop planes between more than 16 islands, that almost always require a change of plane (or in some cases an overnight) in Nassau. These flights are often sold out and should be reserved as far in advance as possible.

For those who prefer non-stop service to or between some of the lesser developed yet most beautiful Out Island destinations, a special charter flight may become necessary. The following information is designed to help you figure out the best and easiest ways to fly from one place to another. For further details, contact the specific airline or charter company directly.

Bahamasair

About the best and most affordable way to fly between the islands of The Bahamas is to take **Bahamasair**, the national carrier of the Bahamas. They offer a wide variety of comfortable direct and connecting flights on medium-sized *Dash* and *Shorts* prop planes between Nassau International airport and other destinations such as Grand Bahama, Cat Island, Andros, Eleuthera, Exuma, Abaco, San Salvador, Long Island, and other smaller cays. Their service is either daily or in some cases just several times weekly.

Most of these exceedingly well maintained planes can hold between 24 and 46 passengers each, do not have first or business class sections, and require that confirmed passengers check-in a minimum of one hour early to be guaranteed a seat. The maximum luggage weight per person is 70 pounds, above which additional charges will apply.

The lowest currently published fares to the Out Islands tend to start at between $84 and $204 round-trip from Nassau, depending on the exact location you wish to travel to. A new special "Miami to Nassau + 3 Out Islands" pass allows for travel from Miami to Nassau and then on to any three of their normally serviced Bahamian destinations (excluding Grand Bahama) before returning to Miami for just $350 plus taxes.

Additionally, when traveling with an adult, children under 12 years old may qualify for 50% discounts rates, while infants under 2 years of age sitting on an adult's lap may be entitled to travel for free. There are a limited number of discounted seats per flight, special advance purchase requirements, specific dates of validity, and cancellation & revision penalties that may apply to all of the above, so call Bahamasair reservations (open 7 days a week) or your travel agent, for exact details.

The overall service and comfort level offered to all passengers on Bahamasair flights is good. Make sure your checked luggage tags are marked to the correct final destination, and in the event of lost baggage you may be entitled to as much as a $600 per person automatic insurance coverage.

• **Bahamasair Reservations in North America**, *(800) 222-4262*
• **Bahamasair Reservations in Nassau**, *(242) 377-8222*
• **Bahamasair Reservations in Freeport**, *(242) 352-8341*

Charter Flights Between Islands

As I mentioned above, there are several routes from either Florida to the Out Islands or between Bahamian island destinations that are either not serviced by Bahamasair on the necessary day, or require an overnight in Nassau to complete. In these cases it may be a good idea to check with your host Out Island hotel or the Out Islands Promotion Board for details about arranging a special charter flight.

The following is a brief listing of some of the most popular charter flight companies that tend to charge anywhere between $80 to $450 per person for customized on-demand or scheduled semi-charter flight services on small to mid-sized single and twin engine planes.

• **Cleare Air**, *Tel. (242) 377-0341*
• **Congo Air**, *Tel. (242) 377-5382, Fax (242) 377-7413*
• **Falcon Air**, *Tel. (242) 377-1700*
• **Fernandez Bay**, *Tel. (305) 474-4821, Fax (242) 474-4864*
• **Hawks Nest**, *Tel. (242) 357-7257, Fax (242) 357-7257*
• **Island Express**, *Tel. (305) 359-0380, Fax (305) 359-7944*
• **Island Air**, *Tel. (305) 359-9942*
• **Pinder's Charters**, *Tel. (242) 377-7320*

· **Reliable Air Svc.**, *Tel. (242) 377-7335, Fax (242) 377-8910*
· **Sky Unlimited**, *Tel. (242) 377-8993*
· **Small Hope Bay**, *Tel. (305) 359-8240, Fax (242) 368-2015*
· **Stella Marris**, *Tel. (305) 359-8236, Fax (305) 359-8238*
· **Taino Air**, *Tel. (242) 352-8885, Fax (242) 352-5175*

Private Planes

An increasing number of private planes find their way to the various islands of The Bahamas each and every year. With landing fees ranging around $6 and parking costs averaging about $5.50 a day, this is a rather affordable proposition. Just be sure to fill out the all the appropriate customs and immigration forms.

The best sources for general information about the conditions, fees, specifications, and regulations for flying around down here is via the *AOPA Bahamas Flying Kit*, as well as *The Pilot's Guide to The Bahamas and Caribbean* by Tom Jones. These can be ordered from any FBO or major book shop in North America and the Bahamas.

BY BUS

There are no government buses in The Bahamas. All of the jitney buses that operate along the main roads of Nassau and Freeport are privately owned and have a limited amount of passenger liability insurance. Details about bus travel can be found in each destination chapter throughout this guide.

BY CAR

Unlike some other countries in the region, The Bahamas is a relatively easy place to drive around. To begin with, the steering wheel and all other controls are placed exactly where they would be in your own car at home. The only hitch is that like many former British colonies, **you must drive on the left side of the road!** The odd thing is that unlike Britain, most cars here are US models that still have their steering wheel on the left side as well. While automatic shift vehicles are most common, you can also get a manual transmission jeep or sport utility vehicle if available. Ask the rental car company or your hotel's front desk to give you detailed directions to your next location, as maps may not point out serious construction delays. Typical speed limits are about 45 miles per hour on highways and 30 miles per hour on smaller roads.

A small percentage of Bahamians seem to drive faster than necessary. Expect a few other cars to pass on blind curves and sometimes even pull multiple lane changes at high speeds. If you drive very carefully, remember to bear left, and stay in the appropriate lane for your desired velocity, you should be just fine. All of the roads here are in rather good condition, with no tolls to worry about (except for the ridiculous $2 fee on the Paradise Island Bridge), and have international road signs. Official speeds are always posted in miles per hour and the use of seat belts and child seats is mandatory. While they exist, speed traps and radar have not been put into widespread use here.

Gasoline is expensive in The Bahamas. At press time, gas costs approximately $2.35 per gallon. Since most of the rental vehicles on New Providence and Grand Bahama are rather small, typical fuel efficiency is very high. On the Out Islands the cars are older, bigger, and may use twice the gas per mile. Over the last several years, many 24-hour 7 days a week service stations complete with repair shops and mini-markets have popped up throughout Nassau and Freeport and accept most major credit cards. Normal service station hours are from 8am until 7pm Monday through Sunday, but a small percentage of gas stations may close on Sundays.

There is no official automobile club representative in The Bahamas for members of the AAA and the CAA auto clubs. The only advice I have is to buy a good road map, and get the local phone numbers for your rental agency's emergency assistance offices. In the event of an accident, you should call the police to come to the scene of the accident, write down the license plate of the other car(s) involved, and if possible hand-copy his license and insurance information. If no police arrive on the scene within 45 minutes or so, pay a visit the closest police station, report the accident, and ask them to give you a copy of the accident report or the report number. Call your car rental company as soon as possible after you have obtained the required documentation.

Perhaps the only major drawback to driving through The Bahamas is the severe daily rush hours in and around big cities, the left-hand driving regulations (especially difficult at traffic circles), and the expense and difficulty of parking. It seems that there are at least four cars for every available parking space Nassau and Freeport. Parking spots are typically indicated by a sign, and some of the street side parking spots use coin meters. Tickets and tow trucks are often used for illegally parked cars, and can cost you upwards of $50 per infraction (and much, much more if you are towed).

Several private and municipal parking lots (found by following the white "P" signs with blue backgrounds) can be found in each city, but some close rather early. Most of these garages cost about $2 per hour and somewhere around $10 per 24 hours. Hotels usually have free valet or self-park facilities that are free of charge for their guests.

BOOKING CAR RENTALS

Almost all major airlines arrive at either **Nassau International Airport** or **Freeport International Airport**. For those of you who want to immediately pick up a car upon arrival at these airports, an abundance of well-known international rental car companies operate both airport kiosks and resort area or downtown offices all over New Providence and Grand Bahama islands. Avis, Budget, Hertz, and several smaller companies maintain airport hours from early each morning until the early evening 7 days a week.

On the Out Islands there are no major rental car company offices, and you are usually at the mercy of a limited number of local merchants that have older (and much less well maintained) used American cars. International drivers licenses are not required for North Americans driving in The Bahamas, but it's not a bad idea to visit the CAA or AAA offices and get one for about $17.50. All that is required for car rental documentation is a driver over the age of 25, a major credit card, a cash or credit card security deposit of between $300 and $500, a passport, and your valid US or Canadian drivers license.

If you intend to use a rental car on New Providence or Grand Bahama, it is advisable to book well in advance from North America so that you can save up to 25% of the normal locally available Bahamian rates. If you decide to rent a car only once you have arrived in The Bahamas, rentals can be arranged from any local travel agency or car rental company office. I strongly advise those desiring to rent a car on the Out Islands to to confirm the rental at least a couple of days in advance, so that you can arrange a free pickup, or inexpensive taxi transfer, from the airport of arrival to the typically distant car rental establishment.

It is also important to call your credit card company before you leave to determine if any insurance is automatically included for car rentals there. Most forms of insurance (collision damage waiver with a $250 deductible, vehicle theft, personal accident injury insurance, property theft insurance) will be offered upon your pickup of the car and may add up to well over $16 per day additional. Make sure that you are covered one way or another, or else you may wind up with a big problem.

With advance booking from the US or Canada, non-inclusive prices in the Nassau and Freeport area usually cost below $295 per week for a small 2-door automatic transmission air conditioned car (Suzuki Swift hatchback or similar), plus insurance. On some of the Out Islands you may sometimes have no choice but to pay upwards of $80 a day and $425 per week for a gas eating 4-door 1980s sedan with automatic transmission and bad tires, with a $500 deductible on the collision insurance. I have only listed the best Out Island rental agencies with the most reliable cars in this book. There is no tax on car rentals in The Bahamas.

Major Car Rental Companies in North America
- **AutoEurope in the US**, *(800) 223-5555*
- **AutoEurope in Canada**, *(800) 223-5555*
- **Avis in the US**, *(800) 331-1084*
- **Avis in Canada**, *(800) 879-2847*
- **Budget in the US**, *(800) 527-0770*
- **Budget in Canada**, *(800) 268-8900*
- **Hertz in the US**, *(800) 654-1101*
- **Hertz in Canada**, *(800) 263-0600*

Scooter Rentals

While motor scooters may be rented on several Bahamian islands by those 18 and older with a major credit card and a valid drivers license, I strongly suggest that you do not use motorized scooters (mopeds) on New Providence and Grand Bahama due to the high amount of serious accidents involving scooters. If you intend to ignore my advice, expect to spend between $35 and $50 per day for the rental of these vehicles including insurance, plus gas.

BY FERRY

There are a still more than a few ferry lines that run between various islands and cays in The Bahamas. The most utilized ferry services are the small private boats that run from Prince George's Dock behind downtown Nassau's Straw Market and head over **from Nassau to Paradise Island** at the bridge or Casuarina Drive. These run 7 days a week every 30 minutes in each direction between 9:30am and 6:00pm, and cost $2 per person each way.

Additionally there is private ferry service between the 3 Island Dock **from Eleuthera to Harbour Island** at the Government Pier just of Bay Street. The price for this service is $4 per person including luggage, and there are almost always boats available for immediate departure in both directions from about 7am until about 7pm every day of the week. Other major ferries and water taxis include the run **from Abaco to Green Turtle Cay** and back three times every day for $8 per person, and the ferry **from Abaco to Hope Town (Elbow Cay)** twice a day at just $8 per person each way.

BY MAILBOAT

For those of you with plenty of time and are looking for an unusual and affordable way to go, I suggest buying tickets for one of the many Mail and Freight Boats that service the nation. Adventurous travelers can either book a cabin, sleep on bunk beds, or in some cases sack out right on the open air decks of these somewhat noisy diesel powered vessels, and arrive many hours later at the scheduled destination. The prices listed below do not include an optional cabin that usually costs a little bit more, and must be reserved as far in advance as possible.

Since these boats are used mostly by locals, its a great way to meet interesting Bahamians. Make sure to pack plenty of food and drinks for the voyage! Below is a list of the most popular mailboat rides for those island hopping in The Bahamas, but many others exist. Since these schedules are both incomplete and known to change frequently due to weather conditions, I strongly suggest calling the **Nassau Harbour Master's offices**, *Tel. (242) 393-1064.*

Most of these ships depart from Nassau's bustling Potter's Cay Dock just east of the Paradise Island Bridge:

- **Bahamas Daybreak III** - Departs Nassau each Monday at 5:00pm for a 5+ hour trip to the **Eleuthera** destinations of Rock Sound, Davis Harbour, and South Eleuthera. Returns to Nassau from Eleuthera on Tuesday at 10:00pm. Price is $20 each way.
- **Lisa J. II** - Departs Nassau each Wednesday at 3:30pm for a 5+ hour trip to the **Andros** destinations of Nicholls Town, Mastic Point, and Morgans Bluff. Returns to Nassau from Andros on Tuesday at 12noon. Price is $30 each way.
- **Mia Dean** - Departs Nassau each Tuesday at 8:00pm for a 12+ hour trip to the **Abaco** destinations of Marsh Harbour, Treasure Cay, Green Turtle Cay, and Hope Town. Returns to Nassau from Abaco on Thursday at 7:00pm. Price is $45 each way.
- **Sherice M** - Departs Nassau each Tuesday at 1:00pm for a 15+ hour trip to the **Long Island** destinations of Salt Pond, Deadman's Cay, and Seymour's. Returns to Nassau from Long Island on Thursday. Price is $45 each way.
- **Abilin** - Departs Nassau each Tuesday at 12noon for a 17+ hour trip to the **Long Island** destinations of Clearence Town and then heads for **Inagua**. Returns to Nassau from Inagua on Saturday. Price is $45 one way.
- **Eleuthera Express** - Departs Nassau each Monday at 7:00pm for a nearly 6 hour trip to the **Eleuthera** destinations of Governor's Harbour and Spanish Wells. Returns to Nassau from Eleuthera on Tuesday at 8:00pm. Price is $20 each way.
- **Current Pride** - Departs Nassau each Thursday at 7:00am for a 7 1/2 + hour trip to the **Eleuthera** destinations of The Current and The Bluff. Returns to Nassau from Eleuthera on Tuesday at 10:30am. Price is $20 each way.
- **Champion II** - Departs Nassau each Tuesday at 8:00pm for a 11+ hour trip to the **Abaco** destinations of Sandy Point, Moore's Island, and

Bullock Harbour. Returns to Nassau from Abaco on Thursday at 11:00am. Price is $25 one way.

- **North Cat Island Special** - Departs Nassau each Wednesday at 1:00pm for a 14+ hour trip to the **Cat Island** destinations of Arthur's Town, Bennett's Harbour, Bluff, and The Bight. Returns to Nassau from Cat Island on Saturday at 6:00am. Price is $40 one way.
- **Sea Hauler** - Departs Nassau each Tuesday at 3:00pm for a 7+ hour trip to the **Cat Island** destinations of Smith's Bay, The Bught, and Old Bight. Returns to Nassau from Cat Island on Sunday. Price is $30.
- **Grand Master** - Departs Nassau each Tuesday at 2:00pm for a 12+ hour trip to the **Exuma** destination of George Town. Returns to Nassau from Exuma on Friday at 7:00am. Price is $35.

TOURIST INFORMATION CENTRES

Several islands of The Bahamas have an extremely convenient government-run **Tourist Information Centre** available to all visitors. Typically operated by The Bahamas' powerful **Ministry of Tourism**, these are the best places to pick up hundreds of free brochures about that island's attractions. The friendly and knowledgeable staff members at these information centers can also provide tourists with extremely useful detailed maps of all the local sights and beaches, help you book all sorts of excursions, arrange private customized tours and talented guides, put you in touch with recommended charter boat and fishing trip operators, and give you great advice on where to find some of the off the beaten path sights that only a local would ever know about.

Most, but not all, of these information offices are open during regular retail business hours, so on Saturday afternoons and all day on Sundays they are usually closed. The following is a listing of where you can find these Tourism Information Centres. Islands without separate tourist offices may have some of the same types of assistance and brochures available at one of their Island Commissioner's offices.

- **Nassau, New Providence**, *(Rawson Square), Bay Street, Tel. (242) 326-9781*
- **Nassau, New Providence**, *(Main Airport Arrivals Terminal), Tel. (242) 377-6806*
- **Freeport, Grand Bahama**, *(International Bazzar), Tel. (242) 352-8044*
- **Governor's Harbour, Eleuthera**, *(Queen's Highway), Tel. (242) 332-2142*
- **Harbour Island, Eleuthera**, *(Bay Street), Tel. (242) 333-2621*
- **George Town, Exuma**, *(Queen's Highway), Tel. (242) 336-2430*
- **Marsh Harbour, Abaco**, *(Main Road), Tel. (242) 367-3067*

10. SPORTS & RECREATION

The following is a brief description of the kinds of sports and recreational activities you can expect to enjoy in The Bahamas. Check with local tourist information offices on each island for the locations and specific information regarding venues and outfitters for all types of sports.

BEACHES & SWIMMING

With thousands of miles of secluded coastline, there are hundreds of small, medium, and large beaches to enjoy in The Bahamas. While only a few offer changing rooms, life guards, or other services, the following are what I consider to be the finest, easily reached beaches in the country. Please let me know what other places you feel should also be considered for inclusion in future editions of this book.

Most of these beaches are easily accessible by foot, car, or taxi, and have great offshore snorkeling possibilities:
• **Pink Sand Beach**, *Harbour Island, Eleuthera*
• **Tropic of Cancer Beach**, *Little Exuma, Exuma*
• **Little Twin Beach**, *James Cistern, Eleuthera*
• **Cabbage Beach**, *Paradise Island, New Providence*
• **Town Beach**, *Hope Town, Elbow Cay, Abaco*
• **Lighthouse Beach**, *Bannerman Town, Eleuthera*
• **Fernandez Bay Beach**, *Fernandez Bay, Cat Island*
• **Ocean Beach**, *Green Turtle Cay, Abaco*
• **National Park Beach**, *East End, Grand Bahama*
• **Cable Beach**, *Cable Beach, New Providence*

BICYCLE RIDING

The Bahamas is a truly wonderful place to ride bicycles, especially since much of it is flat. Most hotels have basic one speed to more fancy 21 speed bicycles for rent at around $10 per day.

BOATING

For those interested in casual sailing during their vacation, most seaside hotels and resorts rent out Hobie Cats, Sunfish, and wind-surfers at around $25 per day. If a more serious sailing experience is desired, there are hundreds of available bareboat and crewed yachts available for charter via any major marina and can cost between $300 and $1,250 per day.

Power boats are also easy to find, and can range in size from Boston Whalers at around $70 per day, to giant luxury cabin cruisers with equally inflated prices. For more specific information, contact the BTO or your travel agent.

Boat Excursions

There are also dozens of excursion operators that run full and half-day trips from New Providence and Grand Bahama aboard schooners, catamarans, glass bottom boats, submarines, party boats, and high speed power boats. Check each island's chapter for a full list of excursion operators offering day trips on all sort of boats – even submarines.

FISHING

With well over 5,400 square miles of sea surrounding the islands of The Bahamas, there is plenty of superb deep sea and reef fishing. Grouper, marlin, snapper, tuna, billfish, barracuda, bonefish, and wahoo are among the many fish commonly caught here. No special fishing license is required for visiting anglers here, and there are well over 1,500 skippers that would be quite happy to take you out for a half day (about $300) or full day (about $550) on a private fishing charter with all the necessary gear and bait.

An assortment of local fishing operators also offer 3 to 4 hour scheduled fishing trips aboard their boats when they can get at least 5 other individuals to go, and they charge around $40 per person for the trip. The most famous deep sea fishing destinations are the Out Islands of **Bimini**, **Abaco**, **Cat Island**, and **Andros**, while there are also excellent bonefishing spots in the shallow flats of **Eleuthera** and **Exuma**. But there is plenty of good sport fishing off just about every other island. There are 28 regularly scheduled tournaments each year, most of which are open to visitors and residents alike.

For further details on fishing outfitters, charter boats, inexpensive fishing boat trips, and marina services, please check each island's listings.

GOLF

There are several fine 9 hole and 18 hole championship golf courses in The Bahamas. Green fees average around $60 per person per round, plus about $30 for cart rentals. Reservations are required, and many hotels have either discounts at these clubs, or offer complimentary green fees in their all-inclusive rates.

On New Providence Island, you can golf at:
- **Cable Beach Golf Club**, *18 holes, 7,040 yards/par 72. Tel. (242) 327-6000*
- **South Ocean Golf Resort**, *18 holes, 6,707 yards/par 72. Tel. (242) 362-4391*
- **Paradise Island Golf Club**, *18 holes, 6,770 yards/par 72. Tel. (242) 363-3000*

On Grand Bahama Island, you can golf at:
- **Lucaya Country Club**, *18 holes, 6,824 yards/par 72. Tel. (242) 373-1444*
- **Emerald Golf Course**, *18 holes, 6,679 yards/par 72. Tel. (242) 352-6721*
- **Ruby Golf Course**, *18 holes, 6,750 yards/par 72. Tel. (242) 352-6721*
- **Fortune Hills Golf Club**, *18 holes, 6,560 yards/par 72. Tel. (242) 373-4500*

On Eleuthera, you can golf at:
- **Cotton Bay Golf Club**, *18 holes, 7,068 yards/par 72. Tel. (242) 334-6101*

On Abaco, you can golf at:
- **Treasure Cay Golf Club**, *18 holes, 6,985 yards/par 72. Tel. (242) 365-8578*

HORSEBACK RIDING

Unfortunately, there are a limited number of horseback riding trips offered in The Bahamas. The best trips I have experienced have been with **Happy Trails Stables** in the Coral Harbour section of New Providence Island at *Tel. (242) 362-1820*. For about $30 a person (including free hotel pick-up service from Nassau or Paradise Island) you can enjoy a great ride through the trails and the beaches of the island's south coast.

Over on Grand Bahama, about $35 can get you a nice hour long ride through forest trails and deserted beaches with the folks at **Pinetree Stables** on North Beachway Drive at *Tel. (242) 373-3600*. Kids can get pony rides at **Cantalupa Riding School** near Carmichael Road on the south shore of New Providence Island at *Tel. (242) 361-7101*.

JET SKIING

Jet Skis are available for around $30 per half hour along Cable Beach and Paradise Island on New Providence, as well as at Taino, Lucaya, and Xanadu beaches on Grand Bahama Island. Hotels are not allowed to offer this sport due to insurance and safety reasons, so there are no jet skis offered as part of any all-inclusive package anywhere in The Bahamas.

SCUBA DIVING

There are several great dive sites off of virtually every island here. While the immense Barrier Reef (the third largest in the world!) just off of **Andros** is perhaps the most well-known dive in The Bahamas, there are also exciting adventures to be found near Eleuthera, Cat Island, Abaco, Bimini, Long Island, San Salvador, Grand Bahama, and the south shore of New Providence Island. You can find plenty of fish-filled coral reefs, wrecks of all vintages, high velocity tidal currents, shark feeding sights, and sea walls.

If you wish to dive here you must first present a valid PADI or NAUI certification. If you are not already certified and wish to learn how to enjoy this fascinating sport, you have two choices. Most major resorts offer complimentary 1 hour "resort courses" in their swimming pool for beginners. From there you can take a supervised shallow (25' or so) one tank ocean dive for around $45 a person, and perhaps be allowed to take a much deeper dive (65' or so) the next day with the same operator. If you prefer to become certified here, it takes about 4 to 5 days in a row of comprehensive instruction and first-hand underwater training, including mandatory theory classes, and costs about $450 a person.

Once you are certified, you can expect to pay somewhere around $40 for a 1 tank dive, $60 for a 2 tank dive, and $50 for a 1 tank night dive including rental gear, a diving master, and transportation to and from the sight via boat. Rentals of gear, underwater cameras, and special private trips can be easily arranged by all local dive operators. Check each chapter for listings of suggested local dive shops.

SNORKELING

In many cases, all you need to do to enjoy fantastic snorkeling in The Bahamas is just find a nice beach and jump in the water. For a more unusual experience you may want to consider spending about $25 for a half-day snorkel excursion offered by many area dive shops, tour operators, and hotel guest services desks. These trips require no special skills or licenses from their participants, and often go to secluded beaches and deserted islands.

Other available trips include a full day of snorkeling on several locations with a lunch of fresh speared lobster for around $60 per person. I have listed many of these excursions in each island chapter, and most scuba centers also offer snorkeling trips daily.

These are my picks for the five best snorkel trips you can take:

- **Jean Michel-Cousteau Out Islands Snorkel Program**, *see sidebar on page 90*
- **Lincoln Jones Tours**, *Green Turtle Cay, Abaco, Tel. (242) 365-4223*
- **Small Hope Bay**, *Andros, Tel. (242) 368-2014*
- **Rainbow Inn**, *Eleuthera, Tel. (242) 335-0294*
- **Fernandez Bay Village**, *Cat Island, Tel. (954) 474-4821*

THE BEST DIVE PROGRAMS

Small Hope Bay Lodge, Andros, Tel. (242) 368-2014

Stuart Cove's Dive Center, New Providence, Tel. (242) 362-5227

Underwater Explorers Society, Grand Bahama, Tel. (242) 373-1250

Dive, Dive, Dive, New Providence, Tel. (242) 362-1143

Stella Maris Resort, Long Island, Tel. (242) 336-2106

Dive Abaco, Abaco, Tel. (242) 367-2887

Bimini Undersea Adventures, Bimini, Tel. (242) 347-3089

Exuma Fantasea Scuba, Exuma, Tel. (242) 336-3483

Walker's Cay Undersea, Abaco, Tel. (242) 352-5252

Valentine's Dive Center, Harbour Island, Tel. (242) 333-3483

Unexso, Grand Bahama, Tel. (242) 352-3811

Brendal's Dive Shop, Abaco, Tel. (242) 365-9941

Nassau Scuba Center, New Providence, Tel. (242) 327-8150

Ramora Bay Dive Shop, Harbour Island, Tel. (242) 333-2323

Fernandez Bay Village, Cat Island, Tel. (954) 474-4821

TENNIS

You can play at private tennis centers and courts in many hotels and resorts in The Bahamas. If your hotel doesn't have tennis facilities, you can check with another hotel that offers courts for the exclusive use of their guests, but sometimes can be persuaded to welcome others. If you are looking for lessons or court time, you can inquire at either the front desk of your hotel, or at a local tourist information office for details and suggestions. Typical court fees are about $15 per hour outdoors, and $25 per hour on an indoor court.

JEAN-MICHEL COUSTEAU
BAHAMAS OUT ISLANDS SNORKELING ADVENTURES

A special new program created for the Bahamas Out Island Promotion Board in conjunction with marine biologist Jean-Michel Cousteau (son of famed scuba inventor Jacques Cousteau) has started on several locations in The Bahamas. The program includes a full day of intensive snorkeling at several coral reefs, wreck sights, and sea caverns off the island that you are staying on. Your guide for this event will not only open your eyes to the abundance of fish and marine life in The Bahamas, but will also educate you about underwater ecology and local history.

Among the coral reefs and wrecks you may encounter countless grouper, star fish, silverslides, sea cucumbers, striped grunts, snapper, stingrays, angelfish, sea urchins, porcupine fish, eels, lobster, sergeant majors, eagle rays, sponges, parrot fish, barracuda, and many more. The program is offered to visitors traveling to the Out Islands of Abaco, Andros, Bimini, Cat Island, Eleuthera, Exuma, Harbour Island, Long Island, and San Salvador. The price for this unique adventure, which includes two guided snorkeling trips and a souvenir T-shirt, starts at $97 per person (or $240 per person including your very own set of professional quality US Divers snorkeling gear to keep). This is the most intensive program of its type in the country.

For specific details and a full list of participating hotels and resorts, please contact the Bahamas Out Island Promotion Board toll-free at Tel. (800) 688-4752 before you depart from North America.

11. FOOD & DRINK

FOOD

There are several interesting dishes that have been a staple of the local diet for many centuries. Since the nation is surrounded by water, many of these native dishes are based on seafood, but several more are made with farm-raised animals that are common here. If you're the least bit adventurous, be open minded and try some odd sounding dishes. Every city has at least several great restaurants in all price ranges.

COMMON BAHAMIAN DISHES

chicken souse - a thick stew of chicken, peppers, onion, and spices
baked crab - a land crab stuffed with bread crumbs, crab meat, and vegetables
cracked conch - flattened conch meat that is breaded and lightly deep fried
coconut tart - a small pie baked with a sweetened and shredded coconut filling
conch fritters - bite-sized deep fried balls of dough with small pieces of conch
conch salad - marinated raw conch, onion, hot sauce, tomatoes, and peppers
fish chowder - made with rum, sherry, celery, tomato, and fish
               (usually grouper)
guava duff - a baked dough with eggs, butter, and the pulp of sweet guava
grouper fingers - deep fried strips of grouper fillet with tartar or cocktail sauce
Johnnycakes - a small stove-top cooked wheat bread
minced lobster - shredded lobster meat cooked in onions and tomatoes
peas & rice - rice cooked with pigeon peas, salt pork, tomatoes, and spices
steamed fish - usually grouper steamed and then smothered in Creole sauce
turtle soup - a spicy thick stew made with vegetables, spices, and turtle meat

---

DRINK

Throughout the islands, you will find the same selection of soon-familiar beverages. During breakfast, the most common drink is **coffee** at around $1 a cup, and is usually served along with either milk, condensed milk, or with cream in some better hotels. The **tea** here costs about the same amount as coffee and is offered in both regular and herbal varieties and is quite good. In the large hotels, you can also order an espresso or cappuccino for around $2.75 each, while decaffeinated instant coffee is available in most larger cities and resort areas.

As the day progresses, a much more varied selection of beverages will be available for consumption. Even though the **water** is officially safe to drink, tap water in any foreign country can have its risks, so I suggest always drinking bottled water. In The Bahamas there are many brands of great tasting local and European bottled waters. These waters cost about $1.75 per liter in a store and as much as $3.50 per liter in a restaurant. There is also an assortment of carbonated **soft drinks** like Coca Cola, Fanta orange and grape, ginger ale, and locally made Goombay Punch that cost about $1 per can in stores, and around $1.75 per glass in most restaurants. Fruit juices such as apple or orange are a bit more expensive here (around $2 for a small can) since they must be imported, and are usually from concentrate.

There are also some famous brands of Bahamian, American, and European **beer**. The most common types are pilsner and is close to what you normally can find at home. This medium strength (3.5% to 5% alcohol) beer typically costs between $3 and $5.50 per glass on tap or in a bottle, and includes Bahamian-brewed **Kalik** and a locally brewed version of Heineken. Some establishments may also offer Budwiser, Becks, and perhaps even Guinness stout. For a stronger kick, try a locally-made *Kalik Gold* at almost double the alcohol content for the same price.

Rum has always been a major beverage of choice in The Bahamas, and several varieties locally produced by companies such as Barcardi, Ricardo, and Todd Hunter can be found at any bar or restaurant. Imported liqueurs are found everywhere, and specialty drinks such as Goombay Smashes, Mud Slides, Kamikazes, Planter's Punch, Bahama Mamas, Pina Coladas, and Yellow Birds can cost between $4 and $6.50 each depending on where you order them.

Imported wine from France, Italy, Spain, Chile, and California is commonly available anywhere you go in The Bahamas. A bottle of good house wine or table wine should cost under $19 in a normal restaurant. Fancier labels start at around $38 in a gourmet restaurant, and about half that much in stores. The finest restaurants such as Graycliff and Buena Vista in Nassau offer rare auction-quality vintages costing upwards of $7,500 each!

EATING OUT

There are many good eating establishments in all price ranges. In almost every city chapter of this book you will see listings of several restaurants that I have enjoyed and can fully recommend, but I still suggest that you try to find a few gems on your own. It is easy to find great restaurants serving either regional or various forms of international cuisine by simply asking several locals or your hotel's front desk for a suggestion. Many restaurants accept Visa and Mastercard and will put their logo on the front door. American Express is not as widely accepted.

Breakfast is served from 7:00am until 10:00am and usually consists of eggs, toast, bacon or sausage, grits, and in a real Bahamian place there will also be Johnnycakes and several types of fish available. Lunch is normally taken somewhere between 12noon and 2:00pm and may range from a deli style sandwich to a serious seafood or meat meal. Dinner is a leisurely event that takes place somewhere between 6:00pm and 9:00pm and is when most locals and visitors prefer to take multiple courses such as thick soup, a fancy salad, and a main dish followed by rich desserts and strong coffee.

Restaurants come in many types, each with a different typical ambiance. All cities will have dozens of good or great place to eat. You can choose between a full service restaurant, a reasonably priced cafe where a limited menu is served, or a popular and affordable local restaurant that is usually the best bet for informal dining. For a better quality quick bite, head for a conch stand, a fast food place like Subway, or one of several great delicatessens and pizza joints that can be found in every downtown and tourist related sector in the country.

Usually an American style breakfast in a local restaurant with eggs, toast, bacon, and coffee will cost about $6.50. If you instead choose to dine inside a hotel, expect to get hit for about $12.50 for a sit-down meal, or at least $19.50 for a buffet. A simple sandwich type lunch in a small restaurant can set you back between $4.75 and $9.75 a person, while a fancy 4 course gourmet lunch can easily cost upwards of $21 a person. A Bahamian, Chinese, French, or Italian multiple course dinner without wine can cost from $21.50 to well over $65 per person depending again on what you choose and where you eat. In general, expect to spend a bare minimum of at least $42.50 per person per day on dining if you will be eating all three meals each day in mid-priced restaurants.

In most restaurants you can find selections that are either totally a la carte, 2 or 3 course daily specials, and cheaper combination plates (tourist menus) with fixed prices. Vegetarians will have an extremely limited selection, but can always find something in just about every restaurant and café in The Bahamas. Several restaurants offer their shellfish items by the pound.

When you have finished your meal and receive the bill you will notice that a charge has added in. **There are no taxes on meals and drinks from any restaurant, but most will include a 15% service charge.** If you have had a great meal, consider an additional 5% tip for good service and a 10%

tip for extraordinary service to be left in cash on the table when you depart. If you put a tip on your credit card, I can assure you that your waiter will never get it.

I have included brief descriptions in each regional chapter of nearly 70 of the restaurants throughout The Bahamas that I have enjoyed and can appropriately review. I have listed each destination's eating establishments in up to four separate price categories reflecting the average price per person of a full meal, not including tax, wine, or tip. Within each of the price categories, I've listed the restaurants from top to bottom in the order of my preference. All included menu selections and prices are subject to frequent change without notice.

12. THE BEST PLACES TO STAY

After staying in or visiting more than 125 different hotels, resorts, inns, villas, guest houses, and bed and breakfasts throughout The Bahamas, these are the places I will never forget. I have based my selections on a combination of aspects including overall beauty, location, quality of service, value for the money, cuisine, special features, attitude of the staff, and my own sense of what a hotel should offer.

Of course, there are plenty of other fine hotels throughout the country, but these were the places that I feel would help anyone have a great experience. I have listed these hotels in a few different categories, listing them in the order in which I would suggest them to a good friend. Not all of these fine properties are expensive, but most tend to be in the middle to upper end of the price range. Full reviews of the majority of the following selections can be found in their corresponding chapters.

VERY EXPENSIVE

SANDALS ROYAL BAHAMIAN, *Cable Beach, Nassau. Tel. (242) 327-6400, Fax (242) 327-6961. US & Canada bookings (Unique Vacations) 1-800-SANDALS. Low season rack rates from $545 per double room per night (A.I.). High season rack rates from $590 per double room per night (A.I.). 3 night minimum stay. Special package rates may also be available. Couples Only. All major credit cards accepted.*

After visiting many different properties in The Bahamas, I have easily come to the conclusion that the Sandals Royal Bahamian resort and spa is by far the most impressive. This magnificent new couples-only property is a perfect getaway for couples of all ages that want to share their vacation in a remarkably romantic setting on the sea. Built on 13 acres of luscious grounds landscaped with exotic flowering plants and trees, this new flagship of the well known Sandals hotel chain operates as an "Ultra All-Inclusive" resort, where unlimited fine dining, top shelf cocktails, fine imported wines, scuba diving, golf, tennis, live evening entertainment, dozens of daily activities, special services, airport transfers, as well as all taxes and gratuities are included in one of several package prices.

This wonderful new hotel now boasts 196 of the region's most lavish rooms and suites, in an impressive 7 floor ocean-side Manor House wing and 10 luxurious secluded villa buildings. All of the rooms here contain huge private marble and terra-cotta bathrooms with gold plated fixtures, the finest quality hair and skin care products, individually controlled air conditioning systems, opulent hand-crafted teak and mahogany furnishings, remote controlled satellite color televisions with several movie channels, direct dial telephones, plush designer fabrics and custom woven carpets, awesome private balconies or patios, mini-safes, hair dryers, some of the world's most comfortable king size 4-poster beds, and stunning views of the turquoise sea or beautifully maintained sub-tropical gardens.

Those fortunate enough to select one of over 50 stunning suites and special honeymoon accommodations may also find several additional amenities, such as fully stocked marble wet bars, video cassette players, separate sitting rooms, retractable make-up mirrors, oversized Jacuzzis, semi-private plunge pools, and many special concierge services.

SANDALS ROYAL BAHAMIAN ON CABLE BEACH, NASSAU

While many of the extremely sociable European and North American couples here may prefer to spend most of their well earned vacation just laying in the sun and relaxing on the beach, there are enough adventurous activities here to keep you and your partner busy for several weeks. The property boasts five great fresh water swimming pools, with waterfalls and a serious swim up bar, a piping hot outdoor Jacuzzi hot tub, their own private offshore island with a nice white sand beach and dining facilities, a complete water sports program offering comprehensive scuba diving and water skiing programs (and instruction), several sailboats, ocean kayaks, membership in the nearby 18 hole championship Cable Beach Golf Course, a fantastic 24 hour penthouse health club with state of the art workout equipment, professionally surfaced night-lit outdoor tennis courts, a stunning concert and performance pavilion, and a newly added luxury Spa center where optional massages and relaxing health and beauty treatments are available. For those from European nations, Sofia Snozzi (the hotel's wonderful Swiss multilingual translator and guide) will be more than glad to arrange special trips and help make introductions to several other guests that speak the same language.

There are six great specialty restaurants that each serve delicious meals in casual and semi-formal settings. Food & Beverage director Tony Curtis has created a series of well-designed menus that have something for everybody. Breakfasts here are served either buffet style, a la carte, or via room service and usually consist of cooked to order omelets, crispy bacon, fresh fruit, imported cheeses, exotic fresh fruits, fresh ground coffee, home-made pastries, bagels and croissants, Nova Scotia smoked salmon, popular hot and cold cereals, and a sampling of traditional Bahamian favorites. At lunch time you can choose to dine on assorted pizzas and sandwiches at the pool-side Royal Cafe Grill, feast on a large international buffet and salad bar at Spices Restaurant, or just grab a burger or some freshly caught Bahamian seafood over at the private offshore island's Cafe Goombay.

Throughout the evening, you have several more options for fine dining. Those seeking a romantic ambiance in a beautiful art deco restaurant may reserve a table for two at the intimate semi-formal Baccarat French Restaurant. The more relaxed Crystal Room offers expertly prepared international cuisine and a good selection of imported wines, while the private island's Cafe Goombay lets you sit under the stars for a delicious steak or fish dinner. For a more social and relaxed evening meal, I would suggest enjoying a huge buffet and rotisserie at Spices or perhaps a Tex-Mex meal at the Royal Cafe Grill. Late night people can head over to the authentic 150 year-old Cricketers Pub for light English-styled pub fare and ales until 3:00am.

Additionally there are several open bars that serve fine imported wines, spirits, and fantastic frozen drinks from 11:00am until 3:00am, special excursion and guest services desks, a full service boutique and tobacconist, fine English billiard tables, Ping-Pong tables, dozens of daily scheduled activities, fun contests for free gifts, full concierge service, and much more. Charming wedding services can also be arranged on the premises if the staff are notified well in advance. The resort's General Manager, Mr. Stephen Ziadie, has assembled an incredible team of staff members that really know how to treat every guest here as a VIP. Sandals Royal Bahamian resort and spa is the finest all-inclusive resort and spa for couples only in this part of the world, and receives my absolute highest recommendation.

PINK SANDS, *Harbour Island, Eleuthera. Tel. (242) 333-2030, Fax (242) 333-2060. US & Canada bookings (Island Outpost) 1-800-688-7678. Low season rack rates from $305 per double room per night (M.A.P.). High season rack rates from $460 per double room per night (M.A.P.). All major credit cards accepted.*

Pink Sands is definitely one of The Bahamas' most luxurious and exclusive smaller luxury hotels. Known around the globe for many years, this picture-perfect hotel and restaurant overlooking miles of wonderful pink sand beach is a remarkable place to stay. The property was originally a nice seaside hotel owned by the Malcolm family, but a few years ago it was all but destroyed by the high winds and pounding waves of Hurricane Andrew. In the hurricane's aftermath, the property was purchased by Island Record's founder Chris Blackwell and painstakingly redesigned and constructed into the newest member of his successful Island Outpost chain of boutique-styled hotels.

There are a total of 26 strikingly designed spacious one and two bedroom air conditioned cottages that either face directly onto the sea or lavish semi-tropical gardens and feature deluxe private bathrooms lined with exotic tiles and stocked with Island Outpost's own line of natural hair and skin care products, remote control color satellite televisions with video cassette recorders, direct dial telephones with computer modem inputs and cordless capability, custom-made hardwood furnishings and tropically inspired decorative arts, unpolished marble floors, audio systems with compact disk players and racks of Island Records CDs, am-fm clock radios, available in-room fax machines, plush embroidered cotton bathrobes, remarkable wet bars with coffee machines and fine English china, private garden or beach-view patios with teak lounge chairs, electronic mini-safes, and much much more.

Pink Sands offers its fortunate guests (many of whom are well-known artists from the motion picture and music industry) Harbour Island's

A ROOM AT THE PINK SANDS HOTEL, HARBOUR ISLAND, ELEUTHERA

most complete array of services and facilities, including amazing gourmet beachfront and garden-side al fresco style restaurants that both specialize in fusing local and international cuisine, a complete health club, a fantastic Club House with a relaxing library that doubles as a state-of-the-art video theater, complimentary laser disc and video cassette rental, three perfectly maintained outdoor tennis courts, a free-form black bottom freshwater swimming pool, room service, available water and land-based excursions, an Island Outpost boutique, and of course direct access to a fantastic stretch of the famous Harbour Island Pink Sand Beach.

Most of the cottages are free-standing and are surrounded by tropical flowering hedges that allow guests to feel they each have their own private villa. During the afternoon and evening the ambiance here is friendly and welcoming, with many guests meeting each other over a drink or a game of billiards. Ever-present managers James and Karen Malcolm have done an excellent job of selecting a staff of friendly locals that have begun perfecting the art of catering to the jet set.

I was thoroughly impressed with Pink Sands, and I strongly recommend it for those who can afford complete luxury and prefer to have the availability of modern day comforts and technology (which no other hotel on Harbour Island offers) in a truly memorable island setting.

EXPENSIVE

BREEZES BAHAMAS, *West Bay Street on Cable Beach, New Providence. Tel. (242) 327-5356, Fax (242) 327-5155. US & Canada bookings (SuperClubs) 1-800-859-7873. Low season rack rates from $220 per double room per night (A.I.). High season rack rates from $270 per double room per night (A.I.). F.A.P. Meal Plan is included. Minimum 2 night stay required. All major credit cards accepted.*

Breezes is one of The Bahamas' most enjoyable all-inclusive resort properties! Situated along a sandy stretch of famous Cable Beach, this resort is among my personal favorites. Breezes' room rates include unlimited meals, water sports, entertainment, top shelf cocktails and beverages, airport transfers, and much more, and is a great example of a well managed resort hotel. All of the 400 large air conditioned rooms feature nice tile bathrooms with hairdryers, ocean-view terraces, extremely comfortable bedding, mini-safe, hardwood furnishings, remote control satellite color televisions, and nice interior designs. Guests here are encouraged to participate in over two dozen daily scheduled events, including free scuba and sailing lessons, kayaking, windsurfing, tennis clinics, island bicycle tours, live music concerts, cabaret shows, standup comedy, fashion shows, aerobics classes, volleyball tournaments, and many other fun activities that run from early morning until late evening each day of the week.

The ambiance here is relaxing, youthful, and exceedingly friendly, with a clientele made up mainly by (but not limited to) 17 to 38 year old singles and couples from major North American and European cities. Among the vast array of facilities here is a picture-perfect beach, three well maintained swimming pools, a powerful Jacuzzi, hundreds of lounge chairs, a water sports pavilion offering a great selection of non-motorized water sports, a popular split level pool-side bar that makes The Bahamas' best frozen cocktails, a lobby bar and concert stage, a disco that stay open till 5:00am nightly, a tranquil piano bar, a fully loaded health club and fitness center with top of the line workout equipment, a beach grill serving snacks and huge burgers, a jogging track, basketball courts, beach-side trapeze and trampolines, billiard and Ping-Pong tables, outdoor tennis courts, large screen televisions, a game room, plenty of 21 speed mountain bicycles, free parking, optional off-sight excursions, and of course lush semi-tropical gardens.

Dining here is simply a fantastic experience with several possibilities. The hotel's casual main Dining Promenade and open air patio offer spectacular buffet breakfasts, lunches, and dinners with over 75 items to choose from, including fine imported cheeses, omelets, grilled steaks, juicy ribs, freshly caught local seafood, grilled chicken, Caribbean specialties, all sorts of pastas, vegetarian dishes, every type of beverage imaginable, and a mouth-watering dessert table. The hotel's cozy little Pastafari restaurant is open daily for Italian inspired dinners (try their famous penne with lobster tails and broccoli). For real power eaters, a midnight snack is also presented every evening.

If you're near the pool you can also hit the Beach Grill for cooked-to-order burgers, wings, and fries during the day, and full barbecue dinners in the evenings. Additionally, there are dozens of self-service frozen pina colada and fruit daiquiri machines all over the hotel, and high quality beer (such as Bass Ale), wine, and liquor generously provided in unlimited quantities.

The staff is what makes Breezes so welcoming, and all the people working here go well out of their way to say hello and see if there is anything at all you need. If you are young at heart and want a vacation you will never forget, I strongly recommend considering Breezes!

GRAYCLIFF, *Nassau, New Providence. Tel. (242) 322-2796, Fax (242) 326-6110. US & Canada bookings (Utell) 1-800-44-UTELL. Low season rack rates from $155 per double room per night (C.P.). High season rack rates from $235 per double room per night (C.P.). All major credit cards accepted.*

For those looking for ultra-deluxe Colonial-style accommodations near the heart of downtown Nassau, Graycliff is the obvious choice. Housed in a 250-plus year-old manor house across the street from the Prime Minister's office and surrounded by lavish gardens, Graycliff has been the most luxurious small inn in the Bahamas for several decades. Currently owned and operated by the gracious Garzaroli family, this fabulous property boasts the nation's finest restaurant, 13 individually decorated rooms and suites, a huge outdoor swimming pool and sun deck, a heath club, a Cuban cigar lounge, several private meeting and reception rooms, and the region's largest wine cellar.

All of the unique rooms and suites are situated in either the main house or a beautiful pool-side wing and contain large opulent private bathrooms with either antique or golden fixtures, air conditioners, a variety of impressive antique furnishings, comfortable bedding, walk-in closets, fine original artwork, remote control satellite televisions, and in several cases even separate sitting rooms, private terraces, mini-bars, Jacuzzis, fine hand-painted tiles, rare oriental vases, and priceless Persian tapestries. The first floor restaurant is a superb place to enjoy formal gourmet meals, and the service here is outstanding. Highly recommended.

SMALL HOPE BAY LODGE, *Fresh Creek, Andros. Tel. (242) 368-2014, Fax (242) 368-2015. US & Canada bookings (Hotel's Florida Offices) 1-800-223-6961. Low season rack rates from $300 per double cottage per night (A.I.). High season rack rates from $330 per double cottage per night (A.I.). Special scuba packages available. All major credit cards accepted.*

This one of a kind seaside inn and scuba resort is among the most casual and welcoming places to stay in the Out Islands. Located just a 10 minute drive from Andros Town airport in the northern reaches of Andros, this world-famous small hotel has been owned and operated by members of the Birch family for over three decades. The property boasts 20 hand-built stone and wooden one and two bedroom cottages just off the sea, each with private bathrooms, ceiling fans, plenty of space, minimalist furnishings, and Androsia brand batik fabrics throughout.

Many of the guests come here to experience some of the world's best scuba activities (including day and night dives to nearby reefs and ocean holes full of exotic marine life), while others just arrive to kick back and do nothing at all except relax. While on vacation at Small Hope Bay, you can enjoy three excellent home-made buffet meals a day, mix your own cocktails, take bicycle rides to quaint settlements and long sandy beaches, make friends with lots of interesting people from all over the globe, work on your tan at the beach, kick back in a hammock, listen to narrated talks about local marine and wildlife, read a fine book from a giant lending library, jump in the open air hot tub, snorkel just offshore, learn how to scuba dive, windsurf along the coastline, hop in a sailboat, or send the kids off on scheduled (and well-supervised) activities, all for no additional charge.

SECLUSION IS YOURS AT SMALL HOPE BAY LODGE ON ANDROS ISLAND!

There are also reasonably priced scuba adventures and certification classes led by expert PADI dive masters, fishing trips, island tours, nature walks, soothing massage treatments, and even chartered air service directly from Florida and Nassau. The guests are a relaxed and informal mixture of singles, couples, and families that wear nothing more formal than swimsuits (even during dinner) and almost all return year after year. After a few nights here, I didn't want to leave!

MODERATE

FERNANDEZ BAY VILLAGE, *New Bight, Cat Island. Tel. (954) 474-4821, Fax (954) 474-4864. US & Canada bookings (Fernandez's Florida Offices) 1-800-940-1905. Low season rack rates from $185 per double private house per night (M.A.P.). High season rack rates from $205 per double private house per night (M.A.P.). Most major credit cards accepted.*

When I first arrived at Fernandez Bay Village, I knew I had finally discovered my own little tropical island paradise! Situated on a beautiful stretch of white sand beach on Cat Island, this small colony of nine striking independent stone and wooden houses is one of The Bahamas' most memorable and romantic hideaways.

ESCAPE TO FERNANDEZ BAY VILLAGE, CAT ISLAND

Each of their nine delightful villas and cottages is unique, but you can expect to find exotic private bathrooms with open air garden showers, antique hardwood furnishings such as 4-poster beds and marble side-tables, chapel-styled sloped wooden ceilings with fans, Mexican tile flooring, mini-refrigerators, unusual Bahamian handicrafts, private terrace areas surrounded by palm trees and hibiscus, incredible beach views, and nice cool breezes from the constant trade winds.

Make full use of their fantastic beach area, enjoy delicious lobster and steak dinners during the superb nightly seaside buffet, mix your own cocktails and cool beverages in a thatched Tiki Bar, pick up a book or one of many magazines from their Clubhouse's lending library, daydream as you rock yourself to sleep with the wind in a hammock, plan an underwater adventure with their PADI dive shop, arrange great fishing trips with expert on-staff guides, jump aboard one of several available sailboats, explore nearby sights and natural wonders by rental car or motor boat, and converse with interesting fellow travelers in all age ranges. On any given day, Fernandez Bay hosts a good mix of European and North American couples in all age ranges, as well as several families with children, who mingle and hang out in nothing more formal than bathing suits and sandals.

Although neither exclusive or luxurious, owners Pam & Tony Armbrister have created an exceedingly comfortable little resort where people can just chill out and have a well deserved break from big city life. Donna and her superb staff of warm-hearted Cat Island natives make sure to greet every guest and make them immediately feel like part of an extended family. For some people this can also be a magically romantic spot, with some couples even arranging the perfect wedding here (including some that met each other for the first time while on vacation at the hotel). I enjoyed my time here so much that I really never wanted to leave, and I am sure that many of you will feel the exact same way! Private charter service to and from Nassau can easily be arranged.

ATLANTIS, PARADISE ISLAND, *New Providence. Tel. (242) 363-3000, Fax (242) 363-3703. US & Canada bookings (Sun International) 1-800-321-3000. Low season rack rates from $130 per double room per night (E.P.). High season rack rates from $140 per double room per night (E.P.). M.A.P. Meal Plans available from $42 per adult per day. Most major credit cards accepted.*

The Atlantis is a magnificent hotel, casino, and entertainment resort alongside one of Paradise Island's finest white sand beaches. Purchased and completely redesigned by Sun International Hotel Ltd. in 1994 for around $250 million, the Atlantis has certainly become the largest and best equipped vacation complex in The Bahamas. There are a total of 1,147 stunning rooms and suites divided into four separate sections of the hotel. While most guests choose to stay in the hotel's beautifully decorated high-rise Coral Towers and Beach Tower wings, the resort also offers a more intimate low-rise section called the Villas and a special VIP area known as the Reef Club.

Accommodations in all sections of Atlantis are fully air conditioned and all contain deluxe bathrooms stocked with fine imported hair and skin care products, remote control color cable televisions with dozens of channels and optional in-room movies, spacious balconies with sun chairs, comfortable double or king size beds, fully stocked mini-bars, electronic security safes, extremely comfortable tropical furnishings, beautiful local lithographs, direct dial telephones with computer data ports, am-fm clock radios, and relaxing pastel colored interiors.

In terms of facilities, there is so much to see and experience while you are here that you really should take a guided tour (offered free to guests three times daily) to decide what to do first. Steps away from the hotel is an amazing 14 acre **Waterscape** that has become the focal point for many guests. The Waterscape (actually the world's largest open air outdoor aquarium) is comprised of giant man-made lagoons and reefs stocked with a vast array of sharks, sting rays, barracudas, sea turtles, parrot fish, angel fish, groupers, a 250 pound Jew fish with an attitude, and over 115 other varieties of colorful native marine life. Open 24 hours a day (and imaginatively back-lit after sunset), the aquarium includes a unique Underwater Tunnel with giant picture windows looking out onto the fish, as well as miles of adjacent tropical walking paths complete with rope bridges and cascading waterfalls.

Scattered throughout the grounds there are also underground caves, five fantastic swimming pools each with its own ambiance, several hundred lounge chairs, exotically designed snack and beverage pavilions, a Lazy River tire tube ride and nearby body slide, various non-motorized water sports, and well over 2,000 exotic trees inhabited by butterflies and wild humming birds. The park and aquarium end at the edge of the calm turquoise colored sea, where a wonderful 2 1/2 mile long sandy crescent beach awaits you. Nearby you can get a great tan, take a free scuba lesson, jump in the sea for a swim, and enjoy various exciting optional activities like para-sailing, jet skiing, deep sea fishing, ocean kayaking, sailing, wind surfing, or water skiing.

Another major attraction is the glittering 30,000 square foot casino (easily the biggest and best in the region) that has 800 slot machines and dozens of blackjack, poker, roulette, craps, and baccarat tables. Alongside the casino there is a showroom featuring a musical revue, a standup comedy club, a cappuccino bar, a sports bar, several designer boutiques, and much more. Additionally, there is both an 18 hole/par 72 championship golf course and nine Har-Tru tennis courts nearby.

Dining here is a real treat, with a total of 10 dining establishments. Among these are the romantic Cafe Martinique serving French cuisine in a semi-formal candle-lit setting, the fabulous Villa d'Este gourmet Italian trattoria, the refined Bahamian Club steak and seafood restaurant, and a couple of rather casual family-style dining rooms such as the Seagrapes international buffet and the trendy Water's Edge Mediterranean restaurant. Those traveling with children between 5 and 12 years of age might want to sign the kids up for the resort's Camp Paradise program that offers supervised fun activities daily. There is, of course, 24-hour room service, express laundry and dry cleaning, a house doctor, several tour and excursion desks, lots of nighttime diversions, optional massages, a state of the art health club, scheduled daily activities, rental bicycles, and free shuttle bus service to the facilities and restaurants you can enjoy over at the super-deluxe Ocean Club and laid-back Paradise, Paradise resorts (also owned by Sun International Hotel Ltd.).

If you are thinking about spending a casual vacation on the pristine beaches of Paradise Island, my first suggestion would be to reserve a room here at the breathtaking Atlantis. As the largest and best equipped major hotel in all of The Bahamas, the Atlantis resort and casino provides its guests with a tremendous array of activities and diversions. This superb full-service property has set a new standard for facilities and customer satisfaction in The Bahamas, and I highly recommend Atlantis for those who are looking for a fun, affordable, and exciting resort with plenty of things to do.

BAHAMAS PRINCESS RESORT & CASINO, *East Sunrise Highway, Freeport. Tel. (242) 352-2542. Fax (242) 352-9661. US & Canada bookings (Princess Hotels International) 1-800-223-1834. Low season rack rates from $95 per double room per night (E.P.). High season rack rates from $120 per double room per night (E.P.). Special package rates available. M.A.P. Meal Plans available from $29 per adult per day. All major credit cards accepted.*

This superb 1,000 acre resort in the heart of Freeport's nicest neighborhood is by far the best hotel on all of Grand Bahama Island. The Bahamas Princess is divided into two separate sections that are located just across the street from one another and surrounded by lush gardens. Families and couples on package vacations tend to stay in the bustling low-rise Princess Country Club section, where there are 565 large and well-equipped rooms and suites, while more upscale or gambling-oriented guests looking for a tranquil luxurious environment often prefer to stay in the opulent 10 story Princess Towers wing that has 400 spectacular rooms and suites.

All rooms on both parts of the resort feature modern tile private bathrooms stocked with imported hair and skin care products, air conditioning, extremely comfortable king or double bedding, remote control satellite color television with pay per view movies, tropical rattan and wooden furnishings, am-fm clock radio, direct dial telephone, nice local artwork, plenty of closet space, and large picture windows looking over an assortment of garden, pool, or island views.

Facilities include Grand Bahama's largest and best equipped casino, giant free-form fresh water swimming pools with cascades and hot tubs, two expertly maintained 18 hole championship golf courses with pro shops and clubhouses, nine professionally surfaced tennis courts, free round-trip shuttle service to nearby Taino and Xanadu beaches where all sorts of water sports can be arranged, room service, boutiques, a car and jeep rental desk, fitness center with sauna, beauty salon, several tour and excursion desks, ice and soda machines, optional in-room mini-safe and refrigerator rentals, express laundry and dry cleaning, available child care, special rooms with full wheelchair access, a full compliment of scheduled daily activities, a children's program, and much, much more.

There are nine great restaurants here, including the wonderfully relaxing La Trattoria for great pizzas and pastas, Guanahani's family-style Bahamian restaurant, The Patio where large buffets are offered three times daily, the Garden Café deli, the Lemon peel coffee shop, Morgan's Bluff seafood restaurant, the open air pool-side John B. snack bar, and more dressy Rib Room and Crown Room gourmet establishments. There are also no less than eight impressive bars and nightlife venues that have either amazing drink specials, glamorous Vegas-style revues, popular happy hours, and live music or dancing nightly.

Guests at the Bahamas Princess arrive daily from all over the globe, and range from singles and couples to newlyweds and families with children. The service here is quite good, with many of the staff members going well out of their way to make sure you'll return again soon. Highly recommended as the best full service resort on Grand Bahama, and the rates are very affordable!

GREAT ABACO BEACH RESORT & MARINA, *Marsh Harbour, Abaco. Tel. (242) 367-2158, Fax (242) 367-2819. US and Canada bookings (Out Island Promo Board) 1-800-688-4752. Low season rack rates from $145 per double room per night (E.P.). High season rack rates from $185 per double room per night (E.P.). M.A.P. Meal Plans available from $32 per adult per day. Most major credit cards accepted.*

Great Abaco is the only deluxe full-service resort hotel on Great Abaco Island. Situated along Marsh Harbour's reef-protected seafront, this modern and extremely well maintained first class hotel is the perfect place to stay for those interested in deep sea fishing, water sports, and boating activities. Those who prefer to sit back and enjoy a stress-free vacation while enjoying all the comforts of home will also be delighted here.

Guests can be accommodated in one of 52 deluxe air conditioned sea-view rooms (several can adjoin for family use) that all have a deluxe private bathroom, remote control satellite television with free movie channels, mini-refrigerators, a coffee machine, direct dial telephone, a wet bar, nice West Indies-style hardwood furnishings, king or double beds, wall to wall carpeting or tiled floors, large French windows that open up onto panoramic balconies, and more space than some other hotel's suites. There are also six free-standing air conditioned villas available near the beach that all come equipped with all the above plus a full kitchen, two bedrooms, and two bathrooms.

The property boasts this country's largest and best equipped marina, hosts several world-class fishing tournaments, and offers a huge array of services and facilities, including a good casual sea-view restaurant, a fun swim up pool-side bar and snack bar, two completely different large freshwater swimming pools, complimentary Sunfish and Hobie Cat sailboats, plenty of available boat rentals and excursions, a convention center, a self-service laundromat, several nice boutiques, a mini-market and liquor store, outdoor tennis courts, a small sandy beachfront with a volleyball court, lots of free outdoor parking, and nice landscaped grounds filled with a variety of flowering plants and trees. I strongly suggest the Great Abaco Beach Resort for families, couples, and sports enthusiasts.

RADISSON CABLE BEACH CASINO & GOLF RESORT, *West Bay Street, Cable Beach, New Providence. Tel. (242) 327-6000, Fax (242) 327-5969. US & Canada bookings (Radisson) 1-800-333-3333. Low season rack rates from $135 per double room per night (E.P.). High season rack rates from $188 per double room per night (E.P.). Lower package prices are often available. "Splash" All Inclusive Plan available. All major credit cards accepted.*

After a wonderful $15 million renovation project, the newly expanded Radisson Cable Beach Casino & Golf Resort has become one of the best places to stay while vacationing in the Cable Beach area! This unusually inviting large beachfront resort hotel is a favorite among North Americans and European singles, couples, and families looking for superb value for the money and a full complement of world-class facilities. For those interested, there are also countless special events, including weekly theme dinners, exciting beach barbecues, manager's cocktail parties, and Junkanoo music and dance events.

Besides offering a large sandy beach area and strikingly landscaped free-form swimming pools with cascades, the Radisson also has a challenging nearby 18 hole championship golf course, more than 10 outdoor night-lit tennis courts, a complete sports center with racquetball and squash facilities, plenty of water sports, and a complete children's activities program directed by experienced counselors. Guests here also can choose from six restaurants with diverse international and local cuisine, enjoy cocktails at three different bars, and directly access the adjacent casino complex. Almost all of the newly redecorated rooms face onto the turquoise sea and have powerful air conditioners, beautifully tiled private bathrooms, remote controlled satellite television with movie channels, mini-bars, mini-safes, direct dial telephones with computer data ports, large panoramic balconies with outdoor furniture, tropical designer fabrics, and either one king or two queen beds.

Not only are the room prices impressively affordable, but for those interested there is an optional "Splash" All Inclusive program that can be purchased before you arrive or selected upon check-in as an upgrade. Splash clients receive three meals a day at any restaurant in the resort, free wine with dinner, as many top shelf cocktails as they desire, golf green fees, tennis and racquetball court fees, plenty of non-motorized water sports, daily scheduled events, round-trip airport transfers, all taxes and service charges, and much more. Service here is prompt, professional, and polite, with a relaxing overall ambiance that helps all the guests to easily enjoy a relaxing vacation.

INEXPENSIVE

THE BLUFF HOUSE, *Green Turtle Cay, Abaco. Tel. (242) 365-4247, Fax (242) 365-4248. Low season rack rates from $90 per double room per night (E.P.). High season rack rates from $100 per double room per night (E.P.). M.A.P. Meal Plans available from $35 per adult per day. Most major credit cards accepted.*

From the moment I stepped inside my room at the Bluff House, I knew I had found a great place! Owner Martin Havill, an English expatriate who fell in love with this charming island some years ago, has created the perfect casual hotel where the guests become friends with one another after their first day. The Bluff House has become one of my favorite places to unwind in all of The Bahamas and the Caribbean. Scattered along the property there is a private marina, a nice little sandy beach area, several lodges with stunningly decorated guest rooms, and the clubhouse where delicious meals and strong yet soothing cocktails are served daily. All of the guests I met here said that they felt as if they were staying in a rich friend's summer house, and I could not agree more.

The hotel features 28 of the largest air conditioned rooms, suites, and villas in a series of charming low-rise structures resting just above the sea. Almost all of the rooms feature amazing terraced sun decks with sweeping views of the adjacent ocean, impressive selections of hand-crafted rattan furnishings, rich fabrics with tropical motifs, chapel styled ceilings with powerful fans, deluxe tiled private bathrooms, lots of closet space, convenient half-size refrigerators, some of the country's most comfortable king or double beds, wall to wall carpeting, and French doors that let in plenty of natural sunlight and the gentle sounds of breaking waves.

Among the many services and activities that you can enjoy here are a nice quiet sandy beachfront, scheduled complimentary round-trip boat trips to the historic and picturesque village of New Plymouth, an outdoor tennis court with racquets and balls, free snorkeling and beach gear, optional bonefishing and reef fishing expeditions, available snorkeling trips and picnics to area lighthouses and deserted islands, a private marina that can arrange boat rentals and custom charters, memorable self-guided hikes to local beaches and New Plymouth, and an infamous Saturday night shuttle boat to a popular nearby nightclub with live music and plenty of local ambiance.

Chef Veronica at the ocean-view Bluff House Restaurant serves up delicious breakfasts and dinners (including weekly open air barbecues and live entertainment), while the relaxed water-front Beach Club offers a good selection of lunch salads and sandwiches. There is also a nightly cocktail hour with hors d'oeuvres served before dinner. The service here is exceedingly friendly, and I highly recommend a few nights at this undiscovered little island inn and fine local restaurant.

BUENA VISTA, *Delancy Street, Nassau, New Providence. Tel. (242) 322-2811, Fax (242) 322-5881. Low season rack rates from $65 per double room per night (E.P.). High season rack rates from $90 per double room per night (E.P.). Special package rates available upon request. All major credit cards accepted.*

The Buena Vista is a beautiful Old World-style 19th-century Bahamian manor house a few blocks above the heart of downtown Nassau's Bay Street. This remarkably charming inn and gourmet restaurant has five delightful large rooms and suites that all have new air conditioners, deluxe private bathrooms, remote control cable televisions with over 25 channels, direct dial telephones, an assortment of antique and period style furnishings, wall to wall carpeting, plenty of closet space, complimentary coffee and tea service with fine English bone china, and even private terraces and working fireplaces in most cases.

This is a great place to stay if you want to rent a car or hop in a taxi for quick rides to the island's best beach areas and boutiques. The staff really try to make each guest a repeat customer. There are also tranquil gardens, luxurious sitting rooms, available continental breakfasts, and lots of peace and quiet. This is a real gem of a small inn, and with all the money that you can save staying here instead of the larger resorts you can easily afford treating yourself to a few gourmet dinners at their own fabulous restaurant. Highly recommended for those looking for unique accommodations and meals presented with lots of charm and class.

BUENA VISTA HOTEL, NASSAU

THE COVE ELEUTHERA, *Queens Highway, Gregory Town area, Eleuthera. Tel. (242) 335-5142, Fax (242) 335-5338. US & Canada bookings (The Cove's USA Offices) 1-800-552-5960. Low season rack rates from $89 per double room per night (E.P.). High season rack rates from $109 per double room per night (E.P.). M.A.P. Meal Plan available for $33 per adult per day. Most major credit cards accepted.*

The Cove is an extremely welcoming small hideaway, located just a mile and a half north of Gregory Town on the upper part of Eleuthera. Owned and operated by Ann and George Mullin, a charming couple originally from New York, this is one of my favorite places in The Bahamas to just settle back and unwind. The unique little inn's seven tropical buildings contain a total of 26 air conditioned rooms, each with a private bathroom, ceiling fan, simple yet comfortable white rattan furnishings, sea or garden-view patios, sloped wooden ceilings, tile floors, local lithographs, and ice chests for cooling soft drinks and beer in the rooms or at the beach.

Service here is really good, with a friendly local staff supervised by office manager Ann MacConnell (a walking encyclopedia of local history and culture). The inn, just a $27, half-hour taxi ride from North Eleuthera Airport, is surrounded by 28 acres of beautiful palm trees and Caribbean gardens inhabited by colorful butterflies and countless humming birds, lamp lighters (lightening bugs), and butterflies.

The Cove is a low keyed inn where guests often arrive to get away from it all, and offers a casual (and affordable) restaurant serving homemade Bahamian and American specialties, a small sandy cove beach with excellent snorkeling, a well-maintained swimming pool, occasional live evening entertainment by gifted local musicians like Dr. Breeze, a poolside bar that makes strong frozen drinks, outdoor tennis courts, free shuttle service to and from nearby Gregory Town and Gaulding's Cay Beach, complimentary kayaks and snorkeling gear, a giant lending library full of books in several languages, a TV room filled with classic and current videos, free bicycles, several hammocks, walking trails, plenty of parking, optional excursions and fishing trips, and memorable sunset views.

While far from luxurious or opulent, this is a great place for those who are content to enjoy nature and the company of their loved ones and other like-minded adventurous travelers.

13. NEW PROVIDENCE & PARADISE ISLAND

Located 159 miles east-southeast of Miami, and with a population exceeding 171,000 – more than 60% of the nation's inhabitants – **New Providence Island** is one of the most important islands of The Bahamas. Besides being home to the capital city of **Nassau**, this is the destination that the majority of tourists visit while vacationing in this nation. The heavily developed tourist areas of **Cable Beach** and **Paradise Island** attract thousands of tourists on any given day, and employ most of the locals. Downtown Nassau is more of a government and insurance and banking town, though there are hundreds of fine boutiques, duty-free shops, restaurants, and attractions to visit.

Even though the island is just 27 miles long and about 7 miles wide, there are several outlying districts that few tourists take the time to explore. New Providence's southern shore remains relatively undeveloped, and is dotted with a few scuba centers, just one major hotel, and plenty of charming villages full of friendly residents. In just a few days you can travel by jitney bus, rental car, or scooter (not recommended) to a vast number of historical sights and attractions and still have the time to hit the great beaches here.

This island is also where the best casinos and nightclubs are found, and dining possibilities are plentiful. Just make sure to get a good map from your hotel's front desk, and avoid venturing into the unsafe area well behind downtown Nassau (known locally as "over the hill").

ARRIVALS & DEPARTURES

Most visitors from North America will arrive either by air at **Nassau International Airport**, or by sea on a cruise line that docks in the **port of Nassau**. Consult Chapter 6, *Planning Your Trip*, and Chapter 8, *Cruising to The Bahamas*, for details on flight and cruise arrangements to The Bahamas.

GETTING AROUND NEW PROVIDENCE

Your main options are taxi, jitney bus, and rental car. To get to Cable Beach, downtown Nassau, and Paradise Island, see *Seeing the Sights* below for details.

If you want to rent a car, contact:

• **Avis Rent a Car**, *Airport, Paradise Island & downtown, Tel. (242) 327-7121*
• **Budget Rent a Car**, *Airport, Paradise Island & downtown, Tel. (242) 377-9000*
• **Hertz Rent a Car**, *Airport, Paradise Island & downtown, Tel. (242) 326-8684*
• **Orange Creek Rent a Car**, *Orange Creek, Tel. (242) 323-4967*
• **Airport Taxi Rank**, *Nassau International Airport, Tel. (242) 327-7106*

WHERE TO STAY

Very Expensive

SANDALS ROYAL BAHAMIAN, *Cable Beach, Nassau. Tel. (242) 327-6400, Fax (242) 327-6961. US & Canada bookings (Unique Vacations) 1-800-SANDALS. Low season rack rates from $545 per double room per night (A.I.). High season rack rates from $590 per double room per night (A.I.). Special package rates may be available. 3 night minimum stay. Couples Only. All major credit cards accepted.*

This magnificent new "couples-only" property has recently become the flagship of the famous Sandals chain of "Ultra All-Inclusive" resorts. All of your meals, top shelf cocktails, water sports, evening entertainment, daily activities, special services, airport transfers, as well as all taxes and gratuities are included in the pre-paid package prices. This fantastic new hotel has 196 lavish rooms and suites in its 7 floor beach-side Manor House and 10 adjacent villa buildings. All rooms contain large private marble and terra-cotta tiled bathrooms, air conditioners, hand-crafted teak and mahogany furnishings, remote controlled satellite color televisions, direct dial telephones, private balconies or patios, mini-safes, hair dryers, king size 4-poster beds, and stunning sea or garden views. Most of the several dozen lavish honeymoon suites also contain fully stocked marble wet bars, video cassette players, sitting rooms, oversized Jacuzzis, plunge pools, and special concierge services.

There are six wonderful specialty restaurants that serve delicious meals in either casual or semi-formal settings, five great fresh water swimming pools, waterfalls, several bars and lounges, a disco and entertainment complex, piping hot outdoor Jacuzzi hot tubs, a private offshore island with a delightful Clubhouse and a white sand beach, a water sports program offering unlimited scuba diving and water skiing, sail boats and ocean kayaks, a nearby 18 hole championship golf course, a penthouse

COMPASS POINT HOTEL, NASSAU

CABLE BEACH, NEW PROVIDENCE

health club with state-of-the-art equipment, night-lit outdoor tennis courts, hand-crafted English billiard tables, table tennis, an antique English pub, live jazz and Calypso music, special theme nights, and a newly added luxury Spa center offering optional massages and treatments.

Sandals Royal Bahamian resort and spa is definitely the finest all-inclusive resort and couples spa in all of The Bahamas! Selected as one of our *Best Places to Stay* – see Chapter 12 for a longer review.

GRAYCLIFF HOTEL, *West Hill Street, Nassau. Tel. (242) 322-2796, Fax (242) 326-6110. US & Canada bookings (Utell) 1-800-44-UTELL. Low season rack rates from $155 per double room per night (C.P.). High season rack rates from $235 per double room per night (C.P.). All major credit cards accepted.*

Graycliff is a small luxury inn situated just across the street from Government House in an historic 250-plus year-old manor house. Owned and operated by the gracious Garzaroli family, this superb inn and restaurant features 13 unique rooms and suites that have lavish private bathrooms, air conditioners, impressive antique furnishings, walk-in closets, rare original artwork, remote control satellite televisions, and in some instances there are also separate sitting rooms, private terraces, mini-bars, Jacuzzis, rare oriental vases, and priceless Persian tapestries.

This wonderful getaway just behind downtown Nassau has been attracting the rich and famous (including many members of royalty and movie stars) for several decades. It still boasts the nation's finest formal gourmet restaurant, a huge outdoor swimming pool and sun deck, a heath club, a Cuban cigar lounge, meeting and reception rooms, and the region's largest wine cellar.

Highly recommended as the most luxurious small property on the island. Selected as one of our *Best Places to Stay* – see Chapter 12 for a longer review.

OCEAN CLUB, *Paradise Island. Tel. (242) 363-3000, Fax (242) 363-3703. US & Canada bookings (Sun International) 1-800-321-3000. Low season rack rates from $310 per double room per night (E.P.). High season rack rates from $470 per double room per night (E.P.). Lower package prices are usually available. Gourmet Meal Plans available from $79 per adult per day. Most major credit cards accepted.*

As one of the most expensive and exclusive resort in all of The Bahamas, the Ocean Club should be a strong contender for those of you who desire luxurious accommodations and serious privacy. Situated along a stunning wide beach in a carefully guarded part of Paradise Island, this hotel has once again become the peaceful hideaway of choice for a select group of rich and famous visitors. All of the 71 rooms, suites, and 2-bedroom private villas feature air conditioning, giant deluxe private bathrooms, marble flooring, hand-crafted hardwood furnishings, large remote control cable televisions with pay per view movies, large patios with cast iron outdoor furnishings and ceiling fans, designer fabrics, and nice garden or ocean views.

Guests at the Ocean Club have access to amazing gardens facing the 14th-century French Cloisters, one of the country's most romantic outdoor gourmet restaurants, a private beach club and bar, a nearby 18 hole championship golf course, an outdoor tennis center, a charming swimming pool, a picture-perfect beach, free parking, 24-hour room service, water sports, optional excursions, and free scheduled shuttle service to the Atlantis resort and casino.

Expensive

ATLANTIS, PARADISE ISLAND, *Paradise Island. Tel. (242) 363-3000, Fax (242) 363-3703. US & Canada bookings (Sun International) 1-800-321-3000. Low season rack rates from $130 per double room per night (E.P.). High season rack rates from $140 per double room per night (E.P.). Lower package prices are usually available. Meal Plans available from $42 per adult per day. All major credit cards accepted.*

This wonderful hotel, casino, and entertainment resort lies on one of Paradise Island's best beaches. Here visitors can reserve a room in one of four separate sections that comprise a total of 1,147 large modern air conditioned rooms and suites. Each comes with private bathrooms, remote control color cable televisions with optional in-room movies, large balconies, mini-bars, electronic mini-safes, tropical furnishings, beautiful local artwork, direct dial telephones, am-fm clock radios, and extremely comfortable furnishings.

Among this fine property's highlights is an amazing 14 acre Waterscape, an open air aquarium with underground viewing tunnels and walking paths that lead past giant man-made lagoons and reefs filled with countless sharks, sting rays, barracudas, sea turtles, and many other varieties of exotic marine life. There are also five fantastic swimming pools, several snack and beverage pavilions, a tire tube ride and body slide, plenty of water sports, and of course a wonderful 2 1/2 mile long sandy crescent beach. Guests can also visit the hotel's tour desks to book excursions and activities such as free scuba lessons, para-sailing, jet skiing, deep sea fishing, submarine adventures, ocean kayaking, sailing, wind surfing, helicopter rides and water skiing.

Additionally, there is a fantastic 18 hole/par 72 championship golf course, nine Har-Tru tennis courts, a fully equipped health club, scheduled daily activities, free shuttle bus service to other points on Paradise Island, and a Camp Paradise children's program that offers supervised fun-filled activities daily.

Another major attraction is the largest and best designed casino in all of the region, with 800 slot machines and dozens of blackjack, poker, roulette, craps, and baccarat tables. Evening entertainment is provided at a showroom featuring Vegas-style revues, a standup comedy club, a cappuccino bar, a sports bar, and much more. Dining here is a real treat, with a total of 10 dining establishments ranging from casual family-style buffet dining rooms to elegant candle-lit semi-formal French and Italian gourmet restaurants. If you are thinking about spending a casual vacation on the pristine beaches of Paradise Island, my first suggestion would be to reserve a room at the breathtaking Atlantis! Selected as one of our *Best Places to Stay* – see Chapter 12 for a longer review.

BREEZES BAHAMAS, *West Bay Street, Cable Beach. Tel. (242) 327-5356, Fax (242) 327-5155. US & Canada bookings (SuperClubs) 1-800-859-7873. Low season rack rates from $220 per double room per night (A.I.). High season rack rates from $270 per double room per night (A.I.). Lower package prices are usually available. Minimum 2 night stay required. All major credit cards accepted.*

Breezes is a great new 400 room "All-Inclusive" resort hotel on Nassau's Cable beach that I liked so much I didn't want to ever check out. Here you can avoid ever reaching for your wallet, as you pay in advance for unlimited meals, activities, cocktails, and entertainment. Everything here is well thought out, providing a seemingly endless array of sports and leisure activities for a relaxed clientele of singles and couples usually between 16 and 38 years old. Each day the extremely friendly and helpful hotel staff lists a schedule of fun activities such as scuba diving, sailing, kayaking, wind surfing, snorkeling, tennis, bike tours, trampoline and trapeze lessons, volleyball tournaments, concerts, and much more.

Breezes does a superb job providing great accommodations, simply outstanding meals, some of the island's most delicious cocktails, and a list of well-designed services and facilities that can easily keep you busy for weeks. All of the 400 sun-drenched rooms are air conditioned and contain large private bathrooms, extremely comfortable bedding, nice furnishings, mini-safes, cable television, am-fm clock radios, plenty of closet space, small sea-view balconies, and direct dial telephones with computer data ports. Besides offering fantastic buffet meals with well over 75 items to choose from during breakfast, lunch, and dinner, there is also an intimate pasta bar and a pool-side snack bar.

Also on the property are three beautiful pools, a great Jacuzzi, two bars serving unlimited top shelf cocktails and soft drinks, Hurricanes disco, a concert stage, billiard tables, a game room, a gift shop and newsstand, inexpensive shuttle bus service to downtown Nassau, free airport transfers, an activities desk, optional excursions, and perhaps the best and most friendly staff of any major resort on the island. For those looking for an unforgettable wedding in The Bahamas, with advance notice, Breezes can arrange a spectacular ceremony on the premises at no additional charge.

I strongly recommend Breezes to those of you looking for lots of fun, a bit of loud Caribbean music, plenty of sunshine, a youthful and casual ambiance, and great value for your hard-earned money. Book you reservation well in advance, as they sell out quite often, even during the low season! Selected as one of our *Best Places to Stay* – see Chapter 12 for a longer review.

RADISSON CABLE BEACH CASINO & GOLF RESORT, *West Bay Street, Cable Beach. Tel. (242) 327-6000, Fax (242) 327-5969. US & Canada bookings (Radisson) 1-800-333-3333. Low season rack rates from $135 per double room per night (E.P.). High season rack rates from $188 per double room per night (E.P.). Lower package prices are often available. "Splash" All Inclusive Plan available. All major credit cards accepted.*

The newly enhanced Radisson Cable Beach Casino & Golf Resort is a good place to stay while vacationing on sun-drenched Cable Beach. This unusually inviting medium-sized beachfront resort hotel is an excellent value for the money and has a full compliment of exciting facilities and services, including a large sandy beachfront, three giant fresh water swimming pools, two open air Jacuzzis, an 18 hole championship golf course, several outdoor tennis courts, an indoor racquetball and squash center, plenty of water sports, a fully equipped sports center, and a complete children's activities program directed by experienced counselors. Guests can also choose from six restaurants with diverse international and local cuisine from Europe and the Caribbean, enjoy cocktails at three different bars, and have direct access to the adjacent casino complex.

The vast majority of rooms face directly out onto the sea and have central air conditioning, private bathrooms, remote controlled satellite television, movie channels, mini-bars, direct dial telephones, mini-safes, voice mail, computer data ports, great sea-view balconies, and some of the most comfortable bedding in town. You can also choose to pre-purchase or upgrade to the "Splash" All Inclusive package that includes unlimited meals at any of the hotel's restaurants, as many cocktails as you desire, all golf green fees, introductory scuba lesson, tennis and racquetball court fees, plenty of non-motorized water sports, round-trip airport transfers, and all taxes and service charges.

The staff at the Radisson are all friendly and professional, and the hotel has a wonderfully relaxed ambiance. Especially popular with families, this resort is a great place to vacation at if you want to have lots of fun in the sun at truly affordable prices. Selected as one of our *Best Places to Stay* – see Chapter 12 for a longer review.

COMPASS POINT, *West Bay Street, near Love Beacha. Tel. (242) 327-4500, Fax (242) 327-3299. US & Canada bookings (Island Outpost) 1-800-688-7678. Low season rack rates from $135 per double room per night (E.P.). High season rack rates from $175 per double room per night (E.P.). All major credit cards accepted.*

If you are looking for a great little resort in a tranquil upscale district of New Providence Island, the trendy Compass Point hotel is a great choice. I first came to this spot some years ago when I was still in the music industry and was invited to recording sessions at the state-of-the-art Compass Point Recording Studios that was then frequented by the Talking Heads, Robert Palmer, and many other top rock and reggae bands. Jamaican-based millionaire Chris Blackwell (founding owner of several record companies and film production companies under the "Island" trademark) recently added the dramatic new Compass Point resort to his successful Island Outpost chain of world-class boutique hotels in Jamaica and along Miami Beach's trendy South Beach. Now Compass Point is quietly becoming the home away from home for well-traveled vacationers and the occasional rock star.

Situated a 15 minute ride west of Cable Beach on several acres of palm tree and hibiscus-lined seaside gardens, the resort is actually a series of wonderful multicolored tropical cabanas and villas that are different from any other lodgings offered in The Bahamas. Most of the hotel's 20 rustic-chic one and two bedroom units are fully air conditioned, and all have sun decks (several face directly onto the sea), deluxe private bathrooms stocked with the hotel chain's own "Outpost" brand of natural hair and skin care products, exotic hardwood floors and furnishings, giant beds, remote control satellite color televisions with video cassette recorders, stereo sound systems with compact disc machines, beautiful batik fabrics and tropical interior designs, electronic mini-safe, stacks of Island Records' best CDs, bathrobes, ceiling fans, coffee makers, mini-bars loaded with top shelf liquors and French Champagne, and in some rooms fully stocked deluxe kitchenettes.

Facilities include an oceanfront restaurant, a well-maintained fresh water swimming pool and sun deck, a small beach area, express laundry and dry cleaning, room service, a nice bar area, an Island Outpost boutique, plenty of hammocks, nice gardens, racks of current travel and fashion magazines, complimentary tennis courts, optional snorkeling, jet skiing, water skiing, sailing, deep sea fishing, scuba diving, submarine rides, and many other excursions.

I strongly recommend this hideaway to those who really want to get away from the stress of big city life, but still want to be a short ride away from countless diversions such as casinos, restaurants, duty free shopping, nightclubs, and sporting activities.

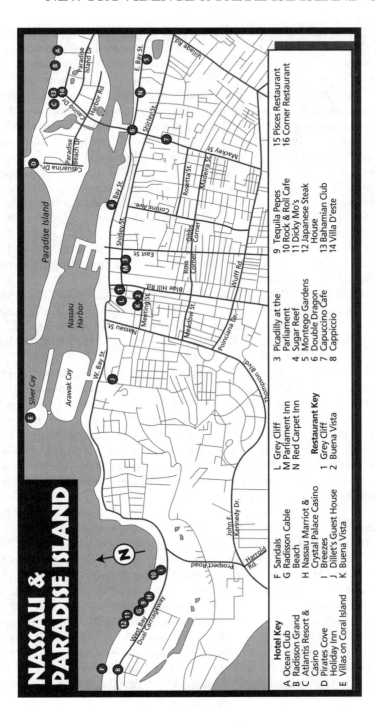

NASSAU & PARADISE ISLAND

Hotel Key

A Ocean Club
B Radisson Grand
C Atlantis Resort & Casino
D Pirates Cove
E Villas on Coral Island
F Sandals
G Radisson Cable Beach
H Nassau Marriot & Crystal Palace Casino
I Breezes
J Dillet's Guest House
K Buena Vista
L Grey Cliff
M Parliament Inn
N Red Carpet Inn

Restaurant Key

1 Grey Cliff
2 Buena Vista
3 Picadilly at the Parliament
4 Sugar Reef
5 Montego Gardens
6 Double Dragon
7 Capuccino Cafe
8 Cappiccio
9 Tequila Pepes
10 Rock & Roll Cafe
11 Dicky Mo's
12 Japanese Steak House
13 Bahamian Club
14 Villa D'este
15 Pisces Restaurant
16 Corner Restaurant

THE VILLAS ON CORAL ISLAND, *Coral Island. Tel. (242) 328-1036, Fax (242) 323-3202. US & Canada bookings (Coral Island) 1-800-324-2111. Low season rack rates from $175 per villa per night (C.P.). High season rack rates from $235 per villa per night (C.P.). All major credit cards accepted.*

This intimate complex of individual seaview villas on Coral Island is a rather good bargain. The property sits just off the coast of Nassau's Cable Beach area and has 22 free-standing air conditioned one bedroom villas that contain private bathrooms, private plunge pools, fully stocked kitchens with microwave ovens and ice makers, dual ceiling fans, hair dryers, mini-bar, remote control satellite televisions and video cassette players, free continental breakfast delivered via room service, daily morning newspapers, nice terraces facing the ocean, comfortable modern wicker furnishings, direct dial telephones, am-fm clock radios, tile flooring, and plenty of space to stretch out in.

Guests here have complimentary access to the famed Coral Island marine life attraction, full use of a nice beach and snorkeling area, and use of the full service restaurant for a small fee.

NASSAU MARRIOTT RESORT & CRYSTAL PALACE CASINO, *Cable Beach. Tel. (242) 327-6200, Fax (242) 327-6459. US & Canada bookings (Marriott) 1-800-228-9290. Low season rack rates from $119 per double room per night (E.P.). High season rack rates from $159 per double room per night. All major credit cards accepted.*

Built to look somewhat like a series of multicolored cruise ships by its former owners (Carnival Cruise Lines), this gigantic modern resort has several towering wings located just off the sea. There are a total of 867 rooms and suites, each with air conditioning, private bathrooms, remote control satellite television, direct dial telephone, and local artwork. The property has a massive 35,000 square foot casino, over a dozen restaurants, several bars, plenty of boutiques, a water sports center, a small beach area, a children's club, a Vegas-style revue, business meeting and convention rooms, and more.

Moderate

BUENA VISTA, *Delancy Street, Nassau, New Providence. Tel. (242) 322-2811, Fax (242) 322-5881. Low season rack rates from $65 per double room per night (E.P.). High season rack rates from $90 per double room per night (E.P.). Special package rates available upon request. All major credit cards accepted.*

This beautiful 19th-century Bahamian manor house is situated just a few blocks above the famed Bay Street shopping district in downtown Nassau. There are five wonderful air conditioned rooms that feature deluxe private bathrooms, remote control cable televisions, direct dial telephones, antique and period style furnishings, fine art on the walls, complimentary coffee and tea services with fine English bone china, and in most cases either private terraces or working fireplaces. Perfect for those with rental cars, from here it is just a six minute drive to most of New Providence Island's best sandy beaches and attractions. The property boasts an amazing gourmet restaurant, business meeting and reception rooms, tranquil gardens, luxurious sitting rooms, optional continental breakfasts, and lots of peace and quiet.

I suggest this wonderful inn for those who have had enough of the large impersonal resort hotels and prefer to get a great deal on a charming room (and still have enough money left over to rent a car and treat themselves to gourmet meals at the Buena Vista's wonderfully romantic restaurant). Selected as one of our *Best Places to Stay* – see Chapter 12 for a longer review.

PIRATE'S COVE HOLIDAY INN, *Paradise Island. Tel. (242) 363-2100, Fax (242) 363-2206. US & Canada bookings (Holiday Inn) 1-800-234-6835. Special year round rack rates from $129 per double room per night (E.P.). All major credit cards accepted.*

This medium-sized family-oriented resort hotel is situated on a tranquil cove beach that is perfect for children. The property has 564 rooms and suites (many are seaview) that all offer private bathrooms, satellite televisions, air conditioning, comfortable furnishings, direct dial telephones, coffee makers, mini-refrigerators, balconies, and lots of sunlight. There is a nice beach area, a one acre free-form freshwater swimming pool with an artificial waterfall and two Jacuzzis, several restaurants and bars, a water sports activity center, and a friendly staff.

SOUTH OCEAN GOLF & BEACH RESORT, *near South Ocean. Tel. (242) 362-4391, Fax (242) 362-4728. US & Canada bookings (Winfare) 1-800-241-6615. Year round rack rates from $110 per double room per night (E.P.). Super Saver rates from $92 per double room per night (E.P.). Lower package prices are usually available. All major credit cards accepted.*

A 30 minute drive away from Nassau on New Providence Island's southern coast, the tropical Colonial-styled South Ocean Golf Resort offers garden-view and seaside rooms at affordable prices. The property was recently purchased by the Canadian-based Winfare group and is currently in the process of a major renovation and upgrade that is expected to make it one of the better equipped affordable hotels on the island. The centerpiece of the hotel is its 18 hole/par 72 golf course that attracts the majority of visitors for its exhilarating fairways and reasonable green fees.

The 250 air conditioned guest rooms are split up into the Club House, overlooking the golf course, and the more impressive seafront Great Houses. Each unit features private tile bathrooms (many with huge Jacuzzis), exotic hardwood furnishings, direct dial telephones, mini-refrigerators, ceiling fans, large patios, mini-safes, color cable televisions, am-fm clock radios, and either double or king bedding. Facilities include a small beach area with complimentary non-motorized water sports, four outdoor tennis courts (free for guests), two restaurants, five bars, a health club, two nice outdoor freshwater swimming pools, a gift shop, inexpensive shuttle service to downtown Nassau and Paradise Island, free golf and tennis clinics, a weekly manager's cocktail party with live music as well as free drinks and hors d'oeuvres, a pro shop, scuba diving and jet skis, a tour desk offering dozens of optional excursions, a brand new beach pavilion with a bar and grill, a supervised children's program, jogging paths, and plenty of free parking.

RADISSON GRAND RESORT, *Casino Drive, Paradise Island. Tel. (242) 363-3500, Fax (242) 63-3900. US & Canada bookings (Radisson) 1-800-333-3333. Low season rack rates from $125 per double room per night (E.P.). High season rack rates from $165 per double room per night (E.P.). Lower package prices are often available. "Splash" All Inclusive Plan available. All major credit cards accepted.*

Situated on a nice stretch of white sand beach on the north shore of Paradise Island, this modern 14 story resort hotel is another good choice for couples and families. The Radisson features 360 medium-sized rooms with great triangular balconies overlooking the beach. All of the rooms are essentially the same style (the upper floors have the most beautiful views) and feature air conditioning, private bathrooms, remote control satellite televisions, direct dial telephones, mini-bars, and nice modern furnishings. The resort also boasts a great beachfront with available water sports, a schedule of daily activities, a nice outdoor pool and sun deck, several restaurants and bars, and business meeting facilities.

Inexpensive

DILLET'S GUEST HOUSE, *Dunmore Ave., Nassau, New Providence. Tel. (242) 325-1133, Fax (242) 325-7183. US & Canada bookings (Charms) 1-800- 74CHARMS. Year round rack rates from $68 per double room per night (C.P.). All major credit cards accepted.*

This great little family owned bed & breakfast on a peaceful residential street is a really good choice for those looking to avoid giant hotels. Dillet's is actually a converted Bahamian mansion in a peaceful upscale residential neighborhood a couple of miles west of downtown Nassau.

Run by the charming Dillet-Knowles family, the inn features seven gigantic suite-style non-smoking guest rooms with nice private bathrooms, air conditioners, white rattan furnishings, local artwork, remote control color cable televisions, extremely comfortable bedding, wall-to-wall tile flooring, separate sitting and/or dining areas, am-fm clock radios, large windows looking out onto fruit-bearing semi-tropical gardens, and fully equipped kitchenettes in most cases.

The inn has a peaceful Old World ambiance and is among my favorite places to unwind. Here you can take advantage of the ground floor fireside sitting rooms, enjoy a complimentary continental breakfast including freshly picked fruits, borrow a good novel from a lending library, enjoy a short stroll down the block to the Ardastra and Botanical Gardens, play a few rounds of table tennis, hike over to Fort Charlotte, and meet plenty of interesting guests from the four corners of the globe who return here year after year. Additional meals and afternoon tea are available on request, and thefacilities include secure on-sight private parking, beautiful gardens with hammocks hanging from exotic fruit trees, nice outdoor patios, and on-demand taxi service. The friendly staff here can help to book optional excursions and special interest tours.

When you want to feel at home while in Nassau, this is one of the best affordable places to do so.

PARLIAMENT INN, *Parliament Street, Nassau. Tel. (242) 322-2836, Fax (242) 326-7196. Year round rack rates from $60 per double room per night (C.P.). Long term rates available upon request. All major credit cards accepted.*

For those looking for nice simple accommodations in the heart of the downtown core of Nassau, this cute inn and restaurant near Rawson Square is the best bet. The family-owned and operated Parliament Inn has six rather pleasant guest rooms that all contain private bathrooms, air conditioners, wall-to-wall carpeting, rattan and wooden furnishings, local artwork, and nice city or courtyard views.

Guests here can take advantage of a really good restaurant serving lunch and dinner every day except Sunday, weekly high season fashion shows and theme nights, two fun bars, adjacent secured private parking, and the close proximity to all the fine duty free shops just a one minute walk away along Bay Street. The staff here are really nice local folks, and can help you reserve rental cars, excursions, sightseeing tours, and all sorts of activities. Highly recommended for singles, businessmen, couples, and families that are on a budget but still prefer to be near all the major sights and attractions.

RED CARPET INN, *East Bay Road, Nassau. Tel. (242) 393-7981, Fax (242) 393-9055. US & Canada bookings (Red Carpet Inns) 1-800-251-1962. Year round rack rates from $63 per double room per night (E.P.). Longer term rates available upon request. All major credit cards accepted.*

The friendly little Red Carpet Inn is among the best full service budget hotels in eastern Nassau's international banking and business district. Owned and personally managed by Michael Duggan (a superb host), this nice 3 star inn has a pair of adjoining low-rise lodges with 36 rooms that feature new private bathrooms, individual air conditioners, double beds, remote control satellite televisions, nice wooden and rattan furnishings, tile and carpet flooring, mini-safes, direct dial telephones, and in several cases even private balconies and kitchenettes stocked with basic utensils.

The entire property has a tranquil ambiance since it is completely surrounded by hundreds of towering wild cherry, gnip, sapodilla, lignum vitae, and sour orange trees. Alongside the rooms is a nice outdoor pool and sun deck, a casual western theme restaurant called The Barn, a poolside grill and open air lounge, plenty of free secure parking, a coin operated laundromat, ice and soda machines, an outdoor gazebo patio, live Calypso music on weekends, and a great staff of local residents that seem to smile effortlessly all the time. While most guests here are budget-conscious young couples and families from Europe and America, there are also many repeat guests that could easily afford much more expensive hotels but understandably prefer to experience the level of personalized service and casual ambiance found through these doors.

There is an adjacent shopping center, inexpensive nearby jitney bus service to the downtown Bay Street boutiques and island beaches, and lots of nicely maintained gardens. Highly recommended for businessmen and vacationers looking for affordable lodging in a quiet and extremely secure neighborhood just outside of Nassau.

SUN FUN RESORTS, *near Cable Beach. Tel. (242) 327-8827, Fax (242) 327-8802. Low season rack rates from $55 per double room per night (E.P.). High season rack rates from $65 per double room per night (E.P.). All major credit cards accepted.*

If your budget is a bit tight but you still prefer to stay in a nice, clean small hotel across the street from a quiet beach, Sun Fun is a good selection. Located about a mile or so west of Cable Beach, this 26 room hotel has an assortment of beautifully maintained rooms and suites that all have air conditioning, private bathrooms, remote control satellite televisions, direct dial telephones, queen sized bedding, ceiling fans, nice simple furnishings, and plenty of natural sunlight. In the slightly more expensive suites there are also wet bars, sofa beds, pool-view patios, and more. The hotel has a nice outdoor swimming pool, a great restaurant, a lounge, a nice staff, and plenty of free parking.

WHERE TO EAT

Very Expensive

GRAYCLIFF, *West Hill Street, Nassau. Tel. (242) 322-2796. Open 7 days a week for dinner and on weekdays for lunch. Dress Code is Smart Casual at lunch, and Jacket and Tie at dinner. All major credit cards accepted.*

Of the hundreds of restaurants I have enjoyed in The Bahamas, Graycliff is without any doubt the finest! The friendly Garzaroli family has made this 250-plus year-old manor house the only 5 star dining room in the nation, and have set the standard for the highest levels of quality and service. Graycliff offers superbly prepared and presented classic French influenced specialties that are truly incredible. The restaurant also features a wine cellar with over 300,000 vintage wines from around the world (it is a multiple winner of *Wine Spectator's* prestigious Grand Award), and a unique Cuban cigar room.

The dinner menu here features a fantastic variety of delicious courses such as Bahamian lobster in puff pastry for $16.50, smoked Scottish salmon with cream cheese at $15.50, escargots in old wine and cream for $15.50, Beluga caviar at $84 per ounce, goose liver pate with truffles for $44, Caesar salads at $7.95, tropical salads for $9.50, baked onion soup at $7.75, lobster bisque for $7.75, tortellini with pesto at $15.75, fettucini with cream sauce and white Italian truffles for $43.75, scallops and grilled shrimp in butter sauce at $36.50, filet of sole in Champagne butter sauce for $34.75, sirloin Angus steak with mushrooms at $32.75, tournedos of lamb in Chablis for $33.75, roasted duckling in Grand Marnier and fruit sauce at $30.50, lobster Graycliff for $36.50, Chateaubriand in Bernaise sauce for two at $77, broiled snapper for $33.75, and a selection of desserts including crepes and homemade cakes starting at $9 each.

You don't have to be a guest to eat here. If you want to save some money, the lunches here are less expensive and only semi-formal. A meal here will definitely give you something to remember for years to come!

COURTYARD TERRACE, *Ocean Club, Paradise Island. Tel. (242) 363-3000. Open for dinner from 7:00pm until about 10:30pm every day of the week. Dress Code is Semi-Formal. Most major credit cards accepted.*

Strikingly situated alongside cascading pools of water in the heart of the ultra-chic Ocean Club hotel, the Courtyard Terrace is certainly the island's most romantic semi-formal restaurant. Executive chef Michael Povaney has created a terrific menu that will appeal to almost anyone who enjoys fine cuisine and superb service. You can enjoy a selection of beautifully presented seasonal items that may include such delicious dishes as baked French onion soup for $8, a rich creamy seafood bisque at $8, amazing crab cakes for $16, Beluga caviar with Stolichnaya vodka at $85, a superb Napoleon of minced lobster for $18, smoked salmon with onions and capers at $14.50, shrimp cocktails for $18, fresh caught lobster prepared in a variety of styles at $42, scampi atop angel hair pasta for $42, breast of free-range chicken at $32, breast of duck with raspberry sauce for $37, tortellini with chicken in Gorgonzola sauce at $32, rack of lamb for two for $92, and a wonderful selection of freshly made cakes and other desserts starting at $6.50 each.

The service here is exceptionally good, and a live band often plays soothing tropical music. Men should make sure to wear a jacket and reservations must be made in advance.

Expensive

BUENA VISTA, *Delancy Street, Nassau. Tel. (242) 322-2811. Open Monday through Saturday evenings. Dress Code is Smart Casual. All major credit cards accepted.*

Housed in a dramatic 19th century manor house a few blocks above downtown Nassau, this outstanding gourmet restaurant is well worth the effort to find! The refined yet welcoming main dining room at Buena Vista overlooks traditional Bahamian gardens and is known all over the region for its huge dinner menu of exceptional European-inspired cuisine.

I returned here recently to find a new menu offering such wonderful treats as an amazing Caesar salad at $6.50, green salad with hearts of palm for $5, smoked Nova Scotia salmon at $12.75, duck pate in puff pastry for $9.50, lobster bisque at $6.50, cream of garlic soup for $5.50, prosciutto (ham) with fresh melon at $10.75, cantaloupe with chilled Port wine for $7.50, oysters Rockefeller at $10.75, escargots in a garlic brandy sauce for $10.25, spinach linguini in creamy white wine at $10.50, cheese ravioli in marinara sauce for $11.50, jumbo shrimp scampi at $32.50, charbroiled Bahamian lobster tails for $34.50, fillet of mahi-mahi in roasted peppers and scallions at $31, black Angus tenderloin with eggplant and mozzarella for $34.50, pan-fried veal scaloppini at $31, broiled chicken breast with rosemary for $29, roasted rack of lamb for two at $70, baked venison and pheasant for $33.50, and an outstanding selection of daily multiple course specials starting at $29.50.

The wine list features well over 125 of the world's best wines at good prices, including Cos d' Estornel, Chateau Talbot, Chateau Margaux, Grand Echezeaux, Chassagne Montrachet, Mondavi Reserve Sauvignon Napa, Lindeman Cabernet Sauvignon Blanc, Marques de Riscal Reserva, and others.

Reservations are suggested but are not always necessary. The service here is warm and friendly, the ambiance cool and comfortable. I strongly suggest this fine establishment for romantic couples, vacationing families, and even groups looking for the perfect spot to hold a private function while in Nassau.

VILLA D'ESTE, *Atlantis Resort and Casino, Paradise Island. Tel. (242) 363-0000. Open 6:00pm until 11:00pm everyday except Wednesdays. Dress Code is Smart Casual. All major credit cards accepted.*

This excellent upscale Italian restaurant creates a mouth-watering array of classic northern Italian dishes that are brilliantly prepared and presented in grand style. The restaurant's interior features marble floors, frescoed ceilings, pastel walls lined with soothing still life paintings, plenty of polished brass and hardwood fixtures, and a refined yet relaxed ambiance infused with Frank Sinatra music.

Once you have been seated, one of the excellent waiters will present you with a freshly baked foccacio bread and a menu offering mixed antipasto for $9.50, an amazing terrine of roasted vegetables with goat cheese at $8.75, beef carpaccio for $9.50, crispy fried calamari at $9, huge garlic grilled portobello mushrooms for $8, a rich 3 bean minestrone soup at $5.25, Caesar salad for $6.25, an outstanding salad of fresh mozzarella cheese and tomato with pesto vinaigrette at $7.50, angel hair pasta with garlic tomato sauce for $18.50, fettucini Alfredo that literally melts in your mouth at $18, giant lobster raviolis for $25.50, grilled lamb chops at $33, charcoal grilled chicken for $24.50, pan-roasted tenderloin steak at $32.50, veal scaloppini with wild mushrooms for $32, fresh jumbo shrimp in pasta with roasted peppers at $32, and great desserts such as semifreddo chocolate and espresso mouse cake at $5.50 and marscapone cheesecake with strawberries at $5.50.

The service is among the finest I have seen in The Bahamas, and the experience is well worth the effort to book a table at least a day or two in advance. Highly recommended as the best gourmet Italian restaurant in the country!

BAHAMIAN CLUB, *Atlantis Resort and Casino, Paradise Island. Tel. (242) 363-0000. Open 6:30pm until 11:30pm daily except Tuesday. Dress Code is Smart Casual. All major credit cards accepted.*

When you're in the mood for a truly memorable steak and seafood dinner on Paradise Island, this is one of the best places to go. Designed with an interior that resembles a cross between a private men's club and an opulent Old World oyster house, the Bahamian Club's white vested waiters really know how to pamper you. The menu features incredibly delicious crab cakes at $11.50, pan-seared tenderloin steak for $11, jumbo shrimp cocktail at $12, oysters with shrimp for $12, a great baked red onion soup at $5.50, club salad for $8.50, asparagus with Hollandaise sauce at $5.25, grilled sweet corn for $4.50, swordfish steak at $34, fresh yellowfin tuna for $34, local grouper at $33, T-bone steaks for $37, tender lamb chops at $36, a huge mixed grill for $33, filet mignon at $36, roasted half chicken for $29, chateaubriand at $40, and steak with lobster for $37. Make sure to call for an advance reservation!

JAPANESE STEAK HOUSE, *West Bay Street, Cable Beach. Tel. (242) 327-7781. Open 4:00pm until 11:30pm daily. Dress Code is casual but neat. Most major credit cards accepted.*

When you want to try something different, head for this great Japanese restaurant near the Radisson. After being seated next to other patrons around one of several large Teppanyaki grill tables, skillful chefs prepare and cook an exotic Asian meal right in front of your eyes. Carefully sautéed or grilled with spices such as sesame oil and ginger, their most delicious dishes include Hibachi chicken for $24.95, Sukiyaki rib-eye steak at $29.95, Hibachi shrimp for $34.95, Teppanyaki New York strip steak at $32.95, grilled grouper for $26.95, baked local lobster Japanese style at $43.95, vegetable fried rice for $9.95, and all sorts of sakes, beers, plum wines, and assorted cocktails.

While a bit more expensive than most other area restaurants, I highly recommend this place. Reservations are suggested.

Moderate

DICKY MO'S, *West Bay Street, Cable Beach. Tel. (242) 327-7854. Open from 7:00am until 12 midnight every day of the week. No Dress Code. Most major credit cards accepted.*

Located between Sandals and the Radisson, this laid-back seafood and steak restaurant is packed almost every night with a good mix of locals and visitors. After sitting at one of the open air tables the friendly waiters here (typically dressed in navy jackets) will help you select the day's best dishes. Their giant menu includes such favorites as shrimp cocktail for $9.95, conch fritters at $4.95, French onion soup for $5.50, Caesar salad at $8.95, local lobster salad for $15.95, sautéed mahi-mahi at $15.95, deep fried sea scallops for $25.95, prime rib of beef at $22.95, stuffed pork chops for $14.95, barbecued baby back ribs at $12.50, rotisserie chicken for $12.50, and plenty of other huge plates that come with vegetables, coleslaw, and fries. This is a good place to enjoy a hearty casual meal!

SUGAR REEF HARBOURSIDE BAR & GRILLE, *Deveaux Street, Nassau. Tel. (242) 356-3065. Open 7 days per week from 11:00am until 10:00pm. No Dress Code. All major credit cards accepted.*

Located just off Nassau's active harbor, about a half mile or so west of the Paradise Island Bridge, this delightful open air eatery is really a great choice for lunch and dinner. Lined with colorful mosaics and unique wooden furnishings, this popular informal seaside restaurant creates rather tasty international dishes like seafood crepes at $6, calamari for $5.75, crab cakes at $9.75, conch chowder for $4.75, Caesar salads at $7, oriental chicken salad for $10.25, pastrami sandwiches on rye bread at $6.25, tuna melts with tomato and bacon for $7.25, blackened mahi-mahi sandwiches with roasted peppers at $8.75, huge bacon cheeseburgers for $6.75, barbecued ribs at $8.75, fried alligator for $6.75, smoked salmon with sun dried tomatoes at $9.75, house salads for $5.50, vegetarian lasagna at $14.75, daily pasta specials for $14.75, grilled Bahamian lobster for $22.95, pan roasted grouper with leeks at $21.25, tempura shrimp for $24.25, grilled stuffed pork tenderloin at $23.25, pepper steak for $23.25, tiramisu at $4.50, Bahamian bread pudding for $3.75, and iced cappuccinos at $3. You can drive, walk, or sail to their pier-side tables and have a remarkably good meal in a welcoming casual ambiance.

MONTAGU GARDENS, *East Bay Street, Fort Montagu area. Tel. (242) 394-6347. Dress Code is Smart Casual. All major credit cards accepted. Closed on Sundays.*

Formerly an 18th century Bahamian mansion, and located just across from the sea, Montagu Gardens has been nicely converted into a good moderately priced steak and seafood restaurant. The relaxed dining room presents lunch and dinner choices like stuffed mushrooms with crab meat at $5.50, nacho chips with minced lobster for $7, stuffed jalepeno peppers at $5, Caesar salads for $5, conch chowder for $5.75, grilled grouper sandwiches at $8, bacon cheeseburgers for $6.50, pasta with tomato basil sauce at $10, fettuccine Alfredo with chicken for $13.50, T-bone steaks at $26.95, N.Y. strip steak for $17, lamb chops with mint jelly at $17, blackened chicken breast for $13.50, baby back ribs at $17, grilled gulf shrimp for $22, and broiled local lobster at $27.50. Reservations are recommended.

PIISCES RESTAURANT, *West Bay Street, Cable Beach area. Tel. (242) 327-8827. Open daily for breakfast, lunch, and dinner. No Dress Code. All major credit cards accepted.*

I had a really good meal in this simple little restaurant in the Sun Fun Resort recently, and for the money it is one of Cable Beach's best values. The menu here showcases a good selection of American and Bahamian specialties, including two eggs any style at $3.50, sardines with grits for $5.50, tuna sandwiches at $3.50, B.L.T.'s for $3.50, grilled cheese at $3.00, cheeseburgers for $4, chef's salad at $5, steamed fish for $8.50, center cut pork chops at $8.50, deep fried shrimp platters for $10.50, cracked conch at $8.50, shrimp cocktails for $7.50, lobster salad plates at $16, surf & turf for $25, filet mignon at $18, half a baked chicken for $10.50, seafood combos at $14, and fresh pies for $2.50 each. Reservations are not necessary here.

ROCK & ROLL CAFE, *West Bay Street, Cable Beach. Tel. (242) 327-7639. Open daily from 12 noon until about 2:00am. No Dress Code. All major credit cards accepted.*

With a prime location just off the beach near the Forte Nassau Hotel, this converted mansion now is home to a Hard Rock-style bar and restaurant. Currently among the most popular eating establishments for visitors, this place is lined with gold records, autographed guitars, and other rock memorabilia. They have several small sea-view dining rooms and a beachfront patio where you can select from a massive menu featuring spicy chicken wings at $5, stuffed potatoes with bacon and cheddar cheese for $2.95, large nachos at $9.95, conch chowder for $3.75, chef salads at $9.75, fettuccini Alfredo for $9.95, fried chicken at $8.95, spicy Cajun shrimp with rice for $17.95, filet mignon at $23.95, grilled porter house steak for $19.95, French bread pizzas at $9.95, pan-fried snapper for $14.95, tuna melt sandwiches at $7.50, B.L.T. sandwiches for $5.50, and all sorts of vegetarian items, desserts, ice cold beverages, and exotic cocktails. While far from gourmet or fancy, this is a fun place to grab a good meal at reasonable prices.

DOUBLE DRAGON, *East Bay Street, Nassau. Tel. (242) 393-5718. Open 7 days a week until at least 10:00pm. Dress Code is Casual. Most major credit cards accepted.*

This is one of the few affordable Chinese restaurants worth visiting in Nassau. Located just off the Nassau side of the Paradise Island Bridge, the simple oriental dining room here prepares classic oriental dishes such as won ton soup at $2.25, seafood and tofu soup for $4.75, egg rolls at $1.50, barbecued spare ribs for $5.25, pan fried dumplings at $5.50, coconut shrimp for $6.50, vegetarian spring rolls at $3.25, stir fried vegetables for $7.95, sweet and sour pork at $8.50, shredded Szechuan style beef for $9.25, chicken low mein at $8.50, Singapore style rice noodles for $8.95, shrimp fried rice at $5.25, lobster chop suey for $11.95, and dozens of other favorites.

TEQUILA PEPE'S, *Radisson Hotel on West Bay Street, Cable Beach. Tel. (242) 327-6000. Open for dinner only every night. Dress Code is Casual. All major credit cards accepted.*

This moderately priced casual restaurant above the Radisson's lobby is the only dedicated Mexican steak restaurant in all of Nassau and serves up large portions of spicy dishes with all the trimmings. At dinner only, you can munch on your favorite south of the border standards such as super nachos at $4.50, chili rellenos for $6.25, spicy chicken wings at $5.50, black bean soup for $4, taco salad with chili at $4.75, grilled chicken breast for $17, Mexicali shrimp at $17, sirloin steak ranchero for $18, chicken and cheese quesadillas at $14.95, vegetable fajitas for $13.40, beef enchiladas at $15.50, twin tacos for $14.50, rice pudding at $3, and fried ice cream for $3.50. This is a fun place to sit back and enjoy a causal meal inspired by well known recipes from just south of the border.

Inexpensive

CAPRICCIO RISTORANTE ITALIANO, *West Bay Street, Cable Beach. Tel. (242) 327-8547. Open from about 12noon until 10:00pm or so every evening. No Dress Code. Most major credit cards accepted.*

I fell in love with this cute little family-style Italian restaurant the moment I walked past the place and smelled that amazing home-made Genovese pesto sauce wafting from the kitchen. This informal restaurant and outdoor cafe at the western edge of Cable Beach is an absolute delight. Many of the dishes served here have been prepared using recipes that Mrs. Pizzichini (the delightful chef and owner) learned from her grandmother in Bologna, Italy when she was a child.

The menu includes traditionally prepared antipasto at $9.50, thick minestrone soup for $4.75, mixed salad at $6.50, Parma ham with melon for $8.50, lasagna at $8.50, a superb pasta with fresh pesto for $10.50, sautéed chicken in white wine sauce at $18.75, deep fried scampi for $12.50, veal scaloppini at $17.50, and the only real espresso in town! This is a great find, where you are invited to bring your own wine. Reservations are not usually required.

PICK A DILLY AT THE PARLIAMEMT INN, *Parliament Street, Nassau. Tel. (242) 322-2836. Open for lunch and dinner from Monday through Saturday. No Dress Code. All major credit cards accepted.*

When I'm a bit exhausted from strolling along downtown Nassau's Bay Street shopping district and want a good affordable lunch or dinner, this is one of my favorite places to head for. The giant menu offers well-prepared Bahamian and international specialties like smoked mahi-mahi at $8.95, beer battered Italian sausage for $5, beer battered shrimp in honey mustard sauce at $8, local chicken wings with blue cheese for $7, Mexican 4 layer nachos at $7, green rice loaf with cheddar for $6.95, conch chowder at $6.95, Greek salad for $7.95, vegetable stir fry at $10.25, chicken satay in peanut sauce for $9.25, grilled garlic shrimp at $14.95, blackened chicken breast for $10.50, New York strip steak at $15.95, pasta with tomato basil sauce for $9, poached salmon at $10.50, tuna salad sandwich for $6.95, Reuben sandwich at $6.75, cheeseburgers for $6.95, barbecued pork ribs at $9, and great desserts like their famous Banana a la Dilly for $4.95.

This is a good casual place to unwind and even meet a few hilarious locals while enjoying cold beers and hot food.

CAPPUCCINO CAFÉ & SPECIALTY SHOP, *Mackey Street, Nassau. Tel. (242) 394-6332. Closed on Sundays. No Dress Code. Most major credit cards accepted.*

This new café, restaurant, and gourmet takeout shop near the Nassau side of the Paradise Island Bridge has a great selection of extremely tasty homemade soups, salads, sandwiches, and specialty platters. Their extensive menu offerings include Caesar salads for $5.95, Bulgarian salads with feta cheese at $7.50, fresh fruit salads for $3.95, Bahamian shrimp and lobster salad at $8.50, roast Angus Beef sandwiches for $5.50, turkey breast sandwiches at $4.25, tuna salad with olives and pimentos on French bread for $6.50, grilled turkey with melted cheddar sandwiches at $5.25, fresh buffola mozzerella cheese and tomatoes with basil for $6.25, BLT's at $4.25, conch pate and imported crackers for $4.50, smoked salmon and cream cheese with capers and caviar at $9.95, and over 20 different coffees and refreshing tropical cocktails.

This is the perfect place to stop before heading off to have a great picnic.

THE CORNER RESTAURANT, *Carmichael Street, Carmichael area. Tel. (242) 361-7445. Open every day of the week for breakfast, lunch, and dinner. No Dress Code. All major credit cards accepted.*

If you are heading off to the island's south shore and are looking for a great meal at affordable prices, this is *the* place to go. The exterior is rather simple, but inside The Corner you will find a beautiful hardwood-lined dining room where they serve up gigantic portions of Bahamian and American specialties. Among the items here are 2 eggs with bacon and grits for $3.50, stewed fish with Johnny cakes at $7, chicken souse for $5, mutton souse at $6, steak dinners for $10, fried grouper meals at $7, pork chop dinners for $6, hot wings at $2.50, cheeseburgers for $3, and plenty of daily specials including side orders of vegetables and rice or coleslaw and macaroni salad. The service is great and they also offer takeout items.

SUBWAY, *Charlotte Street, Madeira Street, Blue Hill Road, East Bay Street, Nassau. Tel. (242) 322-7909). Open 6 to 7 days a week until at least 8pm depending on specific location. No Dress Code. Cash Only - No Credit cards accepted.*

When you're running around downtown Nassau or Cable Beach and want a quick bite to eat, this is a healthy alternative to the other fast food joints. The US-based Subway chain of sandwich shops has franchised four operations here, and they do a great job of making inexpensive 6" and foot long subs on fresh white or wheat bread with your choice of 12 different toppings. Prices for a hunger quenching 12" sub range from $3.39 to $6.99 each, and you can choose roast beef, genoa salami, pepperoni, turkey, ham, bologna, tuna, seafood salad with lobster, steak and cheese, roasted chicken, or just cheese and vegetables.

CABLE BEACH

Getting to Cable Beach

From Nassau International Airport a taxi will cost somewhere around $12 per couple including a few bags. Remember that few taxis use their meters, so make sure to get the price settled before you leave the airport.

From Paradise Island a taxi will set you back about $13 per car load (not per person). You can also walk across the long Paradise Island Bridge and take a 75 cent bus heading down Bay Street until you reach the British Colonial Hotel where you catch another bus running down Bay Street (see below).

From downtown Nassau a taxi will cost roughly $9 per car load to anywhere on the Cable Beach strip. To save some money you can also hop on bus #10 or #38 from the stop across the street from the British Colonial Hotel on Bay Street, and for a fare of 75 cents it will let you off at one of several stops along Cable Beach's main West Bay Street. From the bus stops it is only a one minute walk to the many adjacent hotels and beaches.

ORIENTATION

Located five miles west of downtown Nassau, the **Cable Beach** area is centered around a two mile long crescent white sand beach. The area's name comes from a major transatlantic telephone cable to Florida that was built on this site. This is one of Nassau's most developed tourist resort centers, and is actually a really nice place stay while visiting the island.

There are a great variety of water sports rental facilities, moderately priced international restaurants, a large casino complex, several entertaining bars, a wonderful aqua colored seashore, and a couple of interesting places to shop.

SEEING THE SIGHTS

A Stroll Along Cable Beach, West to East

The best place to start your visit to Cable Beach is to get off the bus at the **West Bay Shopping Centre** on West Bay Street. While far from exciting by American standards, this little mall contains a couple of interesting places like the **Caripelago Cafe & Gallery** where you can enjoy a superb iced Antiguan coffee for a mere $1.50 while staring up at a collection of unusual Afro-Caribbean artwork and folk-art items (all for sale). This same center houses several of Cable Beach's inexpensive fast food joints such as Subway, Domino's Pizza, and a packed TCBY yogurt shop.

From here, carefully cross the street and turn right to follow West Bay Street to the west. A few hundred yards later you will pass by the area's major seaside resorts lining the left hand side of the road. The first large hotel you will pass is the brand new **Sandals Royal Bahamian**, a super-deluxe all inclusive resort. From this point you must keep walking a short distance to reach the public beach areas. If you continue west for another 1/4 mile or so, the sleek facade of the family-oriented **Radisson Cable Beach Resort** will soon appear. From here you walk through the hotel lobby and head down some stairs to easily access a great wide stretch of Cable Beach (or perhaps take a quick dip in their nice big swimming pool). Just across the street is the Radisson-owned **Cable Beach Sports Center** where for a reasonable fee you can play on one of many indoor squash and racquetball courts, or use over a dozen professionally surfaced tennis courts (lit at night).

Just next door you can't miss the strangely colored cement towers that make up the massive **Nassau Marriott Resort**, one of the largest hotels in The Bahamas. After walking through the glittering lobby, head down the escalator, and soon you will enter the bustling **Crystal Palace Casino**. This is a major attraction for thousands of tourists and more serious gamblers each day, with its hundreds of slot machines, dozens of Blackjack and poker tables, several craps games, a new sports betting section, and the more exclusive Baccarat pit. Here you can also grab a hearty sandwich, or catch a Vegas-style revue (complete with elaborately costumed topless dancers) on most evenings. *The Crystal Palace Casino has no admission charge, and for those at least 18 years of age it is open daily from 10:00am to 4:00am, with slot machines accessible 24-hours a day.*

From the Casino you should stroll along the hotel's tranquil seaside boardwalk before departing the Marriott through the main entrance on West Bay Street and turn left to keep heading west. Just across the road on the other side of West Bay Street you can visit the **Covered Crafts Market**, a smaller version of Nassau's famous Straw Market where inexpensive trinkets and hand-made gifts can be bargained for. *The market is open daily from about 10:00am until 6:00pm and costs nothing to enter.*

When you're done at the market, cross back over the road and turn right until you pass the quiet medium-sized **Forte Nassau Hotel**, where a good selection of water sports such as parasailing, jet skiing, and boat trips are offered to the general public on the beach. This is a good spot to take a well deserved dip into the crystal clear Atlantic Ocean and work on your tan! On West Bay Street, alongside the Forte are a couple of interesting entertainment venues, including the youthful **Johnny Canoe Bar** and the rather popular the **Rock & Roll Cafe**, a Hard Rock Cafe-style bar and restaurant with occasional live music events and a huge sea-view patio.

After passing the bars, walk to the wonderful new tree-lined **Tropical Walkway**, dividing West Bay Road, and keep an eye out for the concrete labels embedded into the sidewalk describing many of the exotic flora and fauna planted here. The final full service hotel found along this eastern section of Cable Beach is the outstanding **Breezes** all inclusive resort that can be entered only by registered guests. From here it is just a three minute walk to the fantastic Arnold Palmer-managed 18 hole/par 72 championship **Cable Beach Golf Course** that gives discounted rates and waives the membership fees to all registered hotel guests in the area.

Just East of Cable Beach

Now you can choose to take a taxi or hop on jitney bus #10 or #38 to continue eastward along West Bay Street. About 1 1/2 miles past the end of Cable Beach, the street runs past the small **Saunders Beach**, an extremely popular disco called **The Zoo**, and the huge **Tony Roma's** rib restaurant.

At this point, make sure to tell the taxi or jitney bus driver that you wish to exit on **Chippingham Road**. Once you have turned right down Chippingham Road you will walk about 50 yards until reaching the stone gateway that marks the entrance to the **Nassau Botanical Gardens** on the left side of the road. Here you can tour over 17 acres landscaped with several hundred varieties of plants and trees. While still in desperate need of additional renovations, the lush gardens were built on the site of a former limestone mine and are well worth wandering around for an hour or so on a nice day. There are paved walkways that pass by plaques listing the flora's Latin names, several statues, great lawns, and an oriental lilly pond with a waterfall fountain donated by the government of China. *The gardens are open daily from 8:00am until 4:00pm and cost just $1 per person to enter.*

From the botanical gardens you can keep walking up Chippingham Road for another 50 yards or so until reaching a well-marked turnoff leading another 75 yards to the right towards the entrance to the **Ardastra Gardens & Zoo**. This privately owned attraction is the nation's only zoo and is well worth a visit. Here you will find a path that leads past 5 1/2 acres of tropical landscaping complete with huts, ponds, and cages containing some 300 animals found locally and in Caribbean countries, including several endangered Bahamian parrots, yellow amazon parrots, mandarin ducks, sea turtles, meerkats, iguanas, ocelots, lemurs, cockatoos, peacocks, macaws, capuchin monkeys, snakes, two-toed sloths, jaguars, and other creatures. The main highlight for most people are a band of pink flamingos that have been trained to march in single file during the 11:00am, 2:00pm, and 4:00pm performances. *The zoo is open daily from 9:00am until 5:00pm and costs $10 per person to enter, including admittance to one flamingo show.*

Now retrace you steps back down Chippingham Road and follow it until you reach West Bay Street. Turn right on the street and after about 25 yards bear left to head past a bustling **Outdoor Conch and Fish Market**. The road now leads onto a small island called **Arawak Cay**, where barges from the Out Islands fill up with water. Follow the signs leading to a bridge that heads for **Silver Cay**. At the foot of the bridge you will find a parking lot where you must wait a few minutes for a free shuttle bus that takes visitors to the famous **Coral Island** marine life park and attraction.

Coral Island boasts a great underwater observatory pavilion where you can look through over two dozen huge picture windows some 20 feet below the surface. You'll be treated to great views of native coral reefs teeming with lobsters, grouper, sharks, snappers, hogfish, grunts, trumpetfish, barracudas, chub, rays, yellow jacks, sergeant majors, ballonfish, porcupinefish, and many other swimming and crawling creatures between the rocks. There are also special man-made pools full of captive stingrays and spotted eagle rays that are fed daily at 10:00am and 3:00pm, sharks that are fed at 11:00am and 1:00pm, and an artificial reef tank with creatures that are fed at 2:00pm. Nearby is also a tank loaded with giant green, loggerhead, and hawksbill turtles. For small children there is a pool with starfish and conch that can be touched.

The property also boasts a full service villa-style hotel, a good sea-view restaurant, gift shops, and a private beach area with good snorkeling possibilities and nearby changing rooms. *Coral Island is open daily from 9:00am until 6:00pm, and costs $16 per person to enter, plus an additional $6 per person for optional snorkeling. Free transportation is provided to and from Cable Beach, Paradise Island, and downtown Nassau.*

Now return to West Bay Street and turn left to follow it eastward for a bit less than a 1/2 mile or so until you can turn right onto a small lane called Marcus Bethel Way. The lane curves to the right and proceeds alongside **Clifford Park** where a giant party is held each year on July 10th to commemorate Bahamian Independence Day.

Just above a hill near the park, you can't help but notice the massive 18th-century limestone **Fort Charlotte**. Constructed to defend Nassau's harbor from enemy ships, this is the largest such structure on the island (not a single cannon blast was ever fired from here, by the way). You can walk around this wonderfully restored fortress and see its drawbridge, moat, dungeons, and chambers. *The fort is open Monday through Saturday from 9:00am until 4:00pm and is free.*

DOWNTOWN NASSAU

Getting to Nassau

From Nassau International Airport a taxi will cost somewhere around $17.50 per couple including a few bags. Remember that few taxis use their meters so make sure to get the price settled before you leave the airport.

From Cable Beach a taxi will cost about $8 to just about anywhere in the downtown core. There is also jitney bus #10 or #38 that for 75 cents can get you directly to Bay Street.

From Paradise Island taxis charge around $9 per car to most downtown locations. There are also **Water Taxis** scheduled every 30 minutes between 9:30am and 6:00pm, with service from the island side of the Paradise Island Bridge or Casuarina Road near the entrance to Club Med, to the Prince George Wharf just behind downtown's Straw, for about $2 per person each way. The only other alternative is walk across the Paradise Island Bridge and take a jitney bus ride for 75 cents along Bay Street until you reach the downtown core.

GUIDED TOURS OF DOWNTOWN NASSAU!

*The Bahamian Ministry of Tourism has recently begun offering a new program of "**Professionally Guided Walking Tours.**" These 90 minute tours depart Rawson Square's tourist information office twice an hour between 10:00am and 4:00pm Monday through Saturday, and are guided by self-employed graduates from the government's Bahamahost tourism program. They feature a maximum group of 10 people, and guide you on a leisurely walk while quickly explaining sights such as the Pompey Museum, Junkanoo Museum, Rawson Square, Parliament Square, House of Assembly, Senate, Supreme Court, Garden of Rememberance, Nassau Public Library, Jacaranda, Government House, Queen's Staircase, and Fort Fincastle.*

The exact sights change frequently, so please check with the guides for specific details. The price is only $2 per person (plus admission charges to the museums) and gratuities are greatly appreciated by the guides. For more details contact the Transportation and Tours Unit of the Ministry of Tourism at (242) 322-8634, or stop by their Rawson Square offices.

SEEING THE SIGHTS

The best place to begin your exploration of Nassau is at the beginning of Bay Street near the side of the old British Colonial Hotel. **Bay Street** is the commercial heart and soul of Nassau, and is the best place in the country to pick up great values on all sorts of local crafts and imported duty-free merchandise. As you walk along Bay Street there are also several sights and attractions well worth taking advantage of.

The first block of Bay Street is lined mainly by a series of china, crystal, and jewelry shops, but on the left side of the street just off of the corner of George Street is the **Pompey Museum** located in Vendue House, a former 18th-century auction hall for slaves brought into The Bahamas. This is a small and rather interesting museum dedicated to the hsitory of slavery and its eventual abolishment in the 1830s. There are relics from Africa, photographs of plantation life, video clips of the history and culture of the nation during the slavery era, and a gallery filled with works by famed local artisans. *The Pompey museum is open Monday through Friday from 10:00am until 1:00pm and again from 2:00pm until 4:30pm, as well as on Saturday from 10:00am until 1:00pm, and costs around $2 per person to enter.*

The next block of Bay Street is much more interesting. Besides having several better quality boutiques and perfume shops on both sides of the street, here you will find the famous indoor **Straw Market**. This market is where tourists go to bargain and haggle their way to great deals on

Bahamian straw hats, straw handbags, T-shirts, souvenirs, and other gift items. While the merchants can seem a bit pushy at times, deals are especially good on days when the cruise ships are not in port and business is a bit slow. *The straw market is open daily from around 8:30am until at least 6:00pm with no admission fee.*

If you walk through the Straw Market and exit via the rear, you can make a right turn onto **Woodes Rodgers Walk**. This street faces Nassau Harbour and from here you can see the **Prince George Wharf**. This area is where major cruise ships dock while in Nassau, as well as where you can catch the water taxis to Paradise Island. Besides several inexpensive shops selling souvenirs to cruise ship passengers, and a government licensed open air **Hair Braiding Center** (the official rate is $2 per braid), there are also a few fine sights, the most important of which is on Woodes Rodgers Walk itself – the new **Junkanoo Museum**. This is where many of the best costumes and masks used on the December 26th and January 1st late night Junkanoo parades are kept for public inspection. There are also exhibits on local folk art and traditions. *The Junkanoo Museum is open daily from 10:00am until 4:00pm and costs $1 per person to enter.*

Walk to the east end of Woodes Rodgers Walk near the port's **Harbour Control Tower** and then turn (with your back facing the harbor) to walk a few paces into the heart of **Rawson Square**. The building in the center of this peaceful tree-lined square is the **Ministry of Tourism Information Center**, where you will find all sorts of free maps, brochures, and helpful advice about what to see and do on the islands every day of the week from 9:00am until 5:00pm.

This is also where the inexpensive walking tours of downtown Nassau depart from (see sidebar on the previous page), as well as the place to catch 25-30 minute long **horse drawn carriage rides** through the downtown streets ($10 per couple). The bronze statue in the heart of Rawson Square is the bust of **Sir Milo Boughton Butler** (1906-1979), the first Governor General of the Commonwealth of the Bahamas.

Now walk directly across Bay Street and head directly over to the small complex of antique pink colored government buildings that make up the adjacent **Parliament Square**. The square centers around a statue of Queen Victoria of England, and is flanked by the **House of Assembly** on the right, the **Senate** in the back center, and the **House of the Official Opposition Party** to the left. These buildings house much of the national government's top bureaucracy; owing to security concerns, they cannot be visited by the general public during most days.

Now bear right down Bay Street until you reach the next corner, where you will turn left to head up **Parliament Street**. The large regal building you pass on the left side of this exclusive street is the **Supreme**

Court Building, closed to the public, but hosting a magnificent morning procession before each of the four quarterly opening sessions each year. During this celebration, the country's Chief Justice inspects the guards of honor and is accompanied by a performance of the Royal Bahamas Police Force Band dressed in their white pith helmets and genuine leopard skin trimmed uniforms.

Just across the other side of the same street you will find the wonderful **Parliament Inn** with its fun Pick-a-Dilly bar and restaurant on the left side of the street. The inn was built on the sight of a former sponge cleaning yard, but a devastating fungus in the 1920s wiped out both the sponges and its once thriving export industry, leaving the land vacant until this small affordable hotel and restaurant was built in 1937.

Once you reach the back of the Supreme Court, make a left turn through the **Garden of Remembrance** park. This tranquil park is dedicated to those who died in the World Wars and includes a memorial cenotaph inscribed with the names of Bahamians who did not return after serving in the British armed forces. Also on the monolith are the names of four Bahamian Defense Force soldiers that died when their boat was destroyed by the Cuban military in 1980.

Just behind the park is the **Nassau Public Library**, which was originally built in 1798 as a town jail and converted into a library in 1873. These days it is a regular public library and has a fine historical museum on the second floor where you can see exhibits of Lucayan Indian era relics, Bahamian crafts, and rare philatelic pieces. The top floor has a panoramic lookout with fine downtown views that make for a good photo opportunity. *The library and museum is open Monday through Thursday from 10:00am until 6:00pm, Fridays from 10:00am until 5:00pm, and Saturday from 10:00am until 4:00pm, and the museum costs $1 per person to enter.*

Return to Parliament Street and keep walking uphill while passing several lesser important government buildings. Along the way, on the left side of the next block, you will pass the former sight of the Royal Victoria Hotel, the first major tourist hotel built in The Bahamas way back in 1861. At the far right corner of the same street is **Jacaranda**, a stunning 19th-century mansion that once was home to the disgraced Duke of Windsor (a former Royal Governor of the Bahamas), and was later purchased by Canadian real estate mogul Sir Harry Oakes. In the 1940s, Sir Harry Oakes owned over 7,000 acres of prime Nassau real estate before he was mysteriously murdered. Jacaranda is closed to the public at the present time.

At the next corner you should bear left onto **East Hill Street** and walk across the road to pop inside the massive modern **General Post Office Building**, where you can purchase colorful stamps for all those postcards you've been writing to your friends and families. Another pleasant surprise at the post office is that the vending machines just in front sell ice cold sodas at just 50 cents each (the best deal in town!). *The post office is open Monday through Friday from 8:30am until 5:30pm, and Saturdays from 8:30am until 12:30pm.*

Keep walking along East Hill Street and then make a right turn at the next corner onto East Street, a left turn onto Sands Road, and the next right onto Elizabeth Avenue. After passing the hospital, keep walking towards the **Queen's Staircase Straw Market** and proceed up the 65 step **Queen's Staircase**, a once important military road from downtown Nassau to the fortress above that was cut by slaves out of a limestone hill back in the early 19th century. Once you reach the top of the stairs, make a sharp right turn and head towards the giant 12 story **Water Tower** on Bennet's Hill, which rises to 216 feet above sea level.

Just past the Water Tower there is an entrance to **Fort Fincastle**. The fortress was built by Royal Governor Lord Dunmore in 1793 in the shape of a paddle boat in order to scare off potential invaders. Since it was never actually used to defend Nassau, the fortress eventually was converted into a lighthouse and signal tower. Nowadays it can be visited to see some old English recoil cannons, side chambers, and a wonderful panoramic viewing area out over the entire island. *The fortress is open daily from sunrise to sunset with no admission charges.*

From the fortress, take a small set of stone stairs until making your first right turn down an unmarked lane, and then make a left turn down Sands Road, then a right onto East Street, and finally a left turn onto East Hill Street. This lane will bring you in a few blocks to **Gregory's Arch**, an impressive tunnel cut into a large hill known as Prospect Ridge that still divides the rich downhill sections of Nassau from the "Over the Hill" poor neighborhoods found just on the other (left) side of the arch. East Hill Street then curves to the right and merges into Market Street, where you can catch a glimpse inside the fabulous 19th-century **St. Andrew's Kirk**, a famous Presbyterian church that opened its doors in 1810. *The church is open during most days from sunrise to sunset and costs nothing to enter.*

From Market Street make the first left turn onto Duke Street and continue for a short distance until passing by the facade of the **Government House** on your left hand side. This early 19th-century structure is the official residence of the Governor General, and is mainly used to host visiting dignitaries and diplomats and is almost never open to the public. The most interesting scheduled event that takes place here is the **Changing of the Guard** ceremony held one morning every two weeks. From Government House, make a right hand turn onto George Street and follow it downhill until you reach the 17th-century **Christ Church Cathedral**, which is among the oldest structures in town. From here it's a short walk straight down George Street until you can turn right back onto Bay Street and complete your shopping in the boutiques, or better yet, stop off for a fine lunch or dinner.

Guided City Tours

Other than the Ministry of Tourism Walking Tours (see sidebar on page 139), there are two other guided tour companies in Nassau I'd recommend: **Majestic Tours**, *Tel. (242) 328-0908*, offers a four hour combination city and country tour by bus for around $40 that features stops at Ft. Charlotte, Ft. Montagu, Ft. Fincastle, a walk up the Queen's Staircase, Bennet's Hill Water Tower, Government House, House of Assembly, Parliament, Gregory's Arch, the Straw Market, Retreat gardens, Ardastra gardens, the Bahamas National Trust, and a lunch.

The other outfit is **Bahamas Experience Tours**, *Nassau. Tel. (242) 356-2981*. For $18 a person, this local tour operator will pick you up at your hotel and take you on a good two hour bus tour of Nassau, including stops at Ft. Charlotte, Ft. Montagu, Ft. Fincastle, a walk up the Queen's Staircase, Bennet's Hill Water Tower, Government House, House of Assembly, Parliament, Gregory's Arch, and the Straw Market.

PARADISE ISLAND

Getting to Paradise Island

From Nassau International Airport a taxi will cost somewhere around $22 per couple with a few bags, including the $2 toll across the Paradise Island Bridge. Remember that few taxis use their meters so make sure to get the price settled before you leave the airport.

From Cable Beach a taxi will cost about $13 plus a $2 toll for the bridge per car load (not per person) to just about any point on Paradise Island. Those on tight budgets can also take a 75 cent ride on bus #10 or #38 to Bay Street in downtown Nassau and transfer over to another jitney bus at the corner of Bay Street and Frederick Street for a 75 cent ride up Shirley Street towards the Paradise Island Bridge (see below).

From Downtown Nassau taxis charge about $9 per car load, plus a $2 toll for the bridge, to most locations on Paradise Island. There are also **water taxis** scheduled every 30 minutes between 9:30am and 6:00pm for $2 per person each way. They run back and forth from the Prince George Wharf just behind Nassau's Straw Market, and either dock below the island side of the Paradise Island bridge or at Casuarina Road near the entrance to Club Med.

The only other alternative is to take a bus ride for 75 cents on a jitney bus at the corner of Bay Street and Frederick Street, which heads up Shirley Street to a stop near the Nassau side of the Paradise Island Bridge.

From there it's a long uphill walk across the span and then another hike to the destination of your choice.

ORIENTATION

The 686 acre cay now called **Paradise Island** lies two miles east of downtown Nassau across a harbor via the towering Paradise Island Bridge. Paradise Island is a wonderful privately owned resort

THE UNUSUAL HISTORY OF PARADISE ISLAND

Originally named Hog Island after it was first settled in the 17th century by Eleutherian Adventurer leader William Sayle, for over 200 years it remained a quiet private hideaway. At the turn of this century, American millionaire Joseph Lynch (founder of the famed Merrill Lynch investment firm) built an opulent estate on the island's northern coast. In 1939, Swedish industrialist Dr. Axel Wenner-Gren bought the Lynch estate and began to buy up and beautify as much of the island as possible.

In the early 1960s, Dr. Wenner-Gren sold his property to Huntington Hartford II, the rich American heir to the Great Atlantic & Pacific Tea Company (now the A & P Supermarket chain) for just under $10 million in cash. Mr. Hartford soon realized the potential of Hog Island as a major upscale resort destination and had the government change the cay's name to Paradise Island for obvious marketing reasons. In 1964, he built the small Ocean Club hotel and golf resort and had an authentic 14th-century Augustinian Cloister from France reassembled on the resort's Versailles-inspired formal statue gardens. A few years later the Mary Carter Paint Company bought out most of Mr. Hartford's property and soon established itself as a major hotel and resort developer under the guidance of its new subsidiary, Resorts International. The private Paradise Island Bridge was then constructed, a casino was added, the island was subdivided, and several major hotels began to pop up along the seaside.

The Resorts International property changed hands several times to investors such as Donald Trump and Merv Griffin. The American recession of the late 1980s proved disastrous to the tourist economy of the island and all of The Bahamas. It was not until a few years ago, when South African hotel mogul Saul Kersner and his Sun International Hotels and Casinos Ltd. (developers of the world famous Sun City resort) purchased 70% of Paradise Island and infused the economy with an estimated $250 million to create the stunning Atlantis, the nation's largest and most popular resort hotel and casino. In just seven months, thousands of skilled local workers built the world's largest open air outdoor aquarium for the Atlantis, and Sun International has been responsible for making Paradise Island one of the region's most successful tourist destinations.

development that has become the most popular destination for tourists in The Bahamas. The island's north coast is lined with magnificent sandy beaches and resort hotels, including the incomparable Atlantis resort and casino as well as several others.

The island also features fine dining, plenty of water sports activities, a Dick Wilson designed 18 hole championship par 72 golf course, two small shopping centers, private yacht marinas, a growing international airport, an amazing 14th-century French cloister, and much much more. The number one reason for most tourists visiting Paradise Island is the fantastic beaches and turquoise colored waters that remain unmatched anywhere on New Providence Island.

I suggest three different tours of Paradise Island. Each should take as little as one hour to complete by foot, but expect to spend at least another couple of hours at the various beaches and attractions along the way. If you intend to take a rental bicycle, make sure it is well secured while not in use.

SEEING THE SIGHTS

Towards the West

The gateway to Paradise Island is the infamous **Paradise Island Bridge**. This towering span was designed to allow ships to pass below with ease, and thus reaches a dramatic height at its apex. Each car, taxi, or scooter that crosses this bridge must pay a round-trip visitor's toll of $2 (Bahamians get a discounted fare of 75 cents), while bicycles pay just 25 cents. There is no charge for pedestrians.

Just after crossing the bridge you will reach a major traffic circle that is often host to traffic backups. Here you can turn left to either walk, drive, or bicycle down **Paradise Beach Drive**. A few yards down the left side of this road is a small street leading to a dock where the **Water Taxi** to and from downtown Nassau departs. This is also the area where you can find several excursion operators, such as **Dolphin Encounter** and **Island Ranger Helicopters**.

A half mile further down Paradise Beach Drive, the street ends at the intersection of Casuarina Road. At this intersection you will find the entrance to the rustic **Club Med** resort, but unfortunately non-guests are forbidden to enter the property. Now turn right onto Casuarina Road and continue for a 1/4 mile or so. On the right side of the street is the enjoyable **Pirate's Cove Holiday Inn**, a friendly medium-sized seaside resort with a spectacular sheltered cove called **Pirate Beach** that has no undertow and is perfect for the kids. On the left side of the road you can walk through the Paradise Paradise resort and head for the sandy crescent shaped **Paradise Beach**.

Towards the North

Once you have seen the western side of the island, return back to the traffic circle at the base of the bridge, and this time take the next left turn down Casino Road. Continue for a couple of blocks until you reach the casino entrance to the outstanding **Atlantis** resort hotel on the left side of the street. After passing through the casino and into one of several hotel wings, grab a map from the guest services desk and head for the resort's incredible 14 acre outdoor **Waterscape** open air aquarium, filled with exotic marine life such as sharks, sting rays, sea turtles, barracudas, angel fish, and other creatures that can be viewed via glass enclosed tunnels and underground caves lined with giant windows.

There are plenty of other exciting things to see and do for guests and visitors alike, such as gaming in the region's best and largest casino, dining in one of ten unique restaurants, frolicking on the pristine 2 1/2 mile long white sand **Cabbage Beach**, or just wandering around. *The Atlantis resort, casino, and Waterscape aquarium are all open to the public for free.*

Towards the East

Now retrace your steps back towards the now infamous traffic circle in front of the bridge and this time make the next left turn onto Harbour Road. On the left side of the first block you can pop into the **Paradise Shopping Center** mini-mall, while on the right side is the **Hurricane Hole Plaza** mini-mall, which are both filled with inexpensive souvenir shops, designer boutiques, restaurants, and a couple of dozen other shops. Steps away is the **Hurricane Hole Marina** and yacht harbor area from where sea-based excursions often depart.

After about a 1/4 of a mile, take a left turn down Flamingo Road and follow it for a long block until the road ends at the Comfort Suites hotel, where you will turn right onto Paradise Island Drive. A bit less than half a mile down this road on the left hand side is the main access road to the super exclusive (and equally expensive!) **Ocean Club** hotel, where I recently spotted guests such as Michael Jackson, Meg Ryan, and a former American president. Another block or so along the right side of Paradise Island Drive is a stone stairway that leads straight up to the famous 14th-century French **Cloisters** that were shipped here and reassembled stone by stone. The cloisters (frequented by wedding parties shooting pictures) are among the country's architectural wonders and are well worth a visit.

About the only other points of interest further along the same road is the Dick Wilson-designed 18 hole championship **Paradise Island Golf Course**. Tthe ever growing **Paradise Island International Airport** is also along this road.

NIGHTLIFE & ENTERTAINMENT

Discount admission passes for just about all of these clubs are available at some hotel concierge desks, record shops, and from each club's own staff. I have been able to get coupons that reduce the cover charges to just $10 per person or less using these coupons.

CLUB ENIGMA, *just off West Bay Street, Nassau.*

This brand new elegant seaside disco and club just west of the British Colonial Hotel offers a half dozen separate lounges to party all night in. The music here ranges from jazz and reggae, to house and techno depending on what part of the multilevel club you hang out in. There are also scheduled fashion shows, concerts, reviews, and beach parties. VIPs and club members are entitled to special privileges including an opulent private lounge. They are open until at least 5:00am (and sometimes much later!) on Wednesdays through Saturdays. The dress code here is currently casual elegant (no sneakers, ripped jeans, or T-shirts) and the entrance fee averages $30. This is certainly the best club for visiting singles to hit while in Nassau.

CLUB WATERLOO, *East Bay Street, Nassau.*

This down to earth disco and bar complex near Ft. Montagu is a great place to meet all kinds of Bahamians that are here to have a good time. Open every night from 9:00pm until at least 4:00am, there is a large indoor disco room, a fun rock bar called Shooters, and a few outdoor poolside bars that each have a different crowd. They offer happy hours with $1 and $2 drink specials, live music 5 nights a week, billiard tables, and lots of space to roam around in. The complex charges between $20 and $30 to enter, drinks average about $4.50 each, and the dress code is quite casual.

CULTURE CLUB, *just off West Bay Street, Nassau.*

Filled with a good mix of locals and a few adventurous visitors, people come here for some Caribbean style sounds and dancing. Open from Wednesday through Saturday until 3:00am, and Sunday till midnight, the dress code is not strict. Weekend cover charges can be as much as $25 a person, and drinks average around $6 each.

CAFÉ JOHNNY CANOE, *West Bay Street, Cable Beach. Tel. (242) 327-3373.*

This is a good little outdoor bar in the middle of the Cable Beach area that has live Calypso music Thursday through Sunday evenings from 8:00pm or so until at least 11:30pm. On most nights they serve dinner and drinks until midnight, have no cover charge, no dress code, and reasonable drink prices.

JOKER'S WILD COMEDY CLUB, *Casino Drive, Paradise Island. Tel. (242) 363-3000.*

The Joker's Wild is the only real standup comedy club in The Bahamas. With show times from Tuesday through Sunday at 9:30, you can expect to spend around $25 a person to see a routine from a variety of great comics that have appeared on Letterman, Leno, HBO, A & E, the Comedy Network, and Showtime. Located just off the Atlantis resort's magnificent casino.

KING & KNIGHTS, *West Bay Street, Cable Beach. Tel. (242) 327-5321.*

Located in the heart of the Cable Beach hotel strip, this dinner theater and nightclub offers Nassau's only so-called "Native Revues" featuring fire dancing, glass eating, limbo, steal drum band, comedy acts, and traditional dancers in Junkanoo costume. The show times are 8:30pm and 10:30pm daily, and dinner is optional. The show's cover charge is around $35 including 2 drinks.

ROCK & ROLL CAFÉ, *West Bay Street, Cable Beach. Tel. (242) 327-7639.*

The Rock and Roll is a copy of the Hard Rock Café bar & restaurants that have popped up all over the globe. They serve good hearty foods until around 1:00am each night, and the small bar area gets packed on evenings when they have live concerts, drink specials, karaoke, or sporting events on a big screen television. There is no dress code or cover charge here, and drinks cost about $5.75 each. Open until 3:00am every night of the week. This is a good place to start off the evening.

SILK COTTON CLUB, *Market Street, Nassau. Tel. (242) 356-0955.*

This is one of the few places to go in The Bahamas when you want a relaxing evening out and wish to enjoy the sweet sounds of live Blues and Jazz music. Located just a minute's walk from the Straw Market in downtown Nassau, this small yet cozy club is open on Wednesday through Saturday evenings until way past 1:00am, and features a regularly scheduled series of live concerts at reasonable prices.

THE ZOO, *West Bay Street, Cable Beach. Tel. (242) 322-7195.*

Located a short ride from Cable Beach, this giant dance club and bar gets a good share of the tourists on weekend nights. They play hard hitting rap, house, and reggae music until around 3:00am on most Tuesday through Sunday evenings. The weekend cover charge here is around $35 a person, the dress code is casual yet neat, and drinks average $8.50 each.

SHOPPING

Antiques

• **Marlborough Antiques**, *Marlborough Street at the corner of Queen Street, Nassau. Tel. (242) 328-0502.* A rather good source for antique items such as local oil paintings, English maps, vintage home and office decorative pieces, and old prints.

Art & Crafts

- **Caripelago Café**, *Bay Street off East Street, Nassau, unlisted phone, additional location at West Bay Mall on Cable Beach.* This superb café has a wonderful selection of Bahamian crafts and food products for sale including wood and metal folk art, T-shirts, ceramics, jewelry, and all natural hair and skin care products.
- **The Plait Lady**, *Bay Street off Victoria Avenue, Nassau. Tel. (242) 356-5584.* I love this small shop where every item is made right here in the Bahamas. Their stock includes locally produced straw handbags, artistically created Androsia fabrics, Bahamian sponges, unique wood carvings, local spices and preserves, and jewelry made by talented artisans.
- **Various Straw Markets**, *including Bay Street off George Street, the Queen's Staircase, West Bay Street.*

China, Crystal, Glassware, & Porcelain

- **Treasure Traders**, *Bay Street off Market Street, Nassau. Tel. (242) 322-8521.* Inside this giant store you will find a mind blowing selection of both practical and collectable china, crystal, porcelain, and statuettes. The brands they carry often are available here at around 35% below the typical US suggested retail prices and include Lalique, Lladro, Waterford, Wedgwood, Aynsley, Baccarat, Royal Worcester, Herend, Rosenthal, Swarovski, and more.

Clothing & Swimwear

- **Coles of Nassau Ltd.**, *Parliament Street off Bay Street, Nassau. Tel. (242) 322-8393, additional location in the Mall at Marathon.* This is one of the best places to find high quality imported men's and ladies fashions, swimsuits, shoes, and accessories by Calvin Klein, Jospeh Ribkoff, Oleg Cassini, Betsey Johnson, Adrienne Vittadini, Gottex, Mondi, and Ken Done.
- **The Girls from Brazil**, *Bay Street off Parliament Street, Nassau, Tel. (242) 323-5966.* This great little shop sells their own men's and ladies' swimwear custom manufactured in Brazil. They have hundreds of 1 piece, 2 piece, dental floss, and thong style suits, as well as accessories and cover ups that can be found nowhere else on the islands.

Department Stores

- **John Bull**, *Bay Street corner of Elizabeth Avenue, Nassau. Tel. (242) 322-3328, additional locations at the Mall at Marathon, the Port Shop on*

Woodes Rogers Walk, and the Atlantis Resort & Casino on Paradise Island. Since way back in 1929, this major retail operation has been offering thousands of luxury items such as perfumes by Chanel, Estee Lauder, Yves St. Laurent, Lancome, Calvin Klein, and Clinique, time pieces made by Tag Heuer, Raymond Weil, Rolex, Movado, Swiss Army, Guess, Gucci, Piaget, Phillipe Cahrriol, Swatch, Corum, and Seiko, pens by Cross and Mont Blanc, jewelry by Mikimoto, Tiffany & Co., Kabana, David Yurman, Carrera y Carrera, Roberto Coin, leather goods by Moshino, Hugo Boss, Dooney & Bourke, Prima Class, and De Vecchi, and also sunglasses, cigarette lighters, and travel accessories. The leader in high quality gifts and personal items for those with superb taste.

• **The Nassau Shop**, *Bay Street off Charlotte Street, Nassau, Tel. (242) 322-8405.* This sprawling department store in the heart of downtown Nassau offers a full line of men's and ladies' sportswear, slacks, sweaters, formal wear, suits, shirts, and swimwear as well as cosmetics, European and American perfumes, luggage, Swiss watches, imported jewelry, and assorted souvenirs.

Eye Wear

• **Centreville Optical**, *6th Terrace & Collins Avenue, Nassau. Tel. (242) 322-3094.* While it's far from the fancy part of town, this low priced optical store has frames and prescription lenses that are ready in most cases within an hour. They have products from Giogio, Paco Rabane, Ray-Ban, Perry Ellis, Sophia Loren, Christian Dior, Nina Ricci, Zeiss, Matsuda, Alfred Sung, and others.

• **The Optique Shoppe**, *Parliament Street off Bay Street, Nassau. Tel. (242) 322-3910.* Inside this nice modern optical shop are good values on sunglasses, frames, and accessories by Carrera, Ray-Ban, Vuarnet, Christian Dior, and many other French and Italian designers.

Jewelry & Timepieces

• **Coin of the Realm**, *Charlotte Street off Bay Street, Nassau. Tel. (242) 322-4862.* In my opinion this is the best place to find unique jewelry and one of a kind gift items in all of The Bahamas, including a vast array of antique coins found on shipwrecks, earrings filled with precious stones from around the world, pearl necklaces and bracelets, European crafted gold and silver jewelry, collectable stamps, and lots more.

• **The Columbian**, *Bay Street off Frederick Street, Nassau. Tel. (242) 325-4083.* This well established jewelry shop features Colombian emeralds, South African diamonds, and Oriental ruby laden rings and chains, as well as fine watches by Piaget, Chopard, Movado, Baume &

Mercier, Concord, Longines, and Zodiac.

- **Greenfire Emeralds**, *Bay Street off Charlotte Street, Nassau. Tel. (242) 322-2841, additional location on Paradise Island.* Besides offering a full selection of emerald and other precious jewels, Greenfire also sells plenty of gold and silver, Lalique crystal, Versace and Bally leather goods, and many watches including the magnificent Omega and Patek Philippe brands from Geneva.

- **Little Switzerland**, *Bay Street (Several Shops), Nassau. Tel. (242) 356-6920, additional locations at the Hurricane Hole Shopping Plaza on Paradise Island.* With duty free boutiques all over the Caribbean, this major retailer has great prices on a huge assortment of Swiss and Japanese watches, as well as European and Oriental jewelry, crystal stemware, china, leather handbags, and fragrances. Their lines include watches by Brietling, Ebel, and Rado, Swarovski silver crystal, Lenox china, and many others.

Linens

- **The Linen Shop**, *Bay Street off Frederick Street, Nassau. Tel. (242) 322-4266.* Inside The Linen Shop you will find English, Irish, and Oriental linens, including tablecloths, children's clothing, gowns, bed linens, pillow shams, handkerchiefs, runners, local artwork, and local coin sets.

Leather Goods & Luggage

- **The Brass & Leather Shops Ltd.**, *Charlotte Street off Bay Street, Nassau, Tel. (242) 322-3806.* This is the place to go for upscale leather handbags, wallets, shoes, and other high end accessories as well as jewelry from European manufactureres such as Bottega Veneta, Pierre Balmain, Courreges, Land, Fendi, and many others.

- **Fendi**, *Bay Street off Charlotte Street, Nassau. Tel. (242) 322-6300.* A full line of Fendi leather goods, watches, silk scarves, and accessories.

- **Gucci**, *Bank Lane off Bay Street, Nassau. Tel. (242) 325-0561.* A full line of Gucci leather goods and accessories.

- **The Leather Shop**, *Bank Lane off Bay Street, Nassau. Tel. (242) 325-1454.* Here you can get good prices on leather handbags and other goods from companies including Lancel, Ted Lapidus, Isanti, Piel, HCL, and Lanvin.

- **MCM Factory Outlet**, *Prince George Plaza on Bay Street, Nassau. Tel. (242) 326-7039.* They carry a full line of MCM leather handbags, belts, briefcases, wallets, purses, watches, and other high quality accessories at great prices.

Liquor Stores

- **Burns House Ltd**, *East Street off Bay Street, Nassau. Tel. (242) 322-8843, over 25 additional locations all over New Providence.* You can save up to 40% or more off the North American prices on labels like Frangelico, Malibu, Smirnoff, Glenfiddich, Tequila Sauza, Famous Grouse, Cutty Sark, Tio Pepe, Remy Martin, Chambord, Black Velvet, Galliano, Romana Sambuca, and several varieties of wines and beers (including Kalik). This is a good place to ask about duty free specials.
- **Butler & Sands,** *John F. Kennedy Drive, Nassau. Tel. (242) 322-7586.* This major retailer of wines and spirits carries many leading brands of spirits at good discounts such as Southern Comfort, Jack Daniels, Jose Cuervo, Amaretto di Saronno, Grand Marnier, Martell, Johnnie Walker, Barcardi, Finlandia, Chivas Regal, Asolut, Sandeman, Tanqueray, Seagram's, Vueve Cliquot, Mumm's, and many others. They also have delivery service anywhere in the Nassau area.

Perfume, Cologne, & Cosmetics

- **The Beauty Spot**, *Bay Street corner of Frederick Street, Nassau. Tel. (242) 322-5930.* This is the best place to get good deals on a full line of cosmetics and fragrances by such leading companies as Clarins, Clinique, Aramis, Chanel, Biotherm, Yves St. Laurent, Lancome, Estee Lauder, Elizabeth Ardin, and Prescriptives.
- **The Perfume Shop**, *Bay Street corner of Frederick Street, Nassau,. Tel. (242) 322-2375.* Here you can get great duty free savings on imported scents such as Chanel No. 5, Escape, Dune, Lalique, Shalimar, Giogio, White Diamonds, Coco, Obsession, Amariage, Arpege, Paloma Picasso, and many more.
- **Lightbourn's Perfume Center**, *Bay Street corner of George Street, Nassau. Tel. (242) 322-2095.* This famous establishment sells a large array of well known perfumes and colognes such as Chanel, Gucci, Oscar de la Renta, Van Cleef & Arpels, Carolina Herrera, Liz Clairborne, Givency, Guerlain, Perry Ellis, Fendi, Christian Dior, Aramis, Azzaro, Puig, Lagerfeld, and Ungaro at low, low prices.

Shopping Centers

- **The Mall at Marathon**, *Corner of Marathon Road and Robinson Road, Nassau. Tel. (242) 393-4043.* This is the largest indoor shopping center in The Bahamas, with over 70 different shops and boutiques to enjoy. While mostly locals come here since it is well off the tourist route (it's actually a few miles away from downtown Nassau), the prices can often be much lower on the same items found on Bay Street. There is a convenient shuttle bus that runs every half hour or so from Woodes Rodgers Walk (in front of Kentucky Fried Chicken) to the mall and back for around $1 each way, and a huge free outdoor parking lot. The mall is open Monday to Friday from 10:00am until 8:00pm, Saturday from 10:00am until 9:00pm, and Sunday from 12:00noon until 5:00pm.

• **Towne Centre Mall**, *Corner of Blue Hill Road and Independence Drive, Nassau. Tel. (242) 326-6992.* Frequented mainly by Nassau residents, this large two story mall a couple of miles up Blue Hill Road from downtown offers 63 retail shops in the inexpensive to medium price categories. There is also free covered parking and an adjacent bus stop with service to and from downtown Nassau for 75 cents. It's open every day of the week.

T-Shirts & Souvenirs

• **Big Kahuna**, *Bay Street, Nassau. Tel. (242) 326-2684.* This is where you can get good prices on high quality cotton and cotton blend T-shirts with tropical and surf related themes by companies such as Quicksilver, Guy Harvey, Soul, Billabong, Caribbean Soul, and many others.
• **Various Straw Markets**, *including Bay Street off George Street, the Queen's Staircase, West Bay Street.*

SPORTS & RECREATION

Almost all of these recommended excursion companies will be happy to provide free round-trip transfers to any hotel on the island if contacted a least a day or two in advance.

Boating Adventures

Flying Cloud Catamaran Cruises, *Paradise Island. Tel. (242) 393-1957*
These folks offer a wide variety of cruises and adventures aboard the 57' *Flying Cloud Catamaran* sailboat. Their most popular excursion is a $30 per person half day sailing and snorkeling cruise that departs a few times a week. For 3 1/2 hours, you get to sail to a quiet island beach where you are served tropical drinks and can use snorkeling gear for free to explore the marine life. They also offer a 5 hour full day version on most Sundays that costs $45 per person including lunch, as well as special sunset and dinner cruises on selected dates.

Powerboat Adventure, *East Bay Street, Nassau. Tel. (242) 327-5385.*
If you love excitement and high speed boating, you'll certainly enjoy this unique full day trip to the Exuma Islands via cigarette boat. After departing their Nassau dock you will reach speeds up to 40 miles an hour aboard these streamlined 900 horsepower motorboats until docking at Allan's Cay, where you can spot many giant 4' wild iguanas waiting to greet (or perhaps eat!) you. Then it's off to a nice reef area where you can

snorkel with their expert divemaster, then another hair-raising ride to the secluded beaches of Channel Cay for an outdoor beach barbecue featuring freshly caught fish and side salads. The trip costs $150 per person and includes unlimited cocktails, lunch, snorkeling gear, stingray and shark feeds, and much more. A great experience for those with a sense of adventure.

Barefoot Sailing Cruises, *Nassau. Tel. (242) 393-0820.*

These folks provide a fun-filled getaway aboard their 36', 41', and 56' sailboats and depart for a variety of different half day, full day, and dinner cruises. Their half day sail and snorkel trip leaves daily and for $35 a person includes sailing, reef snorkeling, and refreshments. The full day trip is also offered daily and includes all the above, plus a continental breakfast and full buffet lunch and is $50 per person. They also offer sunset Champagne cocktail cruises on some nights as well.

Calypso Boat Trips, *Nassau. Tel. (242) 363-3577.*

These are the most popular party cruises aboard the 100' three-level *Calypso II* boat. Up to 125 vacationers depart for the Blue Lagoon Island 20 minutes away. On the island you can relax at the beach, use snorkeling gear to check out the fish, take an optional dolphin encounter, or rent paddle boats or water cycles, enjoy a complimentary buffet lunch with wine, hang out at the bar, or just relax in a hammock near the sea. The trip lasts about four hours and costs $35 a person.

Fishing Charters

Try either **Born Free Charters**, *Paradise Island, Tel. (242) 363-2003* or **Brown's Charters**, *Paradise Island, Tel. (242) 324-1215.*

Helicopter Rides

Island Ranger Helitours, *Clubland Drive, Paradise Island. Tel. (242) 363-1040.*

For the most adventurous travelers, this local helicopter tour and charter company can arrange an exciting 20 minute trip above Nassau, Paradise Island, and several small islands for around $95 per person.

Horseback Riding

Happy Trails Stables, *Coral Harbour District, South Shore. Tel. (242) 362-1820.*

For around $25 a person (including free hotel pick-up service from Nassau or Paradise Island), you can enjoy a great ride through the trails and the beaches of the island's south coast.

Cantalupa Riding School, *Carmichael Village District, South Shore. Tel. (242) 361-7101.*

A full service children's riding center and academy featuring horse and pony rides starting at around $20 per hour.

Rawson Square Buggy Rides, *Bay Street, Nassau. No Telephone.*

For around $10 a couple, you can get a 25 minute narrated ride along downtown Nassau's most important side streets and historical areas.

Scuba Diving

Stuart Cove's Diving, *South Ocean District, South Shore. Tel. (242) 362-5227.*

This is unmistakably the finest scuba diving facility on the whole island. Located on the south shore of New Providence, they offer excellent "Discovery Dive" resort courses with a shallow reef dive from $79 a person, snorkel trips with free rental gear at $25, an all day 4 tank diving excursion with lunch for $105, 2 tank dives from $65, wilderness dive trips to various Out Islands from $125, and custom trips at reasonable rates. They rent all kinds of gear including underwater cameras, and are rated as a 5 star PADI training facility and can arrange full certification.

Dive, Dive, Dive, *Coral Harbour District, South Shore. Tel. (242) 362-1143.*

This is also a fantastic place to either learn or perfect your scuba skills. They have all sorts of adventures on some two dozen reef, wreck, and ocean sights all around the island. This dive shop has some of the friendliest and most informative dive masters and instructors in New Providence and they can help to arrange PADI and NAUI certifications at all levels including Nitrox, Open Water, Advanced, Rescue, and Divemaster.

They also offer great 2 tank shark dives with a stop at a 6000' sea wall for $105, 2 tank afternoon dives at $65, 1 tank night dives for $50, and a money saving three day dive package with 2 tank dives each day at $165. For real serious divers, they offer 3 to 7 night packages with accommodations in some very nice private villas at their marina site.

Divers Haven, *East Bay Street, Nassau. Tel. (242) 393-0869* and **Bahamas Divers**, *East Bay Street, Nassau, Tel. (242) 393-5644.*

These are two of the better dive operators on the north shore of New Providence Island and offer daily 1 tank dives at $35, 2 tank dives for $60, 1 tank night dives at $50, resort courses for $60, snorkel trips from $25, certification courses, and private charters.

Submarine Rides

Atlantis Submarines, *South Ocean Area, Tel. (242) 356-3842.*

This unusual three hour adventure includes a brief boat ride off the coast to board an authentic 28 passenger submarine that descends to 100' feet below the surface for a 50 minute narrated tour of the reefs. You can peer out of the circular windows and see plenty of exotic fish, lobsters, wrecks, James Bond movie sights, and an occasional shark during the voyage. Accept no imitations, this is the only real submarine ride in town! The price per person is currently about $75 for adults and $40 for kids under 12.

Seaworld Explorer, *Woodes Rodgers Walk, Nassau, Tel. (242) 356-2548.*

This 45 passenger vessel is not actually a submarine, but its glass window lined air conditioned hull rests 5' feet below the sea's surface. The ride gives visitors a chance to see plenty of fish, coral, and wreck sights along the north shore's Sea Gardens Marine Park. A short ride via catamaran is needed to get from Nassau to the mooring sight, and back again. The cost of this excursion is $29 per adult and $19 per kid.

SWIM WITH THE DOLPHIN PROGRAMS

Dolphin Encounters, Blue Lagoon Island, Tel. (242) 363-1003, offers two different types of Dolphin programs to choose from. For $30 per person, you can touch one of several highly trained Atlantic bottlenose dolphins while you stand in shallow water, or for $85 per person you can actually get to swim in a protected lagoon where the dolphins will swim right next to you and let you touch them for up to half an hour. In either case make sure to bring a waterproof camera, and expect a 15 minute boat ride from Paradise Island or Nassau to their private facility on nearby Blue Lagoon Island.

Underwater Walks

Hartley's Undersea Walk, *East Bay Street, Nassau, Tel. (242) 393-8234.*

This unusual excursion offers visitors a chance to put on an old fashioned waterproof brass diving helmet that has a constant supply of air pumped in from compressors aboard a 57' motor boat anchored just above the water. You step down a 12' ladder and walk around fish-laden reefs and seabed for an hour or so with a small group of other explorers led by Christopher Hartley. The whole trip, including the boat ride to the dive site, takes a few hours and costs $45 per person.

PRACTICAL INFORMATION

- **Nassau Police and Fire Department – Emergencies,** *Tel. 919*
- **Nassau Ambulance Dispatch,** *Tel. (242) 322-2221*
- **Doctor's Hospital,** *Tel. (242) 322-8411*
- **American Embassy,** *Tel. (242) 322-1183*
- **Canadian Consulate,** *Tel. (242) 393-2123*
- **Bahamasair,** *Airport, Tel. (242) 377-5505*
- **Ministry of Tourism Information Center,** *Rawson Square, Tel. (242) 326-9772*
- **Weather Information,** *Tel. (242) 377-7178*
- **Directory Assistance,** *Tel. 916*

14. GRAND BAHAMA ISLAND

Eighty miles long and with an average width of 11 miles, **Grand Bahama Island** is the fourth largest island in The Bahamas and the second most popular tourist destination. Grand Bahama is located 83 miles northeast of Ft. Lauderdale, Florida, and has a population of just over 41,000 people.

Most of the hotels, restaurants, casinos, golf courses, excursions, and shopping centers are in the **Freeport** or **Port Lucaya** districts. These areas are both found just a couple of miles away from each other along the west section of Grand Bahama, and are actually part of a special tax-free trading zone that has been privately owned and operated by the Port Authority since 1955, when it was established by American millionaire Wallace Groves.

The vast majority of visitors come here for a few days via package tours and frequent cruise ships. Unfortunately, many tourists never get to roam around the eastern and western edges of the island. While a quick visit will only reveal tons of commercialized areas full of boutiques and duty free shops, the more remote parts of Grand Bahama are lined with great beaches and nice local villages. I encourage you to explore them if you've got the time.

ARRIVALS & DEPARTURES

Most visitors from North America will arrive either by air at **Freeport International Airport** or by sea on a cruise line docking in **Freeport Harbour** or **Port Lucaya**. Consult Chapter 6, *Planning Your Trip*, and Chapter 8, *Cruising to The Bahamas*, for details on flight and cruise arrangements to The Bahamas.

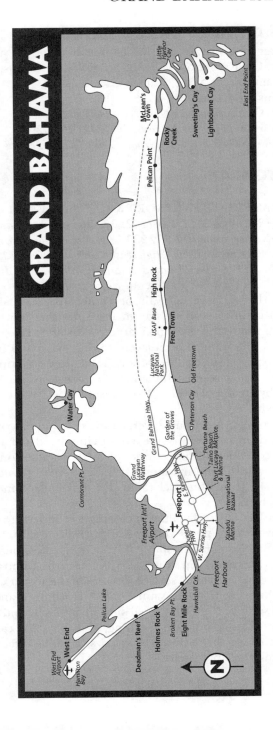

GETTING AROUND GRAND BAHAMA

Your main options are taxi, jitney bus, and rental car. To get to Freeport and Lucaya, see *Seeing the Sights* below for details.

If you want to rent a car, contact:
- **Freeport Taxi**, *Tel. (242) 252-6666*
- **Avis Rent a Car**, *Freeport Airport, Tel. (242) 352-7666*
- **Hertz Rent a Car**, *Freeport Airport, Tel. (242) 352-3297*
- **National Rent a Car**, *Freeport Airport, Tel. (242) 352-9308*

WHERE TO STAY

Moderate

BAHAMAS PRINCESS RESORT & CASINO, *West Sunrise Highway, Freeport. Tel. (242) 352-2542, Fax (242) 352-9661. US & Canada bookings (Princess Hotels International) 1-800-223-1834. Low season rack rates from $95 per double room per night (E.P.). High season rack rates from $120 per double room per night (E.P.). Special package rates available. M.A.P. Meal Plans available from $29 per adult per day. All major credit cards accepted.*

This superb resort is certainly the best hotel on Grand Bahama Island. Families and couples tend to stay in the sprawling low-rise Princess Country Club where there are 565 large rooms and suites, while more upscale guests who want to be adjacent to the casino and International Bazaar tend to prefer the opulent Moorish-style 10 story Princess Towers with 400 spectacular rooms and suites. Both sections of the hotel are surrounded by a total of over 1,000 acres of lavishly landscaped semi-tropical gardens.

All 965 rooms (including several time-share units) of the resort feature nice private bathrooms stocked with imported hair and skin care products, air conditioning, king or double beds, remote control satellite color television with optional movie channels, comfortable rattan and wooden furnishings, am-fm clock radio, direct dial telephone, and either garden, pool, or island views.

There are dozens of facilities including a wonderful casino, giant fresh water swimming pools with cascades and hot tubs, two expertly maintained 18 hole championship golf courses, professionally surfaced tennis courts, free round-trip shuttle service to nearby Taino and Xanadu beaches, water sports, room service, several boutiques, a car and jeep rental desk, fitness center with sauna, beauty salon, tour and excursion desks, ice and soda machines, optional in-room mini-safe and refrigerator rentals, express laundry and dry cleaning, available child care, specially equipped rooms for those with wheelchairs, scheduled daily activities, and even a children's program.

The resort boasts nine great casual and semi-formal restaurants serving a variety of Bahamian and international cuisine, eight impressive bars and nightlife venues, and several business meeting and convention sized rooms. Staff members go well out of their way to make sure you'll return again soon. Guests at the Bahamas Princess arrive daily from all over the world, and range from singles and couples to newlyweds and families with several children.

Highly recommended as the best full service resort on Grand Bahama, and at these prices its a real bargain! Selected as one of our *Best Places to Stay* – see Chapter 12 for a longer review.

CLARION ATLANTIK BEACH RESORT, *Lucaya. Tel. (242) 373-1444, Fax (242) 373-7481. US & Canada bookings (Clarion Hotels) 1-800-252-7466. Low season rack rates from $120 per double room per night (B.P.). High season rack rates from $140 per double room per night (B.P.). Special package rates available. All major credit cards accepted.*

This towering 16 story Swiss-owned resort hotel on the edge of the sea near the Port Lucaya Marketplace is another good choice for vacationers staying on Grand Bahama Island. The property has 175 super clean and comfortable rooms and family style apartments that each come with modern private bathrooms, air conditioning, direct dial telephones, wall-to-wall carpeting, remote control satellite televisions, mini-safes, and either ocean or marina views. The highly recommended 1, 2, and 3 bedroom split level apartments also contain fully stocked and equipped kitchenettes, microwaves, coffee makers, sea-view balconies, and lots of additional space.

Guests here can take advantage of the adjacent beach area, an Olympic-sized swimming pool, a fitness center, optional massages, express laundry and dry cleaning, boutiques, a business center, the nearby 18 hole Lucayan Country Club golf course, four different restaurants, and plenty of optional water sports facilities. The service here is also friendly and professional. This is the about the best full service resort currently operating in the Port Lucaya area.

LUCAYAN BEACH RESORT & CASINO, *Lucaya. Tel. (242) 373-7777, Fax (242) 373-6916. US & Canada bookings (Hotel Direct) 1-800-772-1227. Low season rack rates from $110 per double room per night (E.P.). High season rack rates from $130 per double room per night (E.P.). Special package rates available. All major credit cards accepted.*

The Lucayan Beach is a nice low-rise hotel and casino complex located directly on a pretty stretch of Lucayan Beach. The hotel has a total of 243 rooms and suites that feature marble bathrooms, air conditioning, direct dial telephones, comfortable furnishings, local artwork, and plenty of sea-views. The hotel also has a nice swimming pool, tennis courts, a few decent restaurants, a poorly maintained casino, and a couple of bars.

Inexpensive

SUN CLUB RESORT, *Settler's Way, Freeport. Tel. (242) 352-3462, Fax (242) 352-6835. US & Canada bookings (Hotel Direct) 1-800-327-0787. Low season rack rates from $85 per double room per night (E.P.). High season rack rates from $65 per double room per night (E.P.). Special package rates available. All major credit cards accepted.*

This reasonably priced simple inn a few minutes east of Freeport is a good choice for couples and families on tight budgets. There are 42 rooms and efficiencies that are all air conditioned and contain cable televisions, simple furnishings, and private bathrooms. There is also complimentary shuttle service to a nearby beach, a nice quiet swimming pool, plenty of free parking, and a tennis court. While far from deluxe, this is a friendly little place.

SILVER SANDS SEA LODGE, *Royal Palm Way, Lucaya. Tel. (242) 373-5700, Fax (242) 373-1039. Low season rack rates from $85 per studio apartment per night (E.P.). High season rack rates from $105 per studio apartment per night (E.P.). Special package rates available. All major credit cards accepted.*

Located within easy walking distance to the Port Lucaya area on a quiet side street, this condo complex has several dozen well-maintained studio and 1 bedroom apartments for rent. All of the units are air conditioned and feature private bathrooms, fully equipped kitchens, nice living rooms, and comfortable furnishings. There is a nearby beach, an adjacent jitney bus stop, tennis courts, a restaurant, a snack bar, and daily maid service.

RUNNING MON MARINA RESORT, *Kelly Court, Lucaya. Tel. (242) 352-6834, Fax (242) 352-6835. Low season rack rates from $85 per double room per night (E.P.). High season rack rates from $100 per double room per night (E.P.). Special package rates available. All major credit cards accepted.*

This simple suburban hotel has 32 nice yet rather basic rooms that face their popular marina (with 66 slips) and have air conditioning, private bathrooms, televisions, and refrigerators. There is also a restaurant and free shuttle service to Freeport and Xanadu beach.

WHERE TO EAT

Expensive

THE CROWN ROOM, *Bahamas Princess Casino, Freeport. Tel. (242) 352-9661. Open every evening except Monday. Dress Code is Semi-Formal. All major credit cards accepted.*

The Crown Room is simply the island's most romantic semi-formal gourmet restaurant. A team of talented chefs prepare an outstanding array of classically inspired meat and seafood specialties, including smoked North Atlantic salmon at $12.75, jumbo shrimp cocktails for $13.95, snow crab claws with mustard sauce at $19.75, escargots in basil sauce for $9.75, Coquille St. Jacques at $13.50, Bahamian conch chowder for $4.95, French onion soup for $4.95, clear seafood soup for $7.50, Caesar salads prepared at your table at $7.75, grilled double lamb chops for $29.50, Steak Diane at $29.50, Escalope of Veal piccata for $28.75, Surf & Turf at $39.50, grilled grouper with lemon butter for $24.95, sautéed Dover sole at $31, shrimp scampi for $28.50, Chateaubriand for two at $54, saffron risotto with fresh mushrooms for $18.50, baked Alaska for two at $13, an assortment of pastries for $5.50, and Crepes Suzette for two at $13.50.

The wine list here is exceptionally priced, with bottles from well-known Chilean, South African, Californian, and French vineyards. Wear a jacket and call in advance for reservations.

THE RIB ROOM, *Bahamas Princess Country Club, Freeport. Tel. (242) 352-6721. Dress Code is Semi-Formal. All major credit cards accepted.*

The Bahamas Princess has yet another superb gourmet restaurant, this one just across the street in the Country Club section. The Rib Room features a relaxing dark wood paneled interior and a great menu that offers a delicious assortment of dishes, including baked clams casino for $8.75, lobster salad at $11.75, crab crepes for $9.75, lobster bisque at $5.95, conch chowder for $4.50, Caesar salad for two at $12, filet of grouper with almonds for $19.95, shrimp scampi at $22.95, grilled black Angus strip steak for $29.95, filet mignon at $23.75, steak in pepper sauce for $23.75, rack of lamb for two at $52, grilled chicken breast with wild mushrooms for $19.75, fettuccine with lobster and tomato basil sauce at $23.95, strawberry melba for $4.50, and cherries jubilee for two at $9.50. Reservations are required and jackets are requested.

ARAWAK DINING ROOM, *Lucayan Golf & Country Club, Lucaya. Tel. (242) 373-1066. Dress Code is Semi-Formal. All major credit cards accepted.*

Located in the clubhouse of this beautiful country club, this white glove service restaurant features a seasonally changing menu of imported steak, veal, lamb, duck, seafood, and freshly caught local fish items that cost somewhere around $22.50 each. This is a great place for an affordable casual lunch or a more opulent dinner. Jackets and reservations are required for dinner.

JAPANESE STEAK HOUSE, *International Bazaar, Freeport. Tel. (242) 352- 9521. Open 4:00pm until 11:30pm daily. Dress Code is casual but neat. Most major credit cards accepted.*

After being seated next to other patrons around one of several large Teppanyaki grill tables, skillful chefs will prepare and cook an exotic Asian meal right in front of your eyes. Carefully sautéed or grilled with spices such as sesame oil and ginger, their most delicious dishes include

Hibachi chicken for $24.95, Sukiyaki rib-eye steak at $29.95, Hibachi shrimp for $34.95, Teppanyaki New York strip steak at $32.95, grilled grouper for $26.95, baked local lobster Japanese style at $43.95, vegetable fried rice for $9.95, and all sorts of sakes, beers, plum wines, and assorted cocktails.

While a bit more expensive than most other area restaurants, try this place if you like good Japanese food. Reservations are suggested.

Moderate

ALFREDO'S RESTAURANT, *Clarion Atlantik Beach Resort, Lucaya. Tel. (242) 373-1444. Dress Code is Casual. All major credit cards accepted.*

This dinner-only restaurant features a good selection of internationally inspired dishes such as clam chowder at $3.50, conch chowder for $3.50, consommé at $3, smoked salmon for $9.50, lobster salad with raspberry vinaigrette at $12.50, deep fried mushrooms for $4.50, fresh melon at $4.50, country fried chicken for $8.50, sautéed strips of chicken and shrimp at $12.50, breaded breast of turkey for $9.90, veal cutlets at $14.50, broiled salmon steak for $15.50, broiled Bahamian lobster at $21.50, sautéed shrimp scampi for $18.50, Sirloin pepper steak at $19.50, lamb cutlets for $15.50, frozen chocolate parfaits at $4, and assorted sundaes starting at $4.50.

THE STONED CRAB, *Taino Beach, Lucaya area. Tel. (242) 373-1442. Open 7 days a week from 5:30pm until 10:00pm or so. Dress code is Casual but neat. Most major credit cards accepted.*

This great oceanfront fish and seafood specialty restaurant is another good place to go for grouper, tuna, wahoo, mahi-mahi, swordfish, sole, stone crab, and lobster, as well as steak, chicken, pasta, and salad. The informal indoor and patio dining areas get full on most nights, and expect dinner to set you back about $26 a person plus drinks. Reservations are suggested.

PIER ONE, *Freeport Harbour, Freeport area. Tel. (242) 352-6674. Open every day from 11:00am until 10:00pm. Dress code is Casual but neat. Most major credit cards accepted.*

Known around the globe for its picture-perfect seaside location on stilts above a stone and wooden pier off Freeport Harbour, this highly recommended family-style restaurant is quite good. Here you can feast on Bahamian and American seafood and steak dishes that average around $9.75 at lunch and $20.50 at dinner. The restaurant has indoor and outdoor tables, and daily shark feedings every hour on the hour from 7:00pm until 9:00pm. Reservations are required for outdoor tables.

Inexpensive

LA TRATTORIA, *Bahamas Princess Towers, Freeport. Tel. (242) 352-9661. Open nightly for dinner only. Dress Code is Smart Casual. All major credit cards accepted.*

I really enjoyed my recent dinners at this intimate little Italian restaurant, and I am sure you will too! The extensive and rather affordable menu includes antipasto salads at $6.95, eggplant Caprini for $6.95, fried calamari at $5.75, fresh Buffalo mozzarella with tomatoes and basil for $5.50, oven fresh bruschetta at $4.25, Caesar salad for $4.25, minestrone soup at $3.95, four cheese pizza for $7.25, angelhair pasta with pesto sauce at $8.50, fettuccini Alfredo for $8.95, ziti with clam sauce at $9.25, spaghetti in marinara sauce for $7.95, chicken parmigiana at $11.95, steak pizzaiola for $19.50, veal marsala at $18.50, garlic roasted shrimp for $19.95, and tiramisu at $3.50.

THE PUB AT PORT LUCAYA, *Port Lucaya Marketplace, Lucaya. Tel. (242) 373-8450. Dress Code is Casual. Most major credit cards accepted.*

The Pub is a popular lunch and dinner spot on a marina-view deck near Count Basie Square that has indoor and al fresco dining areas offering a menu that includes fried calamari rings at $6.95, shark strips for $4.50, potato skins at $4.50, fish and chips for $7.95, quiche at $6, barbecued chicken for $9.50, Caesar salad at $3.50, giant half pound burgers for $4.95, seafood linguini at $9.95, hot pastrami sandwiches for $5.50, tuna sandwiches at $4.25, steak and ale pie for $10.50, shepherd's pie at $8.95, and peach melba for $5.

CAFÉ MICHEL, *International Bazaar, Freeport. Tel. (242) 352-2191. Open daily from 7:30am until at least 11:00pm. Dress Code is Casual. All major credit cards accepted.*

This is a good French-style outdoor café that is perfect for an informal yet delicious al fresco breakfast, lunch, or dinner. Here a simple breakfast omelet starts at just $4.75, your choice of over 30 sandwiches and lunch platters start at around $7.75 each, and well-prepared dinner specials of steak, pasta, grilled fish, and poultry cost around $14.25 each.

PIZZA HUT, *Port Lucaya Marketplace, Lucaya. Tel. (242) 373-8383. Dress Code is Casual. Most major credit cards accepted.*

It's just like a Pizza Hut back home, except it faces right onto the marina in the Port Lucaya Marketplace. You have your choice of individual pizzas ranging from $10.80 and up, medium pizzas starting at $13.85 and up, and large pizzas costing upwards of $16.80, as well as pastas at $7.50, salad bar for $3.95, and other side dishes.

FREEPORT

Getting to Freeport

From Freeport International Airport a taxi will cost somewhere around $9 per couple with a few bags. Most taxis here actually use their meters.

From Freeport Harbour a taxi will set you back about $10.50 per car (not per person). You can also take a 75 cent ride on a jitney bus heading down West Sunrise Highway until reaching the International Bazaar and Princess Casino.

From Downtown Freeport taxis charge around $6.50 per car load to most other Freeport locations. Another alternative is to take a bus ride for 75 cents on a jitney bus in front of the Winn Dixie Supermarket off East Mall Drive, which goes past the Princess Towers and its adjacent International Bazaar.

From Port Lucaya a taxi will cost about $10 per car to just about any point in the Freeport area. Those on tight budgets can also take a 75 cent ride on a public bus from across the street at the Marketplace to one of several stops in Freeport, including the International Bazaar, the Princess Casino, and downtown Freeport.

ORIENTATION

Located some five miles inland from the sea, **Freeport** is the largest city on Grand Bahama. The majority of tourists come here to shop till they drop at the **International Bazaar**, play games of chance and skill at the fantastic **Princess Casino**, and perhaps even make a brief visit to the Florida styled **downtown** district, where a few small malls and a great little **Outdoor Fruit Market** can be explored.

While certainly one of the island's most developed tourist resort centers, this is actually a rather nice place stay while visiting the island. There are a great variety of moderately priced hotels, serious shopping possibilities, a large casino complex, and several entertaining bars.

SEEING THE SIGHTS

A Walk Through the Resort Area

The best place to begin your exploration of Freeport is over by the popular **Bahamas Princess Resort & Casino**, a massive resort complex with two sections and nine different restaurants . These two sections make up the largest hotel on Grand Bahama, and tend to attract all sorts of singles, couples, and families from North America. The low-rise Princess Country Club centers around a giant fresh water swimming pool, the fantastic 18 hole championship **Princess Emerald Golf Course**, and several acres of lush semi-tropical gardens.

Just across **West Sunrise Highway** from the country club section is the hotel's Princess Towers, a Moorish influenced high-rise hotel wing that is adjacent to the 18 hole championship **Princess Ruby Golf Course** and is directly connected to the massive **Princess Casino**. This 20,000 square foot gaming facility is a major attraction for thousands of tourists and more serious gamblers, with some 200 regular and progressive slot machines, blackjack and poker tables, craps games, roulette, mechanical horseracing, video poker, a new sports betting section, and the more exclusive mini-baccarat pit. Here you can also grab a gourmet meal or catch a Vegas-style revue on most evenings. *The Princess Casino has no admission charge, and for those at least 18 years of age it is open daily from 10:00am to 4:00am, with slot machines accessible 24 hours a day.*

Just next door to the Princess Casino is one of several entrances to the **International Bazaar**, a huge shopping mall with well over 95 designer boutiques, duty free shops, cafés, international restaurants, and galleries to choose from. Your first stop here should be over at the **Grand Bahama Promotion Board's Tourism Information Office**, located in a small kiosk just off the front of the International Bazaar at West Sunrise Highway. The kiosk is usually open 7 days a week from 9:00am until at least 5:00pm, and can give you all sorts of free maps, brochures, and expert advice on what to see and do while on the island.

After the tourist office, make sure to walk to the nearby corner of West Sunrise Highway and East Mall where you will find the main entrance to the International Bazaar via the Chinese inspired **Torii Gateway**. Once through the gateway you can stroll past dozens of shops on uniquely designed "streets" that have been made to look like foreign destinations including Asian, Middle Eastern, French, South American, Scandinavian, and other regions of the world. The back end of the shopping center is lined by a nice little **Straw Market**, several fast food joints, and souvenir shops. *The International Bazaar is open daily from 8:45am until at least 7:00pm (hours vary with each different retail shop and restaurant), and costs nothing to enter.*

Downtown Freeport

From the back of the International Bazaar, you can hop on a 75 cent jitney bus that goes up East Mall Drive and lets you off in **downtown Freeport** a few minutes later. The downtown section doesn't really look like a city, but it seems much more like a collection of small office buildings, malls, and a few interesting shops scattered along a half mile of wide avenues like East Mall Drive and West Mall Drive, and down a few intersecting side streets like Pioneer's Way.

This district contains many affordably priced boutiques and restaurants that are patronized mainly by locals, and a few luxury item shops are also located here. The major attraction for tourists is the **Outdoor Fruit Vendors' Market** just off West Mall Drive where you can find friendly locals selling all sorts of freshly picked tropical fruits and vegetables, and bottles of home-made hot sauces at great prices. *The Fruit Vendors' Market is open Monday through Saturday from about 9:00am until around 5:30pm, and is free to enter.*

Guided City Tours

There are two services I'd recommend in Freeport that offer city and area tours: **H. Forbes Charter Services**, *Freeport, Tel. (242) 352-9311,* has a good three hour "Super Combination Tour" by bus that costs $16 per person and includes guided tours to the Garden of the Groves, Millionaire's Row, downtown Freeport, The Fruit Vendor's Market, a duty free liquor shop, and the International Marketplace.

The other tour operator based in Freeport and ranging further afield is **Best Island Travel & Tours**, *Tel. (242) 352-4811.* They'll take you on a four hour "West End" tour for $20 per person that visits the off-the-beaten-path western section of the island includin guided tours at Eight Mile Rock, Sea Grape, Holmes Rock, and Deadman's Reef. They also have a full day "Grand Bahama" tour that includes lunch and visits to all of the island's most famous sights and villages for $30 per person.

LUCAYA

Getting to Lucaya

From Freeport International Airport a taxi will cost somewhere around $13.50 per couple with a few bags. Most taxis here actually use their meters.

From Freeport Harbour a taxi will set you back about $13 per car (not per person). You may also hop on a jitney bus for a 75 cent ride heading down West Sunrise Highway and East Sunrise Highway before turning down Coral Road and Royal Palm Way to reach the final stop near the Port Lucaya Marketplace.

From Downtown Freeport taxis charge around $10.50 per car to Port Lucaya. Another alternative is to take a bus ride for 75 cents on a jitney bus in front of the Winn Dixie Supermarket off East Mall Drive, which then turns along East Sunrise Highway before turning down Coral Road and Royal Palm Way to reach its final stop near the Port Lucaya Marketplace.

From Freeport a taxi will cost about $8 per car to Port Lucaya. Those on tight budgets can also take a 75 cent jitney bus ride from behind the International Bazaar that heads down East Sunrise Highway before turning down Coral Road and Royal Palm Way to reach its final stop near the Port Lucaya Marketplace.

ORIENTATION

Situated just off a tranquil narrow sandy strip beach known locally as **Lucayan Beach**, about four miles southeast of central **Freeport**, this area is in the process of reestablishing itself as a major tourist destination. Besides having a handful of hotels and timeshare resorts in close proximity, this district also offers a casino, a great marina, several exciting excursion possibilities, a nearby golf course, a shopping center with over 75 boutiques and restaurants, and a good amount of nightlife. I expect that by the time you read this book, Lucaya will once again be the destination of choice for many vacationers in Grand Bahama.

SEEING THE SIGHTS

A Walk Through the Lucaya Resort Area

As soon as you approach Lucaya via the main road, you will notice that much of the area is sandwiched between sandy **Lucayan Beach** and the nearby **Port Lucaya Marina**. The beach area is a relatively nice place to cool off in the afternoon sun, and several water sports can be enjoyed here. Among the hotels facing the sea are the towering **Clarion Atlantik** that has been wonderfully renovated, and a few others being refurbished at press time, including the **Grand Bahama Beach** and the **Lucayan Beach Resort** with its small and less than impressive **Casino**.

Just across the road from these major hotels is the extremely popular **Port Lucaya Marketplace** shopping center and entertainment area. Located at the edge of a serious marina filled with multimillion dollar yachts from around the globe, this large shopping center contains about 80 fine boutiques, duty free shops, eateries in all price ranges, and bars. The centerpiece of the complex is the marina-front **Count Basie Square** (named for this great jazz player and composer that used to live near here), where local musicians can be found playing live music of all sorts on most afternoons and evenings. *Most of the shops at the Port Lucaya Marketplace are open daily from 9:00am until at least 7:00pm, but the bars and restaurants stay open past 1:00am.*

At the far edge of the International Marketplace is a small **Straw Market**, and this area is also the departure zone for several excursions such as the **Deep Star Submarine** and the world famous **Unexso** dolphin encounter and shark dive adventures. In the general vicinity, you will also find the fine **Lucaya Golf & Country Club**.

NEARBY EXCURSIONS

If you have a day or two to explore Grand Bahama Island, you may find yourself heading for the following unique attractions, parks, beaches, and villages that are best reached by bicycle, taxi, or rental car.

Xanadu Beach

For those looking for a full facility beach and recreation zone with plenty of available water sports and activities, **Xanadu** is close by and easy to reach. Located just 3 1/2 miles south of Freeport, Xanadu is a nicely maintained beach over a mile long and is busy during the winter months. Cool drinks and good hearty meals are available on the premises.

While only an inexpensive taxi ride or quick bicycle ride away from Freeport, those staying at the Bahamas Princess Hotel receive complimentary round-trip bus transportation here and back several times each day.

Taino Beach

Taino Beach is a reasonably nice stretch of white sandy beach lined by a couple of overpriced bars and restaurants, and is among the better nearby places to swim. The beach is roughly three miles east of Port Lucaya, and is an easy place to get to by bike or taxi. Those staying at the Bahamas Princess Hotel receive free round-trip bus service here on a daily basis.

Fortune Beach

Considered among the top beaches on the island, tree-lined **Fortune Beach** is located 5 1/2 miles east of Lucaya. Here you can enjoy miles of soft sand and medium-sized waves, as well as an assortment of seasonal water sports activities. There are also places to buy cold drinks and meals just off the shoreline. This is a good place to take a taxi to on a hot day.

MORE DISTANT EXCURSIONS

The following locations are a bit too far away from Freeport and Lucaya for most people to bicycle to or take a taxi to affordably. I suggest using a car to get here. Contact the rental car agencies listed at the beginning of this chapter for current rates and special deals. Remember to drive on the left in The Bahamas!

Taxis can be hired to get to these places, but keep in mind that the current official taxi rates for this island are $2 for the first 1/2 mile, 30 cents for each additional 1/2 mile, and $2 per person for the third and forth occupant. Taxis may not be an economical way to reach the following places.

Garden of the Groves

Just about eight miles east of Freeport off of Midshipman Road, you'll find a pleasant 12 acre preserve and botanical garden called the **Garden of the Groves**. The garden is named after Wallace Groves, the American millionaire and founder of Freeport who donated this land to the people of the island some years ago. Here you can stroll alongside thousands of exotic plants and trees while keeping your eyes out for a wide variety of wild birds that live here.

There are also ponds, well-manicured gardens, bridges, waterfalls, a local history museum, and a cute little chapel. *The gardens are open daily from 9:00am until 4:00pm, and cost $5 per person to enter.*

Rand Memorial Nature Centre

Operated by the non-profit Bahamas National Trust, this 100 acre nature park off East Settler's Way some three miles northeast of Freeport is a delightful place to visit. There is a 1 1/2 mile nature path that winds its way towards a beautiful pond surrounded by hundreds of semi-tropical plants and inhabited by all sorts of birds (including a flock of flamingos). Special tours are given to bird watchers on the first Saturday of each month, while other special tours are offered to plant enthusiasts on the fourth Saturday of each month.

The nature centre is open Monday through Friday from 9:00am until 4:00pm, Saturdays from 9:00am until 1:00pm, and guided tours cost $5 per person.

Lucayan National Park

Situated about 25 miles east of Freeport off of Midshipman Road, the **Lucayan National Park** is a nice 40 acre park filled with walking paths that wind through a variety of ecosystems. You can see dunes, trees, wildlife, swamps, and huge freshwater caves here, and you can swim on the island's best sandy beach. *The park is open daily from sunrise to sunset, and is free to enter.*

NIGHTLIFE & ENTERTAINMENT

JOHN B. BAR, *Bahamas Princess Country Club, Freeport. Tel. (242) 352-6721.*

Situated alongside the famous free-form swimming pool of the Bahamas Princess Country Club, this great bar has happening music, strong mixed drinks, 2 for 1 happy hour and after midnight specials, and a fun crowd of singles and couples that love to dance and meet other people. This is my favorite place to party in Freeport.

KAPTAIN KENNY'S, *International Bazaar, Freeport. Tel. (242) 351-4759.*

Kaptain Kenny's is among the most popular after-dinner spots to hit for good drinks and live Caribbean music each night. There is no cover charge, and the bar stays open until at least 12 midnight every night. The dress code is completely casual.

YELLOWBIRD NIGHTCLUB, *International Bazaar, Freeport. Tel. (242) 373-7368.*

If you are in the mood to witness a so-called native show that includes fire dancing, glass eating, limbo, steal drum band, comedy acts, and traditional dancers in Junkanoo costume, then this is the place to go. There are two shows each night and dinner is optional. The show's cover charge is around $20, including 2 drinks.

CASINO ROYALE SHOWROOM, *Bahamas Princess Casino, Freeport. Tel. (242) 352-7811.*

This glittering showroom just next to the casino offers a two hour Las Vegas style revue complete with sequined dancers, impersonators, and a variety of local and international entertainers. There are two shows each night except Monday and the cover charge is $25 a person, including two cocktails.

CLUB ESTEE, *Port Lucaya Marketplace, Lucaya. Tel. (242) 373-2777.*

Located near the marina of this busy shopping area, Club Estee is one of the few remaining discos left on the island. The club's massive dance floor gets crowded from about 11:00pm until 3:00am from Wednesday through Sunday, the cover charge is around $10, and the dress code is smart casual.

SHOPPING

Antiques

• **Amanda's Antique & Thrift Shoppe**, *East Mall Drive, downtown Freeport. Tel. (242) 352-7372.* A good source for antique items such as local oil paintings, rare maps, vintage home and office decorative pieces, and old prints.

• **Ye Olde Pirate Bottle House**, *Port Lucaya Marketplace. Tel. (242) 373-2000.* This fun shop and museum displays and sells thousands of antique colorful bottles as well as plenty of souvenirs.

Art & Crafts

• **The Spot**, *Port Lucaya Marketplace, Lucaya. Tel. (242) 373-7950.* Here you can find locally made paintings, arts & crafts, folk art, straw goods, rings, and all sorts of reasonably priced gifts.

• **Various Straw Markets**, *including the ones behind both the International Bazaar and the Port Lucaya Marketplace.*

China, Crystal, Glassware, & Porcelain

• **Island Galleria**, *International Bazaar, Freeport. Tel. (242) 322-8521; addional location at the Port Lucaya Marketplace.* Inside this impressive shop you'll find a great selection of both practical and collectable china, crystal, porcelain, and statuettes. The famous brands they carry are often available at around 30% below the typical US suggested retail prices.

Department Stores

• **John Bull**, *International Bazaar. Freeport, Tel. (242) 352-7515.* John Bull is a major retail operation that sells plenty of luxury items such as perfumes by Chanel, Estee Lauder, Yves St. Laurent, Lancome, Calvin Klein, and Clinique, timepieces by Tag Heuer, Raymond Weil, Rolex, Movado, Swiss Army, Guess, Gucci, Piaget, Phillipe Cahrriol, Swatch, Corum, and Seiko, pens by Cross and Mont Blanc, and jewelry by Mikimoto, Tiffany & Co., Kabana, David Yurman, Carrera y Carrera, Roberto Coin, leather goods, sunglasses, cigarette lighters, and travel accessories.

Jewelry & Timepieces

• **Cartier**, *International Bazaar, Freeport. Tel. (242) 352-5917.* Hidden away in the back of this large open air shopping center, in an opulent palace-style mansion, is the most elegant jeweler in the country. Besides displaying a huge selection of magnificent Italian and French gold jewelry and accessories from the famed Cartier company, they offer a full line of Lalique glass sculptures, fine Swiss watches, and many gift items.

• **The Columbian**, *International Bazaar, Freeport. Tel. (242) 352-5380; additional locations at the Port Lucaya Marketplace, and the Bahamas Princess Resort.* This well established jewelry shop features Colombian emeralds, South African diamonds, and Oriental ruby laden rings and chains, as well as fine watches by Piaget, Chopard, Gucci, Cartier, Corum, Movado, Baume & Mercier, Concord, Longines, and Zodiac.

• **Colombian Emeralds International**, *International Bazaar. Tel. (242) 352-5464; additional location at the Port Lucaya Marketplace.* Besides specializing in a vast array of precious cut and set emeralds in all price ranges, they also sell thousands of different gold and silver chains, unique rings, top quality set and unset gemstones from around the world, and dozens of different watches at good prices. The largest jewelry shop in town.

Linens

• **Linens of Lucaya**, *Port Lucaya Marketplace, Lucaya. Tel. (242) 373-8697.*

- **Far East Traders**, *International Bazaar, Freeport. Tel. (242) 352-9280.* These two affiliated shops sell every type of imported Asian and European linen product imaginable.

Leather Goods & Luggage
- **Fendi**, *International Bazaar, Freeport. Tel. (242) 352-7908.* A full line of Fendi leather goods, watches, silk scarves, and accessories.
- **Gucci**, *International Bazaar, Freeport. Tel. (242) 352-4580; additional locations at the Port Lucaya Marketplace and in the Bahamas Princess Towers.* A full line of Gucci leather goods, clothing, shoes, perfumes, watches, and accessories.
- **The Leather Shop**, *Port Lucaya Marketplace, Lucaya. Tel. (242) 352-5491. Additional locations in the Regent Centre West in downtown Freeport and at the International Bazaar.* Here you can get good prices on leather handbags and other goods from companies including Lancel, Ted Lapidus, Isanti, Piel, HCL, and Lanvin.

Liquor Stores
- **Burns House Ltd**, *International Bazaar, Freeport. Tel. (242) 352-740; over 10 additional locations all over Grand Bahama.* You can save up to 40% or more off the North American prices on labels like Frangelico, Malibu, Smirnoff, Glenfiddich, Tequila Sauza, Famous Grouse, Cutty Sark, Tio Pepe, Remy Martin, Chambord, Black Velvet, Galliano, Romana Sambuca, and several varieties of wines and beers (including Kalik). This is a good place to ask about duty free specials.
- **Butler & Sands**, *Queens Highway, Freeport. Tel. (242) 352-6627; several additional locations on the island.* This major retailer of wines and spirits carries many leading brands of spirits at good discounts such as Southern Comfort, Jack Daniels, Jose Cuervo, Amaretto di Saronno, Goldschalger, Campari, Dewar's, Crown Royal, Grand Marnier, Martell, Johnnie Walker, Barcardi, Finlandia, Chivas Regal, Bailey's, Hennesy, J & B, Absolut, Sandeman, Tanqueray, Seagram's, Stolichnya, Mumm's, and many others.

Perfume, Cologne, and Cosmetics
- **Les Parisiens**, *Port Lucaya Marketplace, Lucaya. Tel. (242) 373-2973; additional locations at the International Bazaar and the Bahamas Princess Hotel.* These large discount fragrance shops sell well known brands from all over the world at up to a 40% discount off US suggested retail prices.
- **The Perfume Factory**, *International Bazaar, Freeport. Tel. (242) 352-9391.* Inside this beautiful colonial mansion you can create your own perfume using their exclusive collection of natural scents. They also

sell fragrances from England, France, Bermuda, and The Bahamas at good prices.

Shopping Centers
- **The International Bazaar**, *Corner of West Sunrise Highway and East Mall Drive, Freeport. Tel. (242) 352-2828.* This is the largest shopping center in Grand Bahamas, offering over 95 different shops, restaurants, cafes, bars, and boutiques. Located just across from the Bahamas Princess Resort & Casino, it is a bustling shopping mall with various streets that have been designed to look like exotic parts of the globe. There are convenient jitney buses that run here from all over the island every fifteen minutes or so. Parking is not always so easy. Most of the shops are open daily from 8:45am until at least 7:00pm.
- **Port Lucaya Marketplace**, *Port Lucaya, Lucaya. Tel. (242) 373-8446.* Located just in front of an active marina, this outdoor mall contains more than 65 shops, bars, boutiques, and restaurants in all price ranges. There is also a great outdoor music area called Count Basie Square, with free concerts each evening (and some afternoons), and a full service marina where several excursions depart. Most of the shops at the Port Lucaya Marketplace are open daily from 9:00am until at least 7:00pm, but the bars and restaurants stay open past 1:00am.

T-Shirts & Souvenirs
- **Bahamas Best Souvenirs**, *International Bazaar, Freeport. Tel. (242) 352-4848.* This is where you can get good prices on high quality cotton and cotton blend T-shirts with tropical island themes, at bargain prices like four T-shirts for $10, refrigerator magnets, postcards, coffee mugs, key chains, pins, and much more at cheap prices.
- **Various Straw Markets**, *including the ones behind both the International Bazaar and the Port Lucaya Marketplace.*

SPORTS & RECREATION
Almost all of the following recommended companies will be happy to provide free round-trip transfers to any hotel on the island if contacted a least a day or two in advance.

Boating Adventures
Kayak Nature Tours, *various locations. Tel. (242) 373-2485*
For those who want a good workout while enjoying the beauty of out-of-the-way Grand Bahama creeks, parks, caves, and beaches, this local firm has two separate full day tours to choose from that cost $75 each and include a picnic lunch and all the necessary gear.

Pat & Diane Cruises, *Lucaya. Tel. (242) 373-8681.*

This company offers a wide variety of cruises and adventures aboard medium-sized motorized catamarans and 57' sailing trimarans. Their most popular excursion is a $49 per person full day "Bootlegger's Beach Party Adventure" party cruise, departing daily to a deserted island beach where you are served unlimited tropical drinks and a native chicken & ribs lunch before you're given snorkeling gear (for free) to explore the marine life. They also offer two hour reef snorkeling cruises daily for $18, as well as special two hour sunset trimaran sailboat rides with dancing, free drinks, and hors d'oeuvres for $25.

Bahama Mama Booze Cruise, *Lucaya. Tel. (242) 373-7863.*

This is a two hour sunset party cruise aboard a 72' catamaran that departs daily and includes dancing, unlimited wine and Bahama Mama drinks, hors d'oeuvres, and lots of blasted participants.

Paradise Princess Glass Bottom Boats, *Xanadu Beach. Tel. (242) 352-2887.*

This company offers a wide array of water sports, but also schedules 90 minute glass bottom boat rides twice a day that move slowly over the reefs and ship wrecks. The price is just $15 a person.

Caving

I recommend **Nautical Adventures**, *Lucaya, Tel. (242) 373-7180,* a small local company that is working hard to create the best cave tours and guided trips on the island. They use comfortable 18 passenger air conditioned mini-buses and offer an "Historic Cave Tour" to the ancient Lucayan Indian caves in Lucaya National Park. They also offer a fun half day guided trip to Gold Rock Beach and several nearby East End villages for just $25 a person each.

Fishing Charters

• **Paradise Charters**, *Xanadu Beach. Tel. (242) 352-2887*
• **Grand Bahama Boat Rentals & Charters**, *Lucaya. Tel. (242) 373-9153*
• **Nautical Adventures**, *Lucaya. Tel. (242) 373-7180*
• **Viva Fishing Cruises**, *Lucaya. Tel. (242) 373-7226*

Horseback Riding

Pinetree Stables, *Freeport. Tel. (242) 373-3600.*

For around $35 a person (including free hotel pick-up) you can enjoy a great 90 minute trail ride through the forests and deserted beaches of the island's south coast. Lessons available, closed on Mondays.

Scuba Diving

Unexso, *Lucaya. Tel. (242) 373-1244.*

The world famous **Underwater Explorers Society** is the best equipped scuba diving establishment on Grand Bahama and offers an excellent series of unique adventure dives and specialty programs for all levels of scuba enthusiasts. Their brand new state of the art facility just behind Port Lucaya's International Marketplace has six custom dive boats, 15 certified dive masters and instructors, a specially designed diving pool, a photography lab, a restaurant, and a great scuba shop full of the most modern underwater equipment for rent and sale. Among the available services are daily $18 snorkeling trips, $89 learn to dive courses with a shallow reef dive the same day, a dolphin encounter program for $29, a 1 tank dive with the dolphin trip at $105, and as many as a dozen reef, shark encounter, and wreck dives each day ranging from $39 to $115 each.

Unexso also offers a **swim with the dolphins** program. For $29 per person, you can take a short boat ride from Port Lucaya to their large facility off Sanctuary Bay and for an in-depth narrative about Atlantic bottlenose dolphins by one of their expert staff members. Once you arrive, six people at a time are asked to stand in 3' deep water and await a pair of trained dolphins to swim in front of you. At that point you can touch the dolphin and interact with it for a couple of minutes. Make sure to bring a swim suit and a waterproof camera, and expect to return to Port Lucaya in about two hours.

Xanadu Underwater Adventures, *Xanadu Beach. Tel. (242) 352-3811.*

This is one of the better scuba diving facilities on Grand Bahama Island. Located at the Xanadu Beach Resort near Freeport, they offer great "Learn to Dive" courses with a shallow reef dive from $79 a person, snorkel trips with free rental gear at $18, 1 tank dives for $32, 2 tank dives for $55, 2 tank night dives for $70, underwater videos of your dive for $35, and PADI open water certifications for only $325.

Skydiving

Tandem Skydive Bahamas, *Freeport Airport, Freeport. Tel. (242) 352-5995.*

Enjoy a thrilling jump off a plane at 11,000' while you are attached to an instructor. Videos of your descent are available as well.

Snorkeling

Fun in the Sun, *Deadman's Cay, West End District. Tel. (242) 349-2677.*

For only $18 a person you are driven to a secluded beach at Paradise Cove, about 25 minutes west of Freeport, to enjoy a half or full day of fun and unlimited snorkeling with free rental gear. They also have a snack bar and lounge on the beach area.

Paradise Watersports, *Xanadu Beach. Tel. (242) 352-2887.*

For about $18 a person, you can cruise to nearby Winky's Wreck and hop off near the reef to snorkel for an hour and a quarter. The trip includes snorkeling gear, instruction, life jackets, and cold beverages.

Submarine Rides

Deepstar Submarines, *Lucaya. Tel. (242) 373-8940.*

This is an unusual one hour adventure aboard an authentic submarine with huge windows that descends 100' feet below the surface. You get a narrated tour of the reefs about a mile and a half off of Port Lucaya. You can peer out of the giant windows and see plenty of exotic fish, lobsters, wrecks, and an occasional shark. This is the only real submarine ride in Grand Bahama. The price per person is currently about $59 for adults and $41 for kids under 12.

Seaworld Explorer, *Lucaya. Tel. (242) 373-7863.*

This 34 passenger vessel is not actually a submarine, but its glass, air conditioned hull rests 5' feet below the sea's surface. The ride gives visitors a chance to see plenty of fish, coral, and wreck sights along Treasure Reef. The cost of this excursion is $29 per adult and $19 per kid.

PRACTICAL INFORMATION

- **Grand Bahama Police Department**, *Emergencies, Tel. 919*
- **Grand Bahama Fire Department**, *Tel. (242) 352-8888*
- **Grand Bahama Ambulance Service**, *Tel. (242) 352-2689*
- **Rand Memorial Hospital**, *Tel. (242) 352-6735*
- **Lucayan Medical Center**, *Tel. (242) 352-7288*
- **Bahamas Air Sea Rescue**, *Tel. (242) 352-2628*
- **Tourism Information Center**, *International Bazaar, Tel. (242) 352-8044*
- **Weather Information**, *Tel. 915*
- **Directory Assistance**, *Tel. 916*

15. THE ABACOS

The **Abacos** are located 11 miles northeast of Grand Bahama Island and 72 miles north of New Providence Island, and are home to about 10,000 Bahamians. The Abaco Islands center around the 86 mile long **Great Abaco Island**, a strikingly lush and mainly undeveloped island dotted with major marina facilities. The most popular Out Island in The Bahamas, this destination is revered for the fine fishing and water-sports that lure visitors here from all over the world. Treasure hunters have also been known to frequent the area in search of the more than 400 **Spanish galleons** that have sunk (mostly due to successful local wreckers) on the reefs just offshore.

Great Abaco is connected to the adjacent 26 mile long **Little Abaco Island** to the northwest, and is flanked by over three dozen beautiful little cays mostly found off the islands' eastern coast, including the wonderful **Green Turtle Cay** and **Elbow Cay**. The S.C. Doodle Highway is the main road in the region and runs for about 130 miles from southern Great Abaco to northern Little Abaco.

Treasure Cay is a small 4 mile long peninsula extending eastward to the sea from from the northern part of Great Abaco Island. This area is home to the Treasure Cay Resort & Marina complex with several hundred townhouses and villas for rent alongside a giant protected marina full of large American fishing vessels. This is the place to head for when you want to tie up your yacht and play golf, dine, scuba dive, or spend the night around like-minded fishing enthusiasts. There is no real town, important historical sights, or worthy attractions to visit in this area.

Marsh Harbour, the third largest city in the country, is a quiet yet industrious town with a growing resort community based on the edge of the sea. Here there are a handful of hotels, rental homes, restaurants in all price ranges, good boutiques, casual bars, and major yachting and charter boat facilities that attract a lively crowd of fishing maniacs.

Green Turtle Cay is a small island just a mile or so east across the sound from Treasure Cay in northern Great Abaco. Life is rather good here, with no serious unemployment, crime, or major social problems to speak of. Popular as a laid-back getaway for couples and families from all over North America and Europe who return year after year, the cay has a few unforgettable inns that provide the perfect ambiance for a relaxing vacation. There are also fine beaches, plenty of rental boats and homes, full service marinas featuring scuba and fishing expeditions, a nearby deserted island, a couple of interesting historical sights, a few boutiques, and lots of friendly locals to help you feel at home from the moment you arrive. It is not at all uncommon to be invited into the house of a complete stranger, and residents often will stop tourists to see if they need a lift. **New Providence**, a sleepy village of some 420 souls, is by far my favorite town in all of The Bahamas to wander around. Make sure to visit the amazing sandy **Coco Bay Beach** and **Ocean Beach** areas that are a long hike (or short ride) outside of town.

Elbow Cay is a delightful little island community five miles off the coast of Marsh Harbour. About 290 mostly white Bahamian residents and vacationers inhabit this quiet community, but hotels and rental villas accommodate another hundred or so well-off visitors from America and Europe during the high season. The main attraction here is the harborfront village of **Hope Town**, a former Loyalist stronghold filled with beautiful 19th-century cottages that in many cases have been converted into restaurants and retail stores. There is also an antique red and white striped lighthouse, a couple of long white sand beaches, a reasonably interesting historical museum, and not much else. While there are several night spots, in general Elbow Cay is a quiet place that can be enjoyed as either a day trip or as a tranquil place to spend a few days.

Abaco's History

Like several other parts of The Bahamas, the Abaco Islands were once occupied by bands of Lucayan Indians who were later enslaved or murdered by Spanish Conquistadors. In the aftermath of the American Revolution of 1776, thousands of those still loyal to English King George III were routinely persecuted, subjected to mob violence, or even sent to the gallows as traitors in the new colonies. After other Loyalists finally repelled the Spanish from The Bahamas, many of these now penniless Tories from the colonies and escaped slaves sailed into the isolated Abacos to start their lives over again.

In 1783, Captain Charles Vane sailed two of his vessels, the *Nautilus* and *William*, all the way from New York to Treasure Cay. Filled with passengers that for the most part had been black slaves in the American colonies, these settlers soon established a small hamlet they called

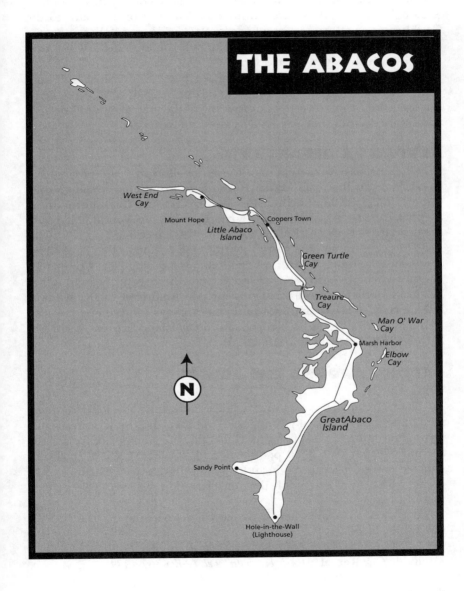

THE ABACOS

West End Cay

Mount Hope

Little Abaco Island

Coopers Town

Green Turtle Cay

Treaure Cay

Man O' War Cay

Marsh Harbor

Elbow Cay

N

GreatAbaco Island

Sandy Point

Hole-in-the-Wall (Lighthouse)

Carleton. Soon after additional Loyalists from the Carolinas started arriving in small numbers. Since the land proved unsatisfactory for agriculture, life on Abaco was difficult for these courageous founders. Although many settlers gave up hope and moved on to south to the Caribbean, a small group of stubborn locals stayed here and became some of the finest fisherman and wooden sailing ship builders in the world, and trade eventually began to prosper.

While many wealthy foreigners have since built lavish seaside residences here in search of a taste of the good life, many of Abaco's residents can trace their roots directly back to some of the first groups of Loyalists and escaped slaves that arrived here over 200 years ago.

ARRIVALS & DEPARTURES

The Abacos have two commonly used small airports. In the center of Great Abaco is the main **Marsh Harbour International Airport**, while some 27 miles further northwest is the tiny **Treasure Cay International Airport**. Be sure to find out which airport is nearest to your hotel, or else the taxi fare may be as much as $45 more than necessary!

These are rather basic airports with small terminals that have snack shops, ticket offices, a taxi rank, and almost nothing else. Companies operating scheduled passenger service into these airports from either Florida or other Bahamian islands include **American Eagle**, **US Air**, **Bahamasair**, **Gulfstream International Airways**, and there are also frequent charter flights on small planes run by **Island Express**, **Twin Air**, **Airways International**, and **Abaco Air**.

GETTING AROUND THE ABACOS

By Rental Car

There are no major rental car agencies here, but some local businessmen have fleets of typically 10 year old (or older) used American sedans, vans, and station wagons for rent. Generally, the going price for a car is around $70 per day, $350 per week, and, for most, CDW (collision damage waiver) insurance is included in the above prices. The insurance carries a $100 or so deductible that must be left in cash or travelers check as a security deposit.

If you need a car anywhere in Abaco, call at least a day in advance. Two reputable places are:
• **H & L Car & Scooter Rentals**, *Marsh Harbour, Tel. (242) 367-2854*
• **Reliable Car Rental**, *Marsh Harbour, Tel. (242) 367-4234*

By Taxi

There are over 150 licensed taxi cabs in the Abacos, and they generally quote similar prices. Unlike most other Out Islands, I have never seen a taxi driver in the Abacos use a government approved rate sheet, or even a taxi meter, to determine the price of a journey. My suggestion is to ask around and find a good driver that will give you the best rates and personalized service.

• **Elegante Limousines**, *Treasure Cay, (242) 365-8053*
• **Lowell Edgecomb**, *Treasure Cay, (242) 365-8276*
• **Macintosh Taxi Service**, *Green Turtle Cay, (242) 365-4309*

WHERE TO STAY

Moderate

GREAT ABACO BEACH RESORT & MARINA, *Marsh Harbour, Abaco. Tel. (242) 367-2158, Fax (242) 367-2819. US & Canada bookings (Out Island Promo Board) 1-800-688-4752. Low season rack rates from $145 per double room per night (E.P.). High season rack rates from $185 per double room per night (E.P.). M.A.P. Meal Plans available from $32 per adult per day. Most major credit cards accepted.*

Great Abaco Beach Resort and Marina is a unique full service resort hotel just steps away from the sea. Popular with families and couples who really enjoy water based adventures such as fishing and yachting, the resort has a superb 185 slip marina, two restaurants, a great swim-up bar, two large outdoor swimming pools, a laundromat, several boutiques, a mini-market and liquor store, outdoor tennis courts, a small sandy beach, complimentary Hobie Cat and Sunfish sail boats, rental boat and charter services, available scuba diving and snorkeling excursions, optional guided island tours and free parking.

All of the 52 deluxe air conditioned rooms face directly out onto the sea and feature deluxe private bathrooms, remote control satellite television with free movie channels, mini-refrigerators, a coffee machine, direct dial telephone, a wet bar, West Indies style hardwood furnishings, large sliding doors that open up onto spacious patios, and more. There are also six free-standing air conditioned villas available near the beach that come equipped with all the above, plus a large fully stocked kitchen, two bedrooms, and two bathrooms. This is a modern and extremely well maintained hotel with all the comforts of home. Selected as one of our *Best Places to Stay* – see Chapter 12 for a longer review.

GREEN TURTLE CLUB, *Green Turtle Cay, Abaco. Tel. (242) 365-4271, Fax (242) 365-4272. US & Canada bookings (Out Island Promo Board) 1-800-688-4752. Low season rack rates from $120 per double room per night (E.P.). High season rack rates from $184 per double room per night (E.P.). M.A.P. Meal Plans available from $36 per adult per day. 3 night minimum stay. Most major credit cards accepted.*

Located on White Sound in Green Turtle Cay, this picturesque New England-style hotel and restaurant is among the most popular places to stay in the Abaco area for wealthier yachtsmen and vacationing couples. The property rests along a nice marina area and consists of 34 well-designed rooms, suites, efficiencies, and villas that have powerful air conditioning, beautiful private bathrooms, hardwood or ceramic floor-ing, fine wooden furnishings imported from North Carolina, clock radios, sea-view patios, ceiling fans, mini-refrigerators, unusual decora-tive art pieces, oriental style rugs, plenty of natural sunlight, and lots of Old World charm.

The club also has a fantastic dining room, an al fresco restaurant area, a nice fresh water swimming pool, a full service marina, optional snorkel-ing and boat charters, a complete dive shop with scuba excursions, a gift shop and boutique, access to nice beaches, a ferry boat landing, a great wood-paneled bar, business meeting rooms, deep sea and bonefishing trips, and much more. This is a nice little place and is well worth the rates. Be advised that they sell out well in advance during much of the year.

TREASURE HOUSES, *Treasure Cay, Abaco. Tel. (954) 525-7711, Fax (954) 525-1699. Low season rack rates from $285 per 2 bedroom apartment per night (E.P.). High season rack rates from $385 per 2 bedroom apartment per night (E.P.). Minimum 3 night stay. M.A.P. Meal Plans available from $34 per adult per day. Most major credit cards accepted.*

Nestled between the beach-front and the 18 hole championship golf course, Treasure Houses are the most deluxe sea-view rental villas available in the Treasure Cay Resort & Marina development. The octago-nal shaped 2 bedroom private homes are clustered around a nice swimming pool just steps from a 3 1/2 mile beach. Each unit comes complete with air conditioning, modern private bathrooms, large patio sun decks, color satellite television, well-equipped full kitchens, and sloped ceilings. The guests have complete access to the golf course, outdoor tennis courts, a modern full service marina, a fun restaurant and action packed bar, and of course the amazing turquoise waters of this part of the South Atlantic Ocean.

Inexpensive

THE BLUFF HOUSE, *Green Turtle Cay, Abaco. Tel. (242) 365-4247, Fax (242) 365-4248. Low season rack rates from $90 per double room per night (E.P.). High season rack rates from $100 per double room per night (E.P.). M.A.P. Meal Plans available from $35 per adult per day. Most major credit cards accepted.*

Owned by Martin Havill, a delightful English expatriate, this great little casual hilltop hotel, restaurant, and full service marina is my favorite affordably priced place to stay in the Abacos. The Bluff House has several small water-view lodges with 28 large and well-equipped air conditioned guest rooms, suites, and villas that have terraced sun decks, hand-crafted rattan furnishings, rich fabrics with tropical motifs, chapel styled ceilings with powerful fans, large modern private bathrooms, lots of closet space, half sized refrigerators, comfortable king or double beds, wall-to-wall carpeting, and French doors that open up to superb sea views. The inn's extra friendly management and staff can be found chatting with guests (usually a mixture of giggling newlyweds and jovial repeat customers) inside the casual Clubhouse Dining Room and water-front Beach House, where delicious home-made meals and strong cool cocktails are typically served.

The services and activities available here are free round-trip boat trips to the charming nearby village of New Plymouth, an outdoor tennis court with racquets and balls, free beach chairs and snorkeling equipment, snorkeling trips and picnics to area lighthouses and deserted islands, a private marina with inexpensive slips and boat rentals, optional bonefishing and reef fishing expeditions, an infamous Saturday night shuttle boat to a popular nearby nightclub with live music and plenty of local ambiance, weekly open air barbecues with live local entertainment, express laundry, and a nice long sandy beach-front. I strongly suggest this inn for those who want to get away from it all but still meet plenty of spirited fellow travelers that love to have a fun time. Selected as one of our *Best Places to Stay* – see Chapter 12 for a longer review.

HOPE TOWN HIDEAWAYS, *Hope Town, Elbow Cay, Abaco. Tel. (242) 366-0224, Fax (242) 366-0434. Low season rack rates from $190 per 2 bedroom villa per night (E.P.). High season rack rates from $250 per 2 bedroom villa per night (E.P.). Reduced weekly rates available. Most major credit cards accepted.*

Hope Town Hideaways are a series of several unique 1 to 5 bedroom harbor-side Loyalist cottages and beautiful luxury homes. Perfect for couples and families who want more privacy and space than other hotels can offer in Hope Town, the Hideaways are a delightful place to spend a relaxing vacation.

All of the free-standing villas feature direct dial private line telephones, nice big bathrooms, fully stocked gourmet kitchens, a variety of extremely comfortable furnishings, strong central air conditioning, large living and dining rooms, cathedral ceilings, huge private decks surrounded by lush tropical gardens and native fruit trees, VHF radio communication systems, direct dial phones and lots of charm.

The villas also come with complimentary dingys to get you effortlessly around Hope Town Harbour, a nearby outdoor swimming pool and brand new harbor-side sun deck, available fishing trips and water-based excursions, nearby long sandy beaches, several fine restaurants not three minutes away, and a property management team of locals that go out of their way to make sure you have an unforgettable stay.

NEW PLYMOUTH CLUB & INN, *Parliament Street, Green Turtle Cay, Abaco. Tel. (242) 365-4161, Fax (242) 365-4138. Year round rack rates from $120 per double room per night (M.A.P.). Most major credit cards accepted.*

The New Plymouth Club is a windswept colonial mansion in the heart of one of the Abacos' most delightful villages. The inn has nine cozy medium-sized air conditioned rooms with private bathrooms, canopy beds in some cases, antiques and Victorian furnishings, patios, and nice garden views. You get a cooked-to-order breakfast and dinner daily, as well as use of the outdoor swimming pool, sun deck, and tranquil public rooms. This is a good choice if you're on a restricted budget looking for good accommodations in a traditional island community.

WHERE TO EAT

Expensive

THE BLUFF HOUSE, *Green Turtle Cay, Abaco. Tel. (242) 365-4247. Dress code is casual yet neat. Most major credit cards accepted.*

When you want to have a great meal and meet plenty of interesting fellow travelers, head for the hilltop sea-view dining room over at The Bluff House. Chef Veronica presents a daily menu with extremely good meat, seafood, and poultry selections that might include their famous blackened grouper, broiled lobster tails, boneless breast of chicken, lamb curry, roasted duck a l'orange, lobster scampi smothered in garlic, chicken Kiev, London broil, cracked conch, stuffed Cornish game hen, leg of lamb, or many other home-made selections. After being seated at either a table for two, or at a large table with complete strangers that all become friends during the meal, you are free to indulge in all the complimentary red and white wine you desire. Dinner here is by reservation only, and costs $31 per person.

GREEN TURTLE CLUB, *Green Turtle Cay, Abaco. Tel. (242) 365-4271. Dress code is smart casual. Most major credit cards accepted.*

Green Turtle Club's indoor dining room is one of the Abaco's most romantic spots for a fine meal. Set back just a few yards from the marina, this lavishly designed restaurant and its adjacent outdoor patio prepare good evening meals based on rotating menus with selected meat, seafood, and fowl entrees. Reservations are mandatory for dinner here and expect to pay around $35 per person for a nice meal – not including wine.

Moderate

MANGOES, *Old Harbour Street, Marsh Harbour, Great Abaco. Tel. (242) 367-2366. Closed on Sundays. Dress code is smart casual. Most major credit cards accepted.*

This popular harbor-side restaurant has seating for over 150 hungry guests in both air conditioned dining rooms and outdoor water-view patios. The more upscale crowd gets here at about 7:30pm to enjoy a full menu with such treats as conch fritters at $5.50, escargot for $6, chicken stuffed with crab meat at $19.50, rack or lamb for $21.50, pasta with seafood in marinara sauce at $18.50, veal picctata in white wine for $17.50, barbecued ribs and chicken plates at $17.50, coconut fried shrimp for $18.50, and grilled grouper at $18.50. They offer a much more affordable lunch menu.

HARBOUR'S EDGE, *Hope Town, Elbow Cay, Abaco. Tel. (242) 366-0292. Closed on Tuesdays. Dress code is casual. Most major credit cards accepted.*

Located on the picturesque Hope Town Harbour, this delightful open air eatery is my favorite place to dine on the entire cay. Clay and Lisa Wilhoyte have created a well-rounded menu of Bahamian and American favorites that include tasty and large dishes like crawfish salad at $8, chicken wings for $6, Caesar salads with fresh fish at $8, nachos for $6, conch chowder at $5.50, grilled grouper burgers for $8, smoked turkey sandwiches at $7.50, cheeseburgers for $8, B.L.T.'s at $7.50, french fries for $2, home-made peas and rice at $2, cracked conch for $19, southern fried chicken at $18, grilled lamb chops with mint jelly for $21, in-season lobster at $22, duck with black current sauce for $22, and all sorts of daily specials. They also have a pool table, pizza on Saturday nights, and occasional live music in the adjacent bar.

SAPODILLY'S RESTAURANT, *Old Harbour Street, Marsh Harbour, Great Abaco. Tel. (242) 367-3498. No Dress Code. Most major credit cards accepted.*

Of all the affordable restaurants in the Abacos, this down to earth local eatery and bar is among my personal favorites. With a dozen or so tables set up below the green and white striped awning, Sapodilly's has a great lunch and dinner menu prepared by local and European chefs that includes conch chowder at $4, chef salads for $8, Caesar salads with grilled chicken at $9, grouper burgers for $8, deep fried shrimp with tartar sauce at $7.50, roast beef sandwiches for $6, aged rib-eye steak dinners at $19, chicken kabobs for $16, burgers at $9, broiled or baked catch of the day for $19, cold beers at just $3.25 each, and a plentiful supply of reasonably priced Cuban cigars. There is also a pool table and a friendly crowd of locals and tourists that like to meet each other.

Inexpensive

GREAT ABACO BEACH SAND BAR, *Old Harbour Street, Marsh Harbour, Great Abaco. Tel. (242) 367-2158. No Dress Code. Most major credit cards accepted.*

Located between the Great Abaco Beach Resort's fine marina and swimming pool, the cute Sand Bar offers an extensive menu of snacks and sandwiches served throughout the day, including local conch chowder for

$3.75, grouper delights at $4.75, coconut mango shrimp for $9.75, fried calamari at $7.25, cheese burgers for $7, grilled chicken burger at $8.75, turkey breast sandwiches for $5.75, Bimini twists at $9.95, grilled grouper salads for $8.95, fresh fruit plates with sherbet at $8.75, cracked conch for $8.75, and some of the island's best frozen drinks made to order for around $5 each. There is live music here on weekends, and lots of friendly vacationers to chat with while casually drinking and dining.

SHARKEES ISLAND PIZZA, *Old Harbour Street, Marsh Harbour, Great Abaco. Tel. (242) 367-3535. Open 11:00am to at least 10:00pm daily. No Dress Code. Cash Only - No credit cards accepted.*

When you are in the mood for a simple inexpensive meal, call this local Marsh Harbour establishment for a reasonably good pizza to eat in, take out, or for delivery directly to area rental homes and hotels. They offer Philadelphia steak subs for $6.50, meatball sandwiches at $5.50, garden salads for $4.50, chef salads at $7.50, personal sized pizzas for $5.75, medium pizzas at $10.75, large pizzas for $13.75, and a full range of toppings starting from $1 per additional topping.

TREASURE CAY

Getting to Treasure Cay

Those arriving here either take their own boat or hop a flight on one of several airlines that service **Treasure Cay International Airport**. From here it's just a 9 minute, $10 taxi ride to the heart of town. If you landed at Marsh Harbour International Airport instead, a taxi here will set you back about $65 one way.

SEEING THE SIGHTS

The Resort Area

This self-contained resort area is home to a major vacation home and low-rise time share apartment development called the **Treasure Cay Resort & Marina**. The complex almost completely surrounds a massive marina where guests either dock their yachts for the season, tie up their fishing cruisers for a brief vacation, or rent an apartment while chartering 17' to 26' vessels.

The complex has a good restaurant, the extremely crowded night spot called the **Tipsy Bar**, the **Diver's Down** excursion operator and scuba shop, several charter and rental boat companies such as **J.I.C.** and **C & C Boat Rentals**, the Jack Nicklaus designed 18 hole championship **Treasure Cay Golf Course**, and lots of rooms and apartments for rent in several different price ranges. Besides the nearby **Ocean Beach**, there is no other major attraction in the general vicinity.

GREEN TURTLE CAY

Getting to Green Turtle Cay

If you fly into **Treasure Cay International Airport**, you can take a 4 minute, $5 taxi ride to the nearby Treasure Cay ferry landing and connect to scheduled ferry service to one of several available stops on Green Turtle Cay. The covered 22 passenger water taxis depart from Treasure Cay daily at 10:30am, 2:30pm, and 4:15pm, while the return trip departs Green Turtle Cay daily at 8:00am, 1:30pm, and 3:00pm. The ferry will also take you to New Plymouth, The Bluff House, or the Green Turtle Club, and bring you back for a fare of around $8 per person each way.

For special charters or additional schedules and current information, contact the **Green Turtle Ferry Service Ltd.**, *Tel. (242) 365-4166*, or hail them on VHF radio via channel 16. You can also get here by private boat.

SEEING THE SIGHTS

Once you have arrived by ferry or private boat to Green Turtle Cay's **Public Dock** in front of New Plymouth, walk straight between the two salvaged antique cannons at the end of the pier's "Welcome to New Plymouth" sign and immediately turn left onto the waterside **Bay Street**. After walking past two blocks of colorfully painted colonial houses and shacks, you will notice two of the village's more popular hangouts. On the left side of the street is the **Wrecking Tree** where simple inexpensive Bahamian meals and cool drinks are served for lunch and dinner. On the right side of Bay Street is the one of a kind **Burt's Sea Garden Club**, a great place to drink a beer and play pool or chat with the locals.

A few yards after Burt's front entrance, make a right turn and head up **Victoria Street**. A few houses up on the right is the world famous **Miss Emily's Blue Bee Bar**, another fine watering hole presided over by a delightful 88 year old woman that invented the secret recipe for the famed "Goombay Smash" cocktail decades ago.

At the next corner, turn right down **Parliament Street** and walk a few steps further until you come to the pink **Old Village Jail**. Marked with the word's "Ye Olde Gaol," the steel barred cells are now filled with cement bags and empty paint cans. After passing by a couple of churches, keep your eyes open for the island commissioner's office and the municipal office building, with a customs office, library, and post office side by side on your left. Next door to the municipal building is the **Albert Lowe Museum**. This restored home contains relics, photos, paintings, scale models, and antiques that relate to the island's colorful history. *The museum is open Monday through Saturday from 9:00am until 11:45am and again from 1:00pm until 4:00pm, with and entrance fee of $3 per person.*

Further along Parliament Street you will find the quaint **New Plymouth Club & Inn** on the left side. Just across from the front of the inn is the entrance to the village's peaceful little **Loyalist Memorial Sculpture Garden**. Opened in 1987 to commemorate the village's bicentennial, this park is dotted with bronze busts of prominent members of several Loyalist families that settled in this area and is centered around a massive statue called "The Loyalists" by artist James Mastin. Make sure to read the plaque below all of these statues to get an idea of the conditions that faced the cay's early settlers. *The sculpture garden is open daily from sunrise to sunset, and while there are no admission fees, donations are greatly appreciated.*

Keep heading down the same road as it then leads past the **Sand Dollar Shoppe & Jewelry Factory** and a **Barclay's Bank** before reaching the water's edge. Now turn right to follow Bay Street back down past **Ole B's** ice cream shop and then head back towards the piers. From here you can continue walking straight for a couple of blocks until merging with the appropriately named **Hill Street**. At the top of the hill, on the right hand side, is the enjoyable Rooster**'s Rest Club & Dance Hall**, where live music and dancing fill the place up on weekend nights.

Also worthy of note in New Plymouth is the unmarked home that used to belong to former English Prime Minister Neville Chamberlain (not open to the public), and, while a nice long hike away, the fantastic **Coco Bay Beach** and **Ocean Beach** areas (make sure to ask a local for good directions) on the cay's eastern coast. From the Public Dock, you should also take a short boat ride up White Sound to the nearby **Green Turtle Club** or the very relaxing **Bluff House** for a fine evening meal or pre-arranged sea-based adventure.

MARSH HARBOUR

Getting to Marsh Harbour

You can get here either by taking your own yacht, or hop a flight on one of several airlines that service **Marsh Harbour International Airport**. From here its just a 7 minute, $10 taxi ride to the heart of town. If you arrived at Treasure Cay International Airport instead, a taxi here will cost about $65 one way.

SEEING THE SIGHTS

Marsh Harbour, the third largest city in The Bahamas, lies 27 miles south of Treasure Cay Airport off the S.C. Doodle Highway. The main drag here is called **Old Harbour Street** by the locals and is lined with a good selection of boutiques, hotels, and resorts. As you enter the commercial section of town via the left exit onto **Don Mackay Boulevard**, you will soon pass the **Royal Bank of Canada**, several service stations, the

Chemist Shoppe drug store, a **CIBC** bank, the **Loyalist Shoppe** gift store, and then **Abaco Treasures** jewelers before reaching the city's only stop light.

At the stop light, make a right turn onto **Queen Elizabath Drive** where you will find the **Commonwealth Bank**, the somewhat helpful **Abaco Tourist Information Center**, a **Batelco** phone company office, and several small shops. From here the road curves around to the left and merges with **Bay Street** (known locally as **Old Harbour Street**) and continues along the harbor-side past **Wally's** restaurant, **Sapodilly's** bar and restaurant, **Mangoes** restaurant and boutique, a branch of the **John Bull** department store, **Sharkee's Island Pizza**, a **Little Switzerland** jewelry store, and the **Great Abaco Beach Resort & Marina**.

From here, you can keep going along the same street as it cuts through an upscale residential neighborhood and then passes **Crossing Beach**, where you will find the **Albury's Ferry Service** piers. From here, a water taxi runs between both Hope Town and Man-O-War Cay daily.

ELBOW CAY

Getting to Elbow Cay

You can either take your own boat all the way, or fly into **Marsh Harbour International Airport**, take an 8 minute, $10 taxi ride to the nearby Marsh Harbour ferry landing, and then connect to scheduled ferry to one of several available stops in Hope Town on Elbow Cay. The covered 36 passenger water taxis depart from Marsh Harbour daily at 10:30am and 4:00pm, while the return trip departs Hope Town on Elbow Cay daily at 8:00am and 1:30pm. The ferry can take you to Hope Town Harbour, (and bring you back) for a fare of around $8 per person each way, or $12 for a same day round-trip.

For special charters or additional schedules and current information, contact **Albury's Ferry Service Ltd.**, *Tel. (242) 365-6010*, or hail them on VHF radio via channel 16.

SEEING THE SIGHTS

After departing the ferry at the main stop in Hope Town, walk along the pier and immediately turn left onto **Harbour Street**, the main street hugging the cay's yacht-filled harbor. A few steps later, turn right up Church Lane and follow it for two blocks until reaching the side of the two mile long **Town Beach**. After visiting the beach for a quick swim or some excellent reef snorkeling, walk back down Church Lane for a block. Now turn left onto **Back Street**. On the left side of the road there are several historic wooden Loyalist cottage buildings that are now home to shops including the **Ebb Tide** boutique and the **Juilette Art Gallery**. On the right side of the block you will soon find the mint green former village jail that now houses the **Post Office**.

Walk along the side of the Post Office and enter the ground floor where you will find one section that has a **Tourist Information Center**, and another section that has information about local dolphin and whale sightings. Further along Back Street, there are some of the **Hope Town Hideaways** rental villas, a beach-lined **Town Garden** filled by unusual trees, and the **Wyannie Malone Historical Museum**. The museum is housed in a well-preserved Loyalist cottage and contains old furnishings, clocks, a timeline of the cay's settlement, information about the 30,000 or so Lucayan Indians that were eventually wiped out by the Spanish, old coins, model ships, photos, information on the wreckers demise in 1863 when the lighthouse was built, and a reconstruction of a traditional kitchen and bedrooms. *The museum is open only when a volunteer is available and costs $1 to enter.*

Now retrace your steps along Back Street past the Post Office and look for the tiny **Clearview Drug Store**, the **Creative Native** T-shirt shop and surfer's art gallery, a well-marked access road to the sandy **North Beach**, and the **Fire Station**. A few yards later bear left at the fork in the road onto **Harbour Street** and keep your eyes open for the **Water's Edge** wood carving studio, more rental villas, the **Harbourview Grocery**, and some restaurants and gift shops.

To get across the water to the **Abaco Lighthouse**, you can either ask for a lift on one of the many pleasure craft in the area, or take an hour walk around to the other side of the harbor. The lighthouse was built over 130 years ago and has a steep circular stairway that leads up to a panoramic viewing platform. *The lighthouse is open from sunrise to sunset daily and is free to enter.*

EXCURSIONS, TOURS, MARINAS, & BOAT RENTALS

You won't go wrong at any of the following places for fishing and boat rentals and excursions:

• **Big Dog Sportfishing**, *Hope Town, Tel. (242) 366-0233, VHF channel 16*
• **Bluff House Scuba**, *Green Turtle Cay, Tel. (242) 365-4247, VHF channel 16*
• **Brendal's Dive Shop**, *Green Turtle Cay, Tel. (242) 780-9941, VHF channel 16*
• **Dive Abaco**, *Marsh Harbour, Tel. (242) 367-2787, VHF channel 16*
• **Donny's Boat Rentals**, *Green Turtle Cay, Tel. (242) 365-4119, VHF channel 16*
• **Great Abaco Marina**, *Marsh Harbour, Tel. (242) 367-2158, VHF channel 16*

- **Island Marine Boat Rentals**, *Hope Town, Tel. (242) 366-0282, VHF channel 16*
- **Linclon Jones Island Excursions**, *Green Turtle Cay, Tel. (242) 365-4247*
- **The Mooring's Yacht Rental**, *Marsh Harbor, Tel. (242) 367-4000, VHF channel 16*
- **Papa Tango Island Tours**, *Marsh Harbour, Tel. (242) 367-3753, VHF channel 16*
- **Rich's Boat Rentals**, *Marsh Harbour, Tel. (242) 367-2742, VHF channel 16*
- **Sand Dollar Excusions**, *Marsh Harbour, Tel. (242) 367-2189, VHF channel 16*
- **Seahorse Boat Rentals**, *Marsh Harbour, Tel. (242) 367-2513, VHF channel 16*
- **Undersea Adventures Scuba Diving**, *Marsh Harbour, Tel. (242) 367-2158*

PRACTICAL INFORMATION
- **Government Health Clinic**, *Marsh Harbour, Tel. (242) 367-2510*
- **Abaco Tourist Office**, *Marsh Harbour, Tel. (242) 367-3067*

16. ELEUTHERA & HARBOUR ISLAND

The beautiful island of **Eleuthera** stretches out for more than 107 miles in length and averages two miles in width. Eleuthera is situated about 74 miles east of New Providence Island, and has a population of 10,500.

Lined on both sides by several spectacular sandy beaches, and inhabited by some of the friendliest people anywhere in the region, this is a great place to get rid of all that big city stress. There are no casinos, duty free shops, billboards, trendy nightclubs, indoor malls, or fast talking trinket salesmen anywhere in Eleuthera. The excitement here is in wandering around quaint hamlets in search of hand-made crafts and some of the most amazing snorkeling imaginable. Most of the population live in simple wooden or cement block homes (many were rebuilt with government assistance after Hurricane Andrew devastated the area a few years ago) and make their living harvesting pineapples and catching abundant fish.

Harbour Island is a narrow 3 1/4 mile long island located about a mile off the eastern coast of northern Eleuthera. Harbour Island is famous for its awesome three mile long pink sand beach (so colored by fragments of invertebrate creatures known as forams) and a wide variety of lavish seaside resorts and seasonal homes frequented by the jet set. The largest community here is **Dunmore Town**, a historic village that is filled with quaint pastel cottages and locals that often stop in the street to say hello to strangers. During the winter months, there are hundreds of wealthy Americans that dock their mammoth yachts nearby and take up residence here.

Local History

Originally occupied by Lucayan Indians, it was not until the late 15th century that passing Spanish galleons came to the Eleuthera area. The

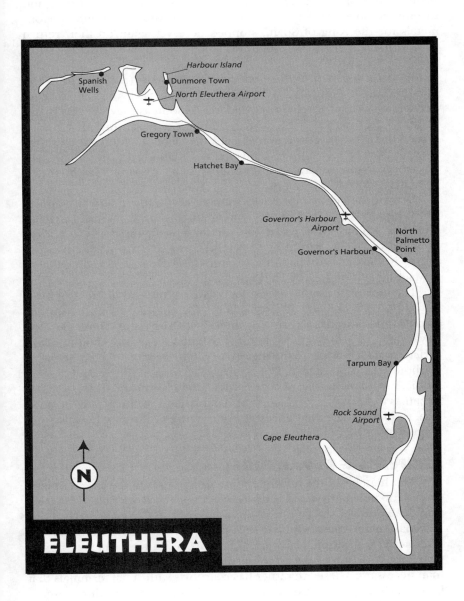

Spanish soon enslaved the entire native Lucayan population and sent them off to work in dreadful conditions at newly established gold and silver mines in South America. These same galleons, laden with precious metals for the King of Spain, stopped here yet again on their return voyages to the Iberian Peninsula and loaded up on potable drinking water from the Spanish Wells area.

In 1648, a group of dissident English Puritans (referred to as the **Eleutherian Adventurers**) led by Captain William Sayles sailed here from Bermuda looking for religious freedom. As soon as they saw this island paradise they named it Eleuthera, after the Greek word that means "Freedom." The Adventurers had many problems, including food short-ages, a lack of proper supplies, and terrible infighting that eventually split the group up into separate communities along Governor's Harbour and Preacher's Cove in Eleuthera.

Fearing the worst, Capt. Sayles soon set sail for the American colonies where he succeeded in obtaining enough provisions from the Massachu-setts Bay Colony to support life on these struggling new outposts. Looking for an easier location to defend themselves from attacks by the aggressive Spanish troops in the region, the Adventurers soon added a new settlement on nearby Harbour Island.

The next major influx of residents came at the end of the American Revolution, when many of those still loyal to the crown left the former colonies and moved here bringing their slaves with them. These so-called Loyalists were also responsible for introducing new ship building and agricultural techniques to the region. In 1783, residents of Eleuthera and Harbour Island, assisted by Col. Andrew Deveaux of the South Carolina militia, forced the retreat of the Spanish from Nassau and the rest of The Bahamas without firing a single shot. To this day, the family trees of many local residents trace their ancestry to a mixture of Puritan, Loyalist, and former slaves bloodlines.

ARRIVALS & DEPARTURES

Eleuthera has three fully operational airports. On the southern part of this 100 mile long island is the newly reopened **Rock Sound Interna-tional Airport**; in the center of the island is the **Governor's Harbour International Airport**; while on the upper part of the island is the **North Eleuthera International Airport**. Make sure to find out which airport is nearest to your hotel, or else the taxi fare can reach as much as $100 more than necessary. These are rather basic airports with small terminals that have snack shops, ticket offices, a taxi rank, and almost nothing else.

Companies operating into some (but not necessarily all) of these airports from other Bahama Islands or Florida include scheduled flights on **American Eagle**, **US Air**, **Bahamasair**, **Gulfstream International Airways**, and scheduled charter flights on small planes run by **Sandpiper Air**, **Falcon Air**, and **Taino Air**.

For Harbour Island arrivals and departures, see pages 210-212.

GETTING AROUND ELEUTHERA

By Rental Car

The best way to get around Eleuthera is by renting a good car. There are still no chain or franchise rental car agencies here, so you must do business with one of several local entrepreneurs that have fleets of typically 10 year old (or older) used American sedans, vans, and station wagons. Unfortunately, these cars are often in bad shape, have bald tires, and very little gas in the tank when you rent them.

Generally, the going price for a car is $60 per day, $280 per week, and the CDW insurance (usually included in the above prices) carries a $100 deductible that must be left in cash or travelers check as a security deposit. Most of the following individuals and gas stations have late model vehicles in unusually good condition, and will both deliver and pick up the car from you anywhere on the island for free. If you need a car at a hotel or airport, make sure to call at least a day in advance.

Try one of the following car rental agencies:
• **Hilton Johnson's Rental Cars**, *Tel. (242) 335-6241*
• **Hilltop Garage Car Rentals**, *Tel. (242) 335-5028*
• **Highway Service Station Rental Cars**, *Tel. (242) 332-2077*
• **Arthur Nixon Car Rentals**, *Tel. (242) 332-1006*
• **James Cash Rental Cars**, *Tel. (242) 335-1096*
• **Stewart's Car Rentals**, *Tel. (242) 335-1128*

By Taxi

There are over 250 licensed taxi cabs in Eleuthera that use standardized government issued rate sheets to calculate fares. These rate sheets can be found posted at the airports and in the possession of every island taxi driver.

The two drivers listed below are the best and most qualified taxi drivers (and Bahamas Host program graduates) that I found working on Eleuthera. For about $150 a day (plus an optional tip), they will be glad to guide you to all the off-the-beaten-path beaches and sights that only locals know about.
• **Hilton Johnson**, *Tel. (242) 335-6241, Fax (242) 335-6356*
• **Arthur Nixon**, *Tel. (242) 332-1006, Fax (242) 332-1006*

WHERE TO STAY

Expensive

PINK SANDS, *Harbour Island. Tel. (242) 333-2030, Fax (242) 333-2060. US & Canada bookings (Island Outpost) 1-800-688-7678. Low season rack rates from $305 per double room per night (M.A.P.). High season rack rates from $460 per double room per night (M.A.P.). All major credit cards accepted.*

Pink Sands is an exclusive little luxury hotel overlooking the island's famous beautiful pink sand beach. Purchased by Island Record's founder Chris Blackwell after it was all but decimated by Hurricane Andrew a few years ago, the hotel was completely rebuilt into a much more modern and elegant resort with several remarkable deluxe cottages.

All of the hotel's 34 one and two bedroom air conditioned cottages have either sea or semi-tropical garden views and come complete with private bathrooms lined with exotic tiles and natural hair and skin care products, unique hardwood furnishings, remote control color satellite televisions with video cassette recorders, direct dial cordless telephones with computer modem inputs, tropical decorative arts, unpolished marble floors, audio systems with compact disk players and racks of Island Records CDs, am-fm clock radios, available in-room fax machines, plush embroidered cotton bathrobes, fully stocked wet bars with coffee machines and fine English china, private garden or beach-view patios, teak outdoor lounge chairs, and electronic mini-safes.

Services and facilities include gourmet beach-front and garden-side al fresco style restaurants, a complete health club, a Clubhouse library with a state of the art video theater, three great outdoor tennis courts, a freshwater swimming pool, room service, optional water and land-based excursions, an Island Outpost boutique, and direct access to the famous beach. James and Karen Malcolm have begun perfecting the art of catering to all their guests (including plenty of rock stars) in this truly memorable island setting. Selected as one of our *Best Places to Stay* – see Chapter 12 for a longer review.

RUNAWAY HILL CLUB, *Harbour Island. Tel. (242) 333-2150, Fax (242) 333-2420. US & Canada bookings 1-800-728-9803. Low season rack rates from $185 per double room per night (E.P.). High season rack rates from $220 per double room per night (E.P.). M.A.P. Meal Plan available for $50 per adult per day. No Children under 16 Permitted. Most major credit cards accepted.*

Carol and Roger Becht's romantic Runaway Hill Club is perched on a tree-lined bluff just above one of the world's finest pink sand beaches. There are a total 10 superbly designed deluxe air conditioned rooms in the main house, a side wing, and an adjacent hilltop cottage that all have large private bathrooms, unique decorations, exotic rattan furnishings, ceiling fan, stone tile flooring, beautiful artwork, stacks of novels, electronic mini-safe, am-fm clock radio, and large windows looking out onto beautiful garden or sea views.

With an ambiance rather like a Cape Cod-style luxury bed and breakfast inn, Runaway Hill is a favored choice for visiting upscale travelers from all over the globe who prefer to avoid having telephones and televisions to disturb them. The grounds are wonderfully landscaped, with Poinciana and Causarina trees, and there is also a nice swimming pool, a rather good restaurant with a nice veranda serving three meals daily, a self-service bar featuring top shelf liquors, and of course direct access to the fantastic pink beach that has made the island so well known. The main house's interior is embellished with a fine collection of unique photographs, water colors by famed local artists, and traditional island handicrafts that make you feel like you are staying in a friend's opulent seaside hideaway.

CLUB MED ELEUTHERA, *Queens Highway, Governor's Harbour area. Tel. (242) 332-2270, Fax (242) 332-2691. US bookings (Club Med Sales Inc.) 1-800-CLUB-MED. Canada bookings (Club Med Sales Inc.) 1-800-363-6033. Low season rack rates from $235 per double room per night (A.I.). High season rack rates from $247.50 per double room per night (A.I.). package prices including airfare are available upon request. Most major credit cards accepted.*

Situated just off a nice long beach outside of Governor's Harbour, this nice French-owned all inclusive resort has been most popular with families traveling with young children, and is not a singles-oriented resort. The "village" consists of several low-rise hotel buildings with over 250 tastefully designed sea or garden view rooms that are just a few minutes walk away from the main clubhouse. The clubhouse itself has an open air theater, a buffet restaurant serving three good meals a day, a bar where pre-purchased beads can be exchanged for drinks, a gift shop, a few ping pong tables, a disco, and an adjacent swimming pool and sun deck.

All of the rooms are air conditioned, have simple yet comfortable furnishings, mini-safes, marble private bathrooms, and absolutely no televisions or telephones. The Club Med features complimentary "Mini-Club" child care and activities programs, a nearby full service water sports center and marina, several professionally surfaced and night-lit outdoor tennis courts, a sprawling golf course, the reservations-only tropical a la carte Terrace restaurant, dozens of friendly multilingual G.O.'s (staff members) from all over the world that can point you in the right direction, and a daily variety of excellent scheduled children's and adult activities. While here, guests have all the meals, soft drinks, activities, airport transfers, child care, and assorted water sports included in their package price (that often includes charter airfare to Eleuthera from major North American cities). A great choice for those looking for a family vacation where the kids have as much fun as the parents.

Moderate

THE COVE ELEUTHERA, *Queens Highway, Gregory Town area. Tel. (242) 335-5142, Fax (242) 335-5338. US & Canada bookings (The Cove's US Offices) 1-800-552-5960. Low season rack rates from $89 per double room per night (E.P.). High season rack rates from $109 per double room per night (E.P.). M.A.P. Meal Plan available for $33 per adult per day. Most major credit cards accepted.*

The Cove Eleuthera is a welcoming little seaside inn just a mile and a half north of Gregory Town. Owned and operated by Ann and George Mullin, a charming couple originally from New York, this is one of my favorite places in Eleuthera to settle back and unwind. The inn's seven tropical buildings contain a total of 26 air conditioned rooms, each with a private bathroom, ceiling fan, simple yet comfortable white rattan furnishings, sea or garden-view patios, sloped wooden ceilings, tile floors, locally produced lithographs, and ice chests for cooling soft drinks and beer in the rooms or at the beach. The inn, just a $27 half hour taxi ride from North Eleuthera airport, is surrounded by 28 acres of beautiful palm trees and Caribbean-style gardens inhabited by colorful butterflies and countless hummingbirds, lamp lighters (lightening bugs), and butterflies.

The Cove offers its guests a casual and affordable restaurant serving homemade Bahamian and American specialties, a small sandy cove beach with excellent snorkeling, a well-maintained swimming pool, occasional live evening entertainment by gifted local musicians like Dr. Breeze, a pool-side bar that makes strong frozen drinks, outdoor tennis courts, free shuttle service to and from nearby Gregory Town and Gaulding's Cay Beach, complimentary kayaks and snorkeling gear, a giant lending library full of books in several languages, a TV room filled with classic and current videos, free bicycles, several hammocks, walking trails, plenty of parking, optional excursions and fishing trips and memorable sunset views.

While far from luxurious or opulent, this is a great place for those who are content enjoying nature as well as the company of other like-minded adventurous travelers. Selected as one of our *Best Places to Stay* – see Chapter 12 for a longer review.

RAINBOW INN, *Queens Highway, Hachet Bay area. Tel. (242) 335-0294, Fax (242) 335-0294. US & Canada bookings (Hotel Direct) 1-800-688-0047. Year round rack rates from $105 per double room per night (E.P.). M.A.P. Meal Plan available for $30 per adult per day. Most major credit cards accepted.*

Located just a 10 mile, $23.50 taxi ride from Governor's Harbour and its international airport, Rainbow Inn is a delightful seaside inn and restaurant that offers some of Eleuthera's most comfortable rental studio apartments and 1-3 bedroom ocean-view homes. The property boasts four spacious air conditioned studio rooms with large private bathrooms, fully stocked modern kitchenettes with microwave ovens and small refrigerators, coffee machines, simple but comfortable furnishings, huge picture windows looking out over either the sea or gardens, large beds, ceiling fans, and plenty of natural sunlight. Additionally there are several nice fully equipped 2 and 3 bedroom private houses on the estate that can be rented by the day, week, or month for extremely reasonable prices.

Owned and operated by former Floridians Ken Keene and Charley Moore, the Rainbow Inn features one of the island's best steak and seafood specialty restaurants, an enjoyable maritime theme bar serving up superb frozen cocktails and occasional live music by gifted locals, one of my favorite swimming pools, an outdoor tennis court, complimentary snorkeling gear and bicycles, several acres of seaside gardens inhabited by hummingbirds and beautiful butterflies, a small adjacent beach area, a world-class bonefishing spot, available snorkeling and fishing trips to spectacular reefs and hidden cove beaches and special discounts on rental cars and various excursions. Ken and Charley make it a point to suggest that their guests explore Eleuthera by car, and provide expert advice on where the most memorable beaches and towns are to be found.

After spending a few days at the Rainbow Inn I really felt like part of an extended family, and didn't want to leave. Everyone is so nice and accommodating here that time seems to drift away much too quickly. For these prices, and the invaluable service by the owners, the Rainbow is a real bargain.

UNIQUE VILLAGE, *off Banks Road, Palmetto Point area. Tel. (242) 332-1830, Fax (242) 332-1838. US & Canada bookings (Out Island Promo Board) 1-800-688-4752. Low season rack rates from $80 per double room per night (E.P.). High season rack rates from $100 per double room per night (E.P.). F.A.P. Meal Plan available for $50 per adult per day. Most major credit cards accepted.*

This nice modern hotel and apartment complex is just a two minute walk to a nice cove beach lining a tranquil subdivision of Palmetto Point. There are 10 spacious and well-maintained ocean-view hotel rooms that all feature strong air conditioners, remote control satellite television (1 channel only), large tiled private bathrooms, ceiling fans, rattan furnishings, large balconies or patios, wood paneling and coffee machines. The management also rents out several fully stocked apartments and houses with complete kitchens in the same area. The complex features a good restaurant with panoramic views serving three meals a day, a small bar, complimentary beach chairs and towels, available snorkeling gear, optional rental cars and more.

HILTON & ELSIE'S ISLAND HOUSE, *Bucaneer Road, James Cistern area. Tel. (242) 335-6241, Fax (242) 335-6356. Year rack rates from $90 per one bedroom apartment per night (E.P.). Long Stay rates available for 3 or more nights. Cash, Check, and Travelers Checks Only - No credit cards accepted.*

Gracious local taxi and tourist guide Hilton Johnson and his wife run a nice little Bahamian style sea-view apartment building in an upscale Eleuthera subdivision with four comfortable units for rent. The apartments are fully furnished and air conditioned, and contain either one or two nicely designed bedrooms, spacious living rooms with comfy sofas, fully stocked large modern kitchens, new rattan furnishings, remote control satellite television, ocean-view terraces with garden furniture, a nearby sandy beach, free parking and plenty of sunlight.

WHERE TO EAT

Expensive

PINK SANDS, *Chapel Street, Dunmore Town, Harbour Island. Tel. (242) 333-2030. Open daily for lunch and dinner. Dress Code is smart casual. Most major credit cards accepted.*

Pink Sands' two outstanding fusion style restaurants (one is on the beach and the other rests in lush gardens) serve what is perhaps the finest and most innovative international cuisine in The Bahamas. While most other restaurants are content to serve up differing versions of the same few local dishes, the kitchen here prides itself on offering something completely different. Feast on gazpacho infused with sesame oil at $4.50, conch chowder with dark rum for $5.50, chicken satay dipped in peanut sauce at $6.95, amazing Caesar salads for $6.75, barbecue jerk chicken salad on mixed greens at $14.75, an amazing lobster salad with exotic tropical fruits for $26, linguini with garlic and crab meat at $11.50, gratinee of grilled marinated vegetables for $10.50, and all sorts of daily specials and devilish desserts.

THE LANDING, *Bay Street, Harbour Island. Tel. (242) 333-2707. No Dress Code. Most major credit cards accepted.*

The Landing is situated in a converted late 18th-century home just across from the Government Dock on Bay Street. A talented French chef prepares dozens of mostly seafood-based international specialties such as octopus salad at $8, smoked salmon for $12, red caviar Romanoff at $20, shrimp risotto for $20, fettuccini with fresh basil and tomato sauce at $18, pasta with mahi-mahi for $20, pasta with lobster chunks at $28, grilled swordfish for $24, grilled shark at $20, mixed grill for two people for $80, T-bone steak at $25, veal in white wine sauce for $28, lamb cardinal at $28, chicken with curry sauce for $20, and several desserts starting at $10 each. The service is pretty good, but the servings are a bit on the small side for these prices.

RAINBOW INN, *Queen's Highway, Hachet Bay area. Tel. (242) 335-0294. Open daily except Sunday in the winter, and Wednesday through Saturday in the summer. No Dress Code. Most major credit cards accepted.*

Rainbow Inn makes some of the tastiest Bahamian-style steak, rib, and seafood dinners on the entire island. Resting on a hill above the sea, all of 20 or so tables look out on to the sea just below Hatchet Bay. Their talented local chef serves up delicious fish chowder at $4, French onion soup for $4.50, escargot at $6, conch fritters for $4.50, poached grouper with local spices at $19, batter-dipped and fried conch strips for $18, shrimp sautéed in garlic butter and wine at $22, seafood crepes for $18, New York strip steak at $19, oven baked chicken with tomato and onion sauce for $15, seafood pasta in white cheese sauce at $14, cinnamon banana fritters for $4.50, and specialty coffees infused with imported liquors starting at $4.50.

They occasionally have live music by well-known local calypso guitarist and singer Dr. Breeze. The Rainbow Inn is also noted for serving some of the best cocktails in The Bahamas!

Moderate

HARBOUR LOUNGE, *Bay Street, Dunmore Town, Harbour Island. Tel. (242) 333-2031. No Dress Code. Most Major credit cards accepted.*

This good seafood restaurant near the Government Dock offers Caesar salad for $7, cracked conch at $8, skewered jerked chicken for $7, spicy chicken wings at $6, conch chowder for $4, lobster salad at $11, charcoal grilled cheeseburgers for $7.50, grouper sandwich at $9, grilled filet of beef for $28, grilled chicken breast at $18, fried grouper for $22, baked local lobster at $28, tasty lamb chops for $28, superb iced cappuccinos for $3.50, and a good wine list including well priced bottles from France, California, Italy, and Australia averaging only $21 each.

THE COVE ELEUTHERA, *Queens Highway, Gregory Town area. Tel. (242) 335-5142. Open daily for breakfast, lunch, and dinner. No Dress Code. Most major credit cards accepted.*

Set on a tree-lined bluff above the sea, this is an exceedingly casual and comfortable restaurant. Their charming local waitresses and cooks serve up great Bahamian and American dishes that include locally grown fruit salad at $6.50, garden salads with your choice of dressings for $3.50, conch chowder at $3.50, soup de jour for $2.75, huge tuna salad sandwiches with pickles and chips at $6, tasty chilled lobster salad for $11.50, BLTs at $5.50, grilled cheese and tomato sandwiches for $4.50, conch burgers at $5.50, cracked conch fried in batter for $10.50, pasta of day at $10, locally caught broiled or grilled Bahamian grouper at $21, boneless grilled chicken breast for $15, delicious lobster tails grilled to perfection at $32, huge New York strip steaks for $18, a marvelous key lime pie at $3, and the world's best coconut pie for $3.

Make sure to check this place out while visiting the northern section of Eleuthera.

HARBOUR VIEW, *Queen's Highway, Rock Sound. Tel. (242) 334-2278. No Dress Code. Cash Only - No credit cards accepted.*

Situated just off the sea, this simple local restaurant is good place to head for a dinner around sunset. Chef Julian Smith and his staff offer a large assortment of well-prepared large portions of island favorites, such as cheese omelets at $3.50, lobster bisque at $5, French onion soup for $3.50, conch salads at $3.50, garden salads for $6, chicken salad sandwiches at $4.50, surf burgers for $4.50, BLT's at $3, grilled cheese for $3, tuna melts at $4.50, conch burgers for $3.75, crack conch at $14, curried mutton for $14, curried chicken at $8, barbecued ribs for $9, grilled steaks at $12, barbecued ribs for $14, pan broiled lobster at $22, a daily sauce for $7, and pineapple tart at $2. On most Fridays and Saturdays, they host an informal "Jerk Out Barbecue" and are open Monday through Saturday from 9:00am until 11:00pm or so.

Inexpensive

MATE & JENNY'S PIZZA SHACK, *off of Queen's Highway, Palmetto Point area. Tel. (242) 332-1504. Open every day except Tuesday from 11:00am until 3:00pm and again from 6:00pm until the last customer leaves. No Dress Code. Visa and Mastercard accepted.*

If you want to try a great down to earth pizza joint and lounge full of friendly locals and adventurous tourists, check out this real gem in Palmetto Point. They serve up delicious individual, medium and large pizzas for between $6 and $20 each with your favorite toppings, as well as lasagna for $14, broiled grouper at $15, baked chicken with special sauce for $12, crack conch at $14, salads for $3, cheeseburgers at $3.40, spicy wings for $3, and the coldest beer around at $3 each. Well worth the effort to find.

DUNMORE DELI, *King Street, Dunmore Town, Harbour Island. Tel. (242) 333-2646. No Dress Code. Cash Only - No credit cards accepted.*

When you're looking for an affordable alternative to high priced restaurants on Harbour Island, this is certainly the best place to go. They offer huge sandwiches made on your choice of breads and rolls ranging from $5 to $8.50 each, featuring either ham, salami, turkey, tuna, lobster salad, roast beef, pastrami, corned beef, and assorted European cheeses. They also offer chef salads at $8, garden salads with popular dressings for $5, an amazing Greek pasta salad with pesto at $8, and Caesar salads with roasted chicken for $8.50. They will even deliver to your hotel room for free.

SAMMY'S PLACE, *off Fish Road, Rock Sound. Tel. (242) 334-2121. No Dress Code. Cash Only - No credit cards accepted.*

For those looking for wonderful inexpensive breakfasts, lunches and dinners in an unpretentious local establishment, Sammy's Place fits the bill. They prepare such dishes as French toast at $5, cheese omelets for $7, conch fritters at $2, chef salads for $5, fish burgers at $5, home made tuna salad for $4, cheeseburgers at $3.50, fried shrimp for $9, pan fried New York strip steak at $14, grouper Creole for $11, barbecue ribs at $10, fisherman's platter for $18, deep fried sea scallops at $14, and serious butterscotch sundaes for $2.50.

CALYPSO CAFE, *North Eleuthera Airport, Lower Bogue. Open early morning through dinner. Tel. Unlisted.*

This cozy airport bar and restaurant offers great home-cooked meals. They have an extensive menu including fresh banana pancakes at $2.50, two eggs any style for $2.25, homemade fruit muffins at $1, hamburgers for $3, tuna sandwiches at $3, bacon turkey clubs for $4, grilled ham and cheese at $4, mutton for $5, seafood salad bowls at $7, sheep's tongue for $4.50, and good pies and tarts for $1.25 each.

SEEING THE SIGHTS

Rock Sound District

There is just one main road that runs all the way up and down Eleuthera, and it is known as the **Queen's Highway**. All the way at the southern tip of this highway is the **East Point Lighthouse**. From here the unpaved Lighthouse Beach Road can take those with jeeps over to **Lighthouse Beach**, one of the island's most beautiful long sandy stretches of coastline. This is certainly a great place to visit, but is exceedingly difficult to reach due to poor maintenance of the narrow access road. Another half mile above the lighthouse is a small spit of land called **Princess Cays** near the hamlet of Bannerman Town. This surprisingly modern and well-equipped port is owned by the government, and has recently been used a few times a week during the summer by Princess Cruise Lines as a port of call for a half day beach barbecue (included in most of their Bahamas-based cruises).

About eight miles further up the highway you will reach a turn-off on your right hand side (there is a sign) that takes you to the **Cotton Bay Club**. This was formerly one of the region's most exclusive hotels, but has since fallen on hard times and is currently closed. The hotel's superb private 18 hole championship **Cotton Bay Golf Course** was designed by Robert Trent Jones and is still open and maintained by some dozen or so wealthy residents that live in multimillion dollar homes along the property's beach. A "Colombian industrialist" has recently purchased the ruined hotel, and plans for a new deluxe resort on this site are supposedly being considered.

Another eight miles north along the highway is the charming community of **Rock Sound**. As you enter town you will notice several nice old colonial-style houses that were once inhabited by infamous local "wreckers," who were known for lighting beacons along the coast to lure unsuspecting ships into the shallow reefs. The treasures and provisions salvaged from these wrecked vessels were so bountiful that the area was formerly known as Wreck Sound.

These days, there is little in the way of excitement here, but there are a couple of great little restaurants and swimming spots scattered around town. As you drive along the highway through town you will pass the outstanding pier-side **Harbour View Restaurant**. If you intend to have lunch here, make sure to grab an extra order of french fries and bring them with you for the next stop (you'll see)!

Just across the street from the restaurant and pier there is a small lane called Fish Road that leads up into town. Take this unmarked road up for a couple of blocks and bear right at the dirt road passing the Masonic Lodge and park your car at the **Rock Sound Ocean Hole Park**. The ocean hole is a large crater filled with fresh ocean water and marine life that enter it via a series of natural underground tunnels. If you stand at the crater's edge and throw in some french fries or strips of bread, a pack of several dozen hungry gray snappers and groupers will jump to the surface and scramble for their lunch. Area teenagers can often be found swimming with the fish here on especially hot days. *Ocean Hole Park is open continuously each day and costs nothing to enter.*

After exiting the crater, return along the dirt road until making the first right turn back onto Fish Road. After passing the town's yellow primary school, bear left onto an unnamed lane. A couple of blocks later turn left and head for **Sammy's Place**, a great little restaurant where huge sandwiches and inexpensive dinners are served to a mainly local crowd. Now leave Sammy's and head further down the same road until making a right turn back onto the northward lane of the Queen's Highway. About a mile or so out of town on the right hand side of the highway is a small modern shopping center called **The Market Place**, where you can stock up on picnic supplies in Eleuthera's best supermarket. Further down the highway you will pass by the newly expanded **Rock Sound International Airport**.

The next major sight lies about 5 1/2 miles north of the airport, where a small road off to the right at the Shell gas station leads to the **Venta Club Eleuthera,** a brand new Italian-owned all-inclusive resort. Bought in ruins from the government for a bargain basement price of $1.6 million, this series of cute attached cottage units has been specially redesigned for the European travel market and looks out onto the beautiful crescent shaped **Winding Bay Beach**.

The Queen's Highway then heads north for another few miles until it reaches the charming town of **Tarpum Bay**. Once you have followed the highway as it curves past the town's sea-front, you will see the stunningly beautiful **Tarpum Bay Anglican Church** with its Adalusian-style white-washed and blue bordered exterior.

The other main attraction here is a strange little half sized replica of a medieval stone fortress that is home to the **Macmillan-Hughes Gallery**. Owned by eccentric ex-pat and artist Peter Macmillan-Hughes, this fine gallery displays a collection of his unique paintings and sculptures. *The castle and gallery are open on most days from 10:00am until around 5:00pm and costs nothing to enter.*

Governor's Harbour District

Return to the highway and follow it further north for 26 miles until reaching the busy little town of **South Palmetto Point**. While no specific tourist attractions are to be found here, a sign-posted road to the left leads to the wonderful **Mate & Jenny's Pizza Shack**, while the same road taken to the right will eventually take you through a church-filled village and over towards the affordable **Unique Village Resort** that rests above yet another fine long beach.

Keep following the Queen's Highway for another five miles until it cuts through **Governor's Harbour**, the largest community in Eleuthera. First settled by the Eleutherian Adventurers in 1648, the town's back streets are dotted with dramatic Victorian houses that were built by wealthy 19th-century merchants and fruit exporters. In town, there are a few small restaurants, a great little movie theater, a couple of banks, a nice shallow beach area, and plenty of tranquil side streets that exhibit the charms of days gone by.

Over an old bridge leading past the left side of town, there is a small peninsula called **Cupid's Cay**. The cay is the sight of the old **Anglican Church**, the massive Island Commissioner's residence, **Ronnie's Hide-a-Way** bar (the island's popular club), and a pier where crowds eagerly await the weekly arrival of the freight boat from Miami. Just above the town itself along the highway is the sprawling **Club Med Eleuthera**, an all-inclusive resort (only guests are allowed through the gates) that is typically packed with families from all over the world, and the busy **Governor's Harbour International Airport**. Just a bit under a mile north of the airport (when you reach the "45 MPH" road sign), turn right down a semi-paved road for 1/4 of a mile to an overgrown walking path. Walk through the brush and onto a superb beach area. A bit further up along the left side of the highway is the unmarked entrance road that goes to the beautiful **Alabaster Beach**.

After another eight miles or so further up the highway, you will pass by the quiet town of **James Cistern**, and then continue six more miles to the **Rainbow Bay** area where you can find the **Rainbow Inn and Restau-**

rant alongside one of the country's best bonefishing zones. Make sure to stop off at either the inn or at any other local establishment and ask directions to the nearby swimming spot known as **Little Twin Beach**, an extremely private area due to the rock cliff cove that completely surrounds it. Also worthy of note is the small hamlet of **Alice Town**, just another couple of miles up, where you can find a fully equipped marina where **Marine Services of Eleuthera** can arrange charter services for large yachts and motor boats.

A 2 1/2 mile drive further along the highway from the Alice Town turnoff will lead you past a series of silos that once belonged to a massive chicken farm, which is now defunct. When you reach the first of these silos, make a left turn on a dirt road and follow it for a short distance until you can park the car and head for a small path leading through the brush. A few steps later you'll descend down some steps that lead directly to the **Hatchet Bay Caves**. Filled with bats, stalagmites, stalactites, and graffiti that dates back over a century in some cases, these remarkable caverns are a great place to explore (assuming you have a strong flashlight). Do not touch the dripping formations as they are still growing and are rather fragile.

Not far from here, there is an unmarked road off to the left side of the highway that takes you to **Surfer's Beach**, where the waves often roll into extreme surfing pipelines during the winter months.

From here it's a few minutes drive up into **Gregory Town**, a charming little seaside community that was among the hardest hit by Hurricane Andrew. Here there are a few hundred souls and a handful of interesting sights and attractions. Soon after reaching the "Welcome to Gregory Town" sign, you will come to a dirt road running uphill to the left that leads to a reasonably long sandy beach area.

Further along on the right hand side of the Queen's Highway as it cuts through town is the **Island Made** boutique, where you can purchase handmade crafts and The Bahamas' own Androsia brand of batik fabrics and clothing at reasonable prices. There is also a small cove full of bonefish and surrounded by small parish churches, including the 19th century native stone **St. Agnus church** and the colorful **Gregory Town All Age Schoolhouse**.

Gregory Town is home to the **Thompson Brothers** supermarket and gas station, the quaint little community cemetery, the great local **Thompson's Bakery**, **Rebecca's Surf Shop** and restaurant (say hello to Pete the Surfer!), **Elvina's** laundromat and bar/restaurant where you can sip some brews with a meal while your clothes soak up the suds, and **Cush's** Bahamian restaurant. About 1 1/2 miles north of Gregory Town is a relaxing hotel and restaurant called **The Cove Eleuthera**.

Some two miles further north from Gregory Town along the left side of Queen's Highway, you'll come across a small hand-painted sign marked "Beach." Turn left at the sign and bear right at the next couple of forks until reaching the impressive **Gauldings Cay Beach**. Besides being a nice remote spot to take a dip into the clear blue water, experienced snorkelers should make a point to swim out to the small island of **Gauldings Cay** to view the world's largest collection of golden sun enemies just off the cay's left side.

The North Eleuthera District

About five miles above Gregory Town is a small cement span called the **Glass Window Bridge**. While built to replace a sturdy bridge that stood here until a couple of years ago, this new structure was severely damaged during one of the infamous "rages" when the waves rose to over 40 feet and knocked it eight feet from its original position. Locals have been trying to walk or drive across this spot for years during these spectacular rages, and some have been swept out to sea in the process. While the bridge is not of any particular tourist interest (it looks like it will fall to pieces any time now), this is a great spot to see the dividing line between the deep blue Atlantic Ocean on the left side and the aqua-colored Caribbean Sea on the right.

The Queen's Highway continues up for another seven miles before passing turnoffs at the village of **Lower Bogue**. These small roads can be followed to either the **North Eleuthera International Airport** or the **Three Islands Dock** where water taxis will be glad to take you to nearby Harbour Island. The highway itself ends a few miles later at a beach-lined fishing community called **The Current**, which was hard hit by Hurricane Andrew and had all of its hotels washed out to sea.

Spanish Wells

This small island is one of The Bahamas' richest fishing communities. It is inhabited mainly by white Bahamians (know locally as *Conchyjoes*) involved in the extremely successful lobster and fishing trade. There are no hotels or major tourist facilities here. Originally a rum runner's haven and outpost, the islanders are seemingly not in any particular mood to deal with visitors to their shores. While water taxis can take you here to see several picturesque old colonial homes, I don't suggest spending any time and effort to visit here.

PRACTICAL INFORMATION FOR ELEUTHERA

- **Eleuthera Tourist Office**, *Governor's Harbour, Tel. (242) 332-2142*
- **Rock Sound Medical Clinic**, *Rock Sound, Tel. (242) 334-2226*

HARBOUR ISLAND

Harbour Island is among the oldest remaining European settlements in The Bahamas, and was founded by William Sayles, a former governor of Bermuda. He had journeyed here in 1648 with fellow Eleutherian Adventurers in search of religious freedom. Once the American Revolution ended, many Loyalists (who favored the crown to the new government of George Washington) left America and settled here along with their slaves. After repelling the Spanish from The Bahamas in 1783, Queen Victoria of England rewarded the Harbour Islanders' bravery by giving them large plots of farming land on nearby Eleuthera which are still in use and are known as the **commanage**.

The 18th and 19th centuries brought prosperity to the island, and ships built at the dockyards here went on to sail the seven seas. **Dunmore Town** was to become The Bahamas' second largest city (after Nassau) for a brief period of time. Locally grown sugar cane was converted to rum, and rum running to America became a major boost to the local economy during Prohibition. By the 1950s, a few wealthy North Americans and Englishmen started building the first of half a dozen or so small hotels on the island and soon began to attract their friends and other socialites to the now famous pink sand beaches found here. While tourism and satellite television have certainly had an effect on the local population, the island was perhaps even harder hit a few years ago by Hurricane Andrew, which destroyed many homes and damaged most of the hotels.

ARRIVALS & DEPARTURES

By Water Taxi

Since there are no airports currently open on Harbour Island, all visitors must get to Eleuthera (by boat or plane) and then connect to Harbour Island by boat. The most common method of reaching the island is by taking a **water taxi**. These motor boats **depart from 3 Island Dock in upper Eleuthera** (a 3/4 mile, $6 taxi ride from North Eleuthera Airport) and ride across the sea for seven minutes. about a mile or so east, to arrive at **Governor's Dock on Harbour Island** just off Bay Street. The price for this service is $4 per person including luggage, and there are almost always boats available for immediate departure in both directions from about 7am until about 7pm every day of the week.

If the weather is extremely bad, the service can be temporarily delayed or suspended. These boats are usually 23 feet long, have a covered seating area, can hold six passengers and their luggage comfortably, and are all privately owned and operated. A taxi from the water taxi landing to any major hotel on Harbour Island costs approximately $6 per couple.

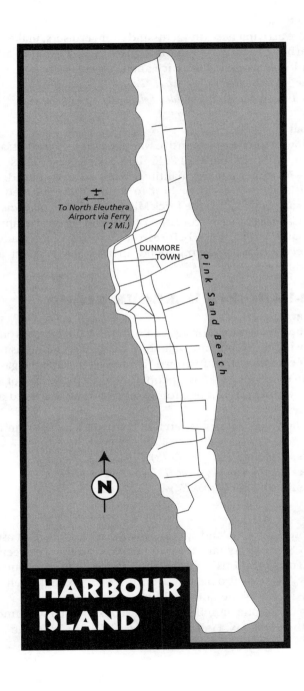

To North Eleuthera
Airport via Ferry
(2 Mi.)

DUNMORE
TOWN

Pink Sand Beach

N

HARBOUR
ISLAND

By Private Boat

If you're arriving here on yachts and cabin cruisers, make sure to call one of Harbour Island's two marinas (listed below) well in advance for important local navigational advice and slip rentals.

• **Valentine's Yacht Club**, *Bay Street, Tel. (242) 333-2645*
• **Harbour Island Marina**, *Bayside, Tel. (242) 333-2427*

By Mailboat

The slowest and least expensive way to get here from Nassau is to use the government's unusual **Mail & Freight Boat** service. These freighters are laden with either a huge quantity of mail or provisions destined for Harbour Island; they try their best to follow the published schedule, which you can get by calling the **Dock Master's Office** *in Nassau, Tel. (242) 393-1064*. Call this office to confirm a space and reconfirm approximate departure and arrival times before you plan this type of adventure. I strongly recommend that you spend an additional $15 if a cabin is available for the journey.

GETTING AROUND HARBOUR ISLAND

By Golf Cart

Even though all the major sights, attractions, and beaches on Harbour Island are within a five minute walk from each other, many visitors prefer to rent **golf carts** to get around town. These well-maintained gas powered vehicles can seat either 2, 4, or 6 people and cost an average of about $50 per day. Any hotel can arrange for a golf cart to be delivered directly to the front desk.

The following companies can also rent you a golf cart in Dunmore Town:

• **Johnson's**, *Princess Street, Tel. (242) 333-2376*
• **Ross's Garage**, *Colebrook Street, Tel. (242) 333-2122*
• **Sunshine Rentals**, *Colebrook Street, Tel. (242) 333-2509*

By Taxi

Taxis on Harbour Island operate on a flat rate system that usually calls for a $6 to $8 one way fare for two people traveling between any two Dunmore Town locations including the hotels, restaurants, and the water taxi landing. You can also negotiate the price for taxi sightseeing services around the island by the hour, half day, and full day.

The main phone numbers for local taxis (usually found parked alongside the water taxi landing) are *Tel. (242) 333-2116* and *(242) 333-2043*.

ORIENTATION

Beautiful **Harbour Island** (sometimes referred to as **Briland** by locals) is a small hilly island about 3 1/2 miles long and about half a mile wide, and is located just off the coast of Eleuthera. Accessible only by water taxi, yachts, and the occasional seaplane, this outstanding destination has been popular with affluent vacationers and seasonal residents for several decades. Most visitors will arrive at the Government Dock water taxi landing off Bay Street in **Dunmore Town**, a delightful village filled with pastel colored Cape Cod-style homes. Although little remains from the days of the Eleutherian Adventurers settlement on this site in the mid-17th century, in many ways a walk through Dunmore Town indeed feels like you're stepping back in time.

What continues to make Harbour Island such a famous getaway for the wealthy is its truly spectacular **Harbour Island Pink Sand Beach**. This is one of the world's prettiest beaches, and stretches for 2 3/4 miles on the island's eastern coast, just a five minute walk from the water taxi landing. There are four higher priced hotels and several dozen exquisite private residences just above the beach on gently sloping bluffs with breathtaking views over the turquoise sea. Although most people believe the beach's famous soft pink sand is a product of eroding pink coral, the tint actually comes from fragments of tiny rose colored invertebrates called forams that live in the reefs just 100 yards off the coast.

Even though all of the most interesting sights are located within a few minutes walk from one another, the majority of visitors (but not me!) rent gas-powered golf carts to effortlessly get around the island. Besides the beach, you can visit over a dozen quiet streets lined with quaint colorful wooden houses, a few simple shops, a miniature outdoor straw market, an extremely limited selection of expensive restaurants, and a few happening nightclubs that are all in or close to Dunmore Town.

Since there are only some 150 or so hotel rooms (most without televisions or telephones in them) and about 50 rental homes available at any given time, the island and its fine beach never seem overcrowded. The spring and summer months are particularly charming and quiet, but during the December through March high season every possible accommodation, marina, bar, and restaurant is filled to capacity (most hotels are booked solid a year in advance at this time). This is a relaxing place, but you will need to bring plenty of money with you to vacation comfortably here for any length of time.

SEEING THE SIGHTS

About the best place to begin a walk around here is to start off at the foot of **Government Dock** near the popular **Seaview Take Away** fast food shack. From the dock make a left turn onto the appropriately named **Bay Street**, one of the larger retail shopping streets in Dunmore Town. On the first block to your left, you will find several wooden kiosks that mark the sight of the tiny **Straw Market** where you can find T-shirts, straw hats, and other inexpensive gifts. Just across Bay Street on the right hand side, you will pass by a couple of boutiques including **The Sugar Mill** where fine local artwork, post cards, T-shirts, and ceramics are available at good prices.

Just upstairs from the Sugar Mill is the **Harbour Island Tourist Office**, where you can pop inside and ask Mr. Tommy Thompson for suggestions, free walking maps, and all sorts of brochures. Their office hours are usually Monday through Friday from 9:30am until 1:00pm and again from 2:00pm until 5:00pm. Further along the right side of the street you will find the **Harbour Lounge** bar and restaurant, and a few charming old houses including the circa 1790 **Loyalist Cottage** (not open to the public).

Make a right turn a couple of blocks down onto **Princess Street** and follow it past some of the prettiest New England-style residences on the island. At the next corner bear right onto **King Street** and on the left hand side are a few great shops, including the fantastic **Dunmore Deli** sandwich shop, the **Briland Androsia Boutique** where you can buy the famed Androsia brand hand-made batik clothing, and the amusing **Piggly Wiggly** grocery store. At the end of the block the street merges into **Dunmore Street**, where on the left side you can pop into the charming **Miss Mae's Tea Room & Fine Things** gift shop and gallery.

After strolling past a few nice old churches and private homes, take a left turn down **Clarence Street** that eventually leads to an access path onto the amazing **Harbour Island Pink Sand Beach**. While all beach chairs and umbrellas found along the beach are for the use of hotel guests only, the entire 2 3/4 mile stretch of pristine sand is public property and may be enjoyed by all. Among the fine hotels that can be found to the left on the bluffs above the sea are the beautiful **Runaway Hill Club**, the stately **Dunmore Beach Club**, and the superb **Pink Sands** resort.

EXCURSIONS, TOURS, MARINAS, & BOAT RENTALS

You won't go wrong at any of the following places for fishing and boat rentals and excursions:
- **Vincent Clear Bonefishing**, *Harbour Island, Tel. (242) 333-2154*
- **Marine Services of Eleuthera**, *Hatchett Bay, Tel. (242) 335-0186*
- **Hilton Johnson Taxi Tours**, *James Cistern, Tel. (242) 335-6241*
- **Greg Thompson Sport-fishing**, *Gregory Town, Tel. (242) 335-5357*

- **Leon Thompson Deep Sea Fishing**, *Harbour Island, Tel. (242) 333-2027*
- **Michael's Cycles Boat Rentals**, *Harbour Island, Tel. (242) 333-2384*
- **Ramora Bay Dive Center**, *Harbour Island, Tel. (242) 333-2323*
- **Rainbow Inn Snorkeling**, *Hatchett Bay, Tel. (242) 335-0294*
- **Sunset Carriage Tours**, *Harbour Island, Tel. (242) 333-2723*
- **Uncle Sam's Snorkeling Trips**, *Harbour Island, Tel. (242) 333-2394*
- **Valentine's Dive Center**, *Harbour Island, Tel. (242) 333-2309*

PRACTICAL INFORMATION FOR HARBOUR ISLAND

- **Harbour Island Tourist Office**, *Above the Sugar Mill, Bay Street, Tel. (242) 333-2621*
- **Harbour Island Police Station**, *Goal Street, Tel. (242) 333-2111*
- **Harbour Island Medical Clinic**, *Church Street, Tel. (242) 333-2227*
- **Harbour Island Post Office**, *Goal Street, Tel. (242) 333-2315*
- **Royal Bank of Canada**, *Murray Street, Tel. (242) 333-2250*

17. CAT ISLAND

Cat Island, population 1,731, is one of the most beautiful and relaxing islands I have ever visited. Although few tourists include this beach paradise in their itinerary, the ones who do are in for a real treat.

Cat Island is in the south-central section of the country, located 48 miles north-northeast of The Exumas and not far from Eleuthera. The island is 50 miles long, with an average width of four miles. There are absolutely no casinos, duty free shops, fancy boutiques, or major resorts here, but instead there are some of the friendliest locals you will ever meet, incredible deserted cove beaches, serious fishing and scuba diving spots, and several small inns and restaurants that will make you feel like staying forever.

Most people come here to enjoy the turquoise waters and kick back, but those with a bit of energy should think about renting a car and visiting the many natural and historical attractions that are well worth the effort.

ARRIVALS & DEPARTURES

Cat Island has four small airports. On the north end of the island is the **Arthur's Town Airport** and in the center of the island is the **New Bight International Airport**. These are both serviced by **Bahamasair** and small charter flights run by Fernandez Bay Village. On the south end of the island is the **Hawks Nest Airstrip**, which can be accessed via charter flights on smaller planes operated by Hawks Nest Hotel.

None of the island's airports offer any passenger services, and there are no taxi ranks on the entire island.

GETTING AROUND CAT ISLAND

By Rental Car

There are no major rental car agencies here, but a few entrepreneurs have built up small fleets of slightly beat-up used American cars. The average fee for a rental car is around $85 per day and $400 per week. The mandatory C.D.W. (collision damage waiver) insurance is included in the

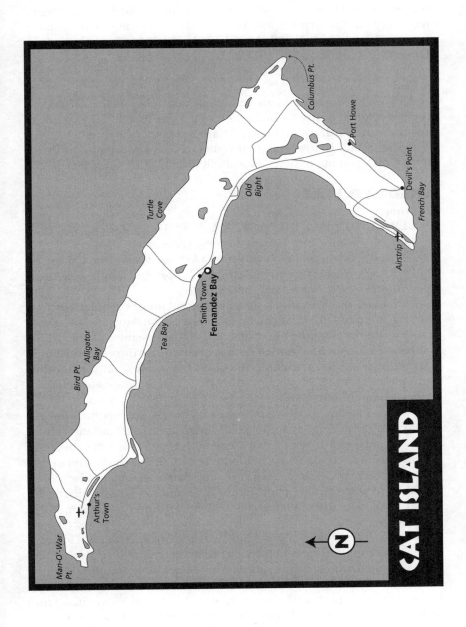

above prices and carries a $200 or so deductible that must be left with the office as a refundable security deposit. Free delivery and dropoff of rental cars at some of the airports may be available if you call well in advance.
•**Jason's Rental Cars**, *New Bight, Tel. (242) 342-3014*
•**Jebon Car Rentals**, *Arthur's Town, Tel. (242) 354-2038*

By Taxi
    As I mentioned above, there are no taxi cabs on Cat Island. To properly arrange transfers, make sure to inform your hotel a couple of days in advance with your scheduled time and point of arrival before you get to Cat Island. In the event that you reach the airport and nobody is there to pick you up, a friendly local will usually offer you a lift!

WHERE TO STAY
Expensive
    FERNANDEZ BAY VILLAGE, *New Bight Area. Tel. (954) 474-4821, Fax (954) 474-4864. US & Canada bookings (Fernandez's Florida Offices) 1-800-940-1905. Low season rack rates from $185 per double private house per night (M.A.P.). High season rack rates from $205 per double private house per night (M.A.P.). Most major credit cards accepted.*
    Fernandez Bay Village is a small inviting colony of several pretty free-standing stone and wooden structures on one of The Bahamas' best sandy beaches. Almost all of the nine villas and cottages feature exotic private bathrooms with open air garden showers, antique hardwood furnishings, 4-poster beds, sloped wooden ceilings with fans, Mexican tile flooring, mini-refrigerators, Bahamian handicrafts, private landscaped terrace areas and superb beach views.
    Facilities at this small casual resort include a great restaurant and dining patio featuring tasty cooked-to-order breakfasts and lunches, as well as an outstanding seaside barbecue buffet each day, a thatched roof seaside Tiki Bar, a tranquil main clubhouse with sitting rooms and a good lending library, a complete PADI dive shop that offers scuba adventures, available deep sea fishing trips, motor boat and car rentals, charter air services, bicycles, and of course a great beach-front lined by hammocks and lounge chairs.
    Fernandez Bay hosts a good mix of European and North American couples in all age ranges, as well as several laid-back families with children. Pam & Tony Armbrister have created an exceedingly comfortable little resort where people can just chill out and have a well-deserved break. Donna and her superb staff of warm-hearted Cat Island natives make sure to greet every guest, and make you immediately feel like part of an extended family. Forget your fancy clothes and just arrive here ready to

wear nothing more formal than bathing suits and T-shirts. Highly recommended! Selected as one of our *Best Places to Stay* – see Chapter 12 for a longer review.

Moderate

HAWKS NEST RESORT & MARINA, *Queen's Highway, Hawks Nest area. Tel. (242) 357-7257, Fax (242) 357-7257. Year round rack rates from $105 per room per night (E.P.). Special packages available. F.A.P. Most major credit cards accepted.*

Hawks Nest is an adorable little resort hotel and marina on over 400 acres of seaside property on the southern tip of Cat Island. The property has 10 impressively designed rooms in a pair of newly renovated lodges just steps away from the marina, the beach, and the Clubhouse. All of the rooms feature powerful air conditioning, new bathrooms, beautiful hardwood furnishings, nice big beds, wall-to-wall tile floors, wooden ceilings with fans, tropical artwork, local handicrafts, large French doors that open up onto private sea-view patios, and in many rooms even half-size refrigerators.

The hotel is exceptionally welcoming and includes a wonderful central Clubhouse with a great restaurant and one of my favorite bars on the island. There are several different cove beaches, a private airport, a full service eight slip marina, an air conditioned fish cleaning hut, complimentary golf cart transportation all over the estate, a boutique selling snacks and locally made straw products, charter air service to and from Nassau, a complete laundromat, available deep sea and bonefishing adventures, optional sightseeing trips, power boats for rent, and plenty more.

The service here is first rate, with special meal requests handled with absolutely no problems (if notified in advance of arrival). Among the more interesting highlights here are its close proximity to superb fishing areas such as Columbus Point and Potter Bank, a tame pet goat that thinks it's a dog, and a husband and wife management team (Anton and Carolyn Hol) who will make sure you can't wait to return. Highly recommended for those looking for good value for the money.

THE BRIDGE INN, *Queen's Highway, New Bight area. Tel. (242) 342-3013. Year round rack rates from $110 per room per night (B.P.). Cash only - No major credit cards accepted.*

The Bridge Inn is a pleasant small family-owned and operated hotel that rents out 14 mid-sized spotless rooms, each with air conditioning, tiled private bathrooms, exposed stone walls and sloped wooden ceilings, brand new wall-to-wall carpeting, color television, simple wooden furnishings and patios. The facilities here include a good restaurant, an outdoor weekend bar and dance club, a nearby beach area, room service, available babysitting, complimentary shuttle bus service to and from downtown New Bight and optional excursions. If you're interested in fishing, they can help you arrange fishing trips.

Inexpensive
HOTEL GREENWOOD INN, *Queen's Highway, Port Howe area. Tel. (242) 342-3053, Fax (242) 342-3053. Low season rack rates from $85 per room per night (E.P.). High season rack rates from $99 per double room per night (E.P.). Special Scuba packages available. F.A.P. Meal Plan for $45 per adult per night. Most major credit cards accepted.*

Greenwood Inn is a simple beach-front hotel and scuba resort owned by a German family that caters to travelers from around the world. There are 20 reasonably sized hotel style rooms in basic one floor lodge buildings with either full or partial sea views, private bathrooms, simple furnishings, comfortable bedding, large open air patios, and local artwork.

Known especially for their comprehensive PADI dive shop and scuba program, the hotel also features an outdoor swimming pool, a full service restaurant, a nice bar area, a television lounge, free use of Hobie Cat sail boats, a long stretch of beach-front, a lending library full of German and English language books, optional fishing and snorkeling adventures, sightseeing trips, available rental cars, and a good staff.

SEA SPRAY HOTEL, *Queen's Highway, Orange Creek area. Tel. (242) 354-4116. Year round rack rates from $85 per room per night (E.P.). Cash only - No major credit cards accepted.*

Those looking for affordabe, comfortable accommodations in the northern reaches of Cat Island should consider this small locally-owned budget hotel on the water's edge. The Sea Spray has 15 simple medium-sized air conditioned rooms in one story lodges. All of the units here have either sea or village views, and come with cable television, private bathrooms, wall-to-wall carpeting, simple wooden furnishings, stucco walls, ceiling fans and adjacent patios.

The inn also has a casual waterside restaurant and bar, free parking, available fishing and scuba trips, and a nice friendly staff.

WHERE TO EAT
Moderate
FERNANDEZ BAY VILLAGE, *Queen's Highway, New Bight. Tel. (954) 474-4821. No Dress Code. Most major credit cards accepted.*

Fernandez Bay's superb chefs concoct some of the best made-to-order lunches and seaside buffet dinners I have found anywhere in these islands. For lunch at the Clubhouse or waterfront Tiki Bar, you can expect to pay about $8.50 a person for overstuffed sandwiches on home-made bread filled with stuffings such as tuna, burgers, ham & cheese, or chicken. Even more impressive are their nightly beach-front buffets dinners that cost around $29.50 a head and include delicious entrees, such as broiled local lobster tails with drawn butter, beef tenderloin that melts in your mouth, freshly tossed salads featuring native and imported vegetables, stuffed potatoes, broccoli au gratin, and hot out-of-the-oven cakes with tropical fruit toppings.

This is a great place to meet lots of interesting people and casually dine in style under the stars. Reservations should be made at least six hours in advance for dinner here.

Inexpensive

BACHELOR'S REST, *Queen's Highway, Knowles area. Tel. (242) 342-6014. Open 7 days a week for lunch and dinner. No Dress Code. Cash Only - No major credit cards accepted.*

Bachelor's Rest is the best place on Cat Island to head for when you're in the mood for freshly caught and prepared Bahamian conch specialties. This simple restaurant offers large portions of mutton souse at $6, conch snacks for $6, chicken snacks at $5, chicken dinners for $7, fish dinners at $8, conch dinners for $10, boiled fish at $6 and several daily specials. Make sure to try their world famous cracked conch at least once before departing the island.

BRIDGE INN RESTAURANT, *Queen's Highway, New Bight area. Tel. (242) 342-3013. Open every day of the week. No Dress Code. Cash Only - No major credit cards accepted.*

Located in the settlement of New Bight near the airport, this large modern restaurant prepares a good selection of breakfast, lunch, and dinner items, including steamed fish with grits and Johnny cakes at $8, four conch fritters for $1, cracked conch at $6, steamed grouper Bahamian style for $9, fried chicken with french fries at $6, barbecued ribs for $10, pizzas at $18, and many other daily specials. The restaurant also features one of Cat Island's best pool tables and a really nice staff that will keep you coming back for more.

SEA SPRAY RESTAURANT, *Queen's Highway, Orange Creek area. Tel. (242) 354-4116. Open from 8:00am until 12midnight daily. No Dress Code. Cash Only - No major credit cards accepted.*

This tranquil white stucco dining room just above the sea has a good menu of Bahamian and American favorites, including stewed fish breakfasts for $8, eggs with bacon and toast at $5, mutton for $7, steamed fish Bahamian style at $7, broiled chicken for $7, fried grouper at $9, conch dinners for $7, pork chops at $7, tender lamb for $7, chicken souse at $6, conch burgers for $5.50, cheeseburgers at $5, and ice cold beers for just $2.75 each.

THE COOKIE HOUSE, *Queen's Highway, Arthur's Town area. Tel. (242) 354-2027. Open daily from 8:00am until 10:00pm. No Dress Code. Cash Only - No major credit cards accepted.*

The adorable little Cookie House restaurant and bakery serves up some good home-made dishes and sweets, such as coconut tarts for $1, cupcakes at $1, meat patties for $1.50, souse at $6, fish and chips for $6, chicken fingers at $5, cheeseburgers for $3, conch patties at $2, hot wings $1, steamed fish at $8, barbecued ribs for $9, conch fitters at $1, soup with dumplings for $6, and many other daily specials. Owner Pat Rolle has also installed a few indoor tables and a nice sunset view dining terrace.

SEEING THE SIGHTS

Northern Cat Island

The island's main road, known as the **Queen's Highway**, commences at the wonderful and desolate **Bain Town Beach**. From here you can follow the highway south along the coast for a few miles until reaching the settlement of **Orange Creek**. Orange Creek is named for its adjacent flats that lead out to sea and are known by sportsmen as excellent bonefishing spots. In this tiny town filled mainly with colorful wood and stone houses and a few churches, you can find the Seventh Day Adventist-managed **Orange Creek Inn** and a more cozy sea-front inn called the **Sea Spray Hotel & Restaurant**.

About two miles further south on the left side of the same road you begin to enter the community of **Arthur's Town**, the capital and largest town on Cat Island. Birthplace of Oscar winning actor Sidney Poitier, this area was once favored by Spanish pirate raiders before being settled by colonial Loyalists who came here with their slaves following the American Revolution.

Just as you enter the town limits, there is a is a well indicated turnoff for the **Arthur's Town Airport**. Keep following the Queen's Highway down through Arthur's Town and soon you will pass by the delightful local **Cookie House** restaurant and bakery on the right side. The sights further along include the yellow Arthur's Town High School, the coral colored government administration building housing the Island Commissioner's office, and a small green police station. Directly across from the government buildings is a small green space known as **Sir Roland Symonette Park**, and behind it stands the inspiring 19th-century **Anglican Church**.

From here the highway curves around through town and leads towards several unusual establishments such as the **Hard Rock Bar and Disco**, open 24 hours a day for cool drinks and billiards, a Batelco phone company building with several working cash and card pay phones, a few miniature **Straw Markets**, the **Big Bull Grocery Store** where you can stock up on simple food stuffs, a small one room local hangout called the **Stuck in the Mud Bar** that is open from 9:00am until 9:00pm only, the **Lone-Some-Me** liquor store that is marked with a sign stating "Licensed to sell intoxicating liquor," and the large **Lover's Boulevard** bar and nightclub with occasional live music and a good pool table. This end of town is dotted with the remains of several old Bahamian stone ovens that have been built away from the houses in order to reduce the possibility of fire.

From the city you will proceed further south along the same road for around 3/4 of a mile as it reaches the outskirts of **Dumfries**. This sector was settled by Loyalists that originally hailed from a Scottish town of the same name and is lined by many antique cottages. Another 2 1/2 miles south is the more impressive former 16th through 18th century pirate haven of **Bennett's Harbour**.

While still known for the adjacent brackish ponds that were used to collect salt for export, this hamlet is also home to a nearby pier where the **Cat Island Special** freight boat unloads its passengers and cargo from Nassau once a week.

Continuing further south, you will zip though a few small villages, such as **Roker's**. About 1/4 of a mile past the sign welcoming visitors to Roker's is a small dirt road off to the right that is sign-posted to "Pidgeon Cay." Those interested can turn down this road and follow it for two miles or so until reaching the spectacular **Pidgeon Creek Beach**.

The Queen's Highway then leads south past settlements like **The Bluff**, and then cuts through a large undeveloped area that is dotted by several slash and burn farms where locals grow melons and tropical fruits. Some 4 3/4 miles past The Bluff is an entrance to the **Industrious Hill Caves**, which are still used by area residents as a shelter from occasional hurricanes. If you intend to explore the caves, make sure to bring a good flashlight.

Central Cat Island

The road now passes a few small former wrecking settlements along the sea, including **The Cove** where locals moved beacons around to purposely shipwreck passing vessels in the old days. One of the more infamous wrecks was that of a schooner called the *Rodegard*, which in 1910 was laden with whisky and kept the townsfolk drunk for many weeks. Keep following the highway a few miles into the settlement of **Knowles** and perhaps take a well-deserved break over at the **Bachelor's Rest** restaurant and bar, where you can get freshly caught conch and other home-made conch specialties at good prices.

From here the highway continues along the edge of **Smith's Bay**. A mile or so after passing the **Smith's Bay Government Clinic** is a small unmarked access road on the left hand side, which leads to a superb series of pink sand beaches all the way across on the island's northeastern shore.

If you keep going south along the Queen's Highway, some of the most noteworthy sights along the way are the amusing **Hazel's Seaside Bar** where locals sip drinks between serious games of dominos, a pier where the ship *Sea Hauler* unloads her passengers and sacks of mail from Nassau once a week, the **Community Packing House** where you can buy fresh fruit at great prices, and the large **Smith's Bay Flats** that is well known for good bonefishing.

Once you have left the Smith's Bay area, you should keep your eyes open for the well marked side road off to the right that leads to the amazing **Fernandez Bay Village** villa colony and restaurant, which offers superb seaside villa accommodations and a wonderful restaurant (reservations required for dinner) resting above a fantastic crescent shaped beach. Around 3/4 of a mile south of Fernandez Bay you will see the **New Bight International Airport**. The highway then continues south into the town of **New Bight**, where you can pop into Iva Thompson's **First & Last Chance Bar and Straw Market**, the well-stocked **New Bight Food Market** grocery store, and the **Bridge Inn** hotel and restaurant.

When you pass alongside the whitewashed facade of the **Holy Redeemer Catholic Church** at the edge of town, you should bear right down a small street that runs along the seaside where the annual **Cat Island Sailing Regatta** takes place. This is a really fun event held for three days in early August and is comprised of handmade wooden "smack boats" competing for trophies. On this same unnamed street, you will first pass the **Sailing Club** weekend disco before it again merges with the Queen's Highway.

Just after merging back onto the highway, keep your eyes open for the pink colored **Government Administration Offices**. Immediately following the government office building is a well-marked unpaved road on the left side of the highway that leads up Como Hill to the amazing **Mt. Alvernia Hermitage**. Park your car at the gate below the hilltop monastery (built on the highest peak in The Bahamas) and walk for five minutes or so along the "Stations of The Cross" pathway to the stone monastery at 206 feet above sea level. This unique structure was built in 1943 by **Fra Jerome**, a famous former architect who renounced his worldly possessions and moved to Cat Island to live here in isolation as a hermit priest.

Make sure to climb up to the top of the bell tower, check out his tiny living quarters, stroll along the miniature cloisters, and peek inside the 5' x 10' chapel. *The Mt. Alvernia Hermitage Monastery is open daily from sunrise to sunset and is free to enter.*

Southern Cat Island

Now return to the highway and keep heading south for some 2 1/2 miles and turn right down a dirt road sign-posted towards Pilot's Harbour. A quarter-mile along this road you will begin to see the sandy shores of **Old Bight Beach**. The highlight of this beach area is the point at which the **Armbrister Creek** lets out into the sea, creating a shallow swimming spot that is hard to beat. If you look to the left as you enter the creek you will find a small heavily forested area where the Lucayan Indians have a sacred burial spot.

When you've had enough time to cool off in the shallow waters, continue along the same road for about 1/3 of a mile, where the road re-merges with the Queen's Highway. Now the highway cuts through the tiny settlement of Old Bight, where you can pop inside a few old churches (including one designed by Fra Jerome), and a few interesting **Straw Markets**.

The next major sight down the highway is a bit more than five miles south at the **Columbus Harbour Roundabout**, lined by conch shells at its base. Bear left at this traffic circle and follow the road as it now leads into the village of **Zonicles**. A few miles further east the road cuts through **Port Howe**, where locals believe Christopher Columbus made his first landfall in the New World in October 1492. Off to the right side of the road, you will see the ruins of the **Colonel Andrew Deveaux Mansion** that was built on land that this national hero of The Bahamas received from the crown after helping to expel the Spaniards from Nassau in 1793. The house was originally built in the Virginia plantation style but is currently in need of some major renovations, and may not be open to the public.

After the mansion, if you keep heading west you will pass the extremely uninviting **Cutlass Bay Nudist Resort** (a bizarre all-inclusive property), and the much more friendly **Hotel Greenwood Inn** beach-front hotel and scuba resort.

Now return to the Columbus Harbour Roundabout and this time head straight ahead towards the west. After about four miles turn right onto an unmarked paved road on the right. This street continues for 7 1/2 miles until it reaches a seaside area called **McQueens**, where you will turn left onto the Hawks Nest Road. Keep going straight until you reach the cute little **Hawks Nest Resort** and marina.

SPORTS & RECREATION

All sports and recreation facilities on Cat Island must be arranged directly at the front desks of hotels such as **Fernandez Bay Village** and **Hotel Greenwood Inn**. Currently, there are no major independent suppliers of any type of excursion, tour, watersports, boating, or fishing trips on this small and mainly undeveloped island.

NIGHTLIFE & ENTERTAINMENT

Most of what nightlife there is on Cat Island, outside your hotel, centers around **Arthur's Town**, the island's capital. As referred to above, you can check out the **Hard Rock Bar and Disco**; the **Stuck in the Mud Bar** (get here early – it closes at 9:00pm); and the **Lover's Boulevard** bar and nightclub, where you can play pool and occasionally hear live music. They are all in town on Queen's Highway.

In **New Bight**, check out the **Last Chance Bar and Straw Market** and the **Sailing Club**, a weekends-only disco. And in the Hawks Nest area, the best bar on the island is located at the **Hawks Nest Resort** (see review above in *Where to Stay*).

18. THE EXUMAS

The Exumas are situated 119 miles southeast of New Providence Island. The Exumas are a chain of 365 or so islands and cays that stretch out for more than 92 miles. Known as a quiet shipbuilding and fishing center with a population of some 3,560 full time residents, this is a fantastic place to boat or drive around in search of some of The Bahamas' most dramatic beaches and best bonefishing.

The largest land masses here are the 40 mile long **Great Exuma Island** and the connecting 12 mile long **Little Exuma Island**, located in the southern portion of the chain. The city of **George Town** (population 461) is a small but active community of friendly descendants of former slaves, several local merchants who have established a few good restaurants, and a small community of Creole-speaking Haitian refugees. While most are busy during the yearly late April **Out Island Regatta**, most North American vacationing yachtsmen and homeowners flock here during the December through April high season.

The Exumas' History

The first permanent settlement of the Exumas began as American colonialists still loyal to King George of England fled here with their slaves in the aftermath of the American Revolution. Although various attempts were made to establish cotton plantations in the early 18th century, the land proved too difficult to cultivate and shipbuilding soon replaced agriculture as the major source of revenue.

ARRIVALS & DEPARTURES

Exuma has only one major passenger terminal at the **Exuma International Airport** on central Great Exuma Island. This is one of the nation's more comfortable small airports and it has a snack shop, working pay phones, airline ticket offices, a full service lounge, and a taxi rank. The carriers operating scheduled passenger service into this airport from Florida or other Bahamian islands include **American Eagle** and

Bahamasair. Charter services to this destination can be booked with small local companies such as **Island Express** and **Airways International**.

GETTING AROUND THE EXUMAS

By Rental Car

There are no major rental car agencies here, but two local businesses in George Town have fleets of used Japanese sedans and American utility vehicles. Generally, the going price for a car is around $60 per day, $300 per week, and C.D.W. (collision damage waiver) insurance is included in the above prices and carries a $200 or so deductible that must be left with the office as a refundable security deposit.

If you need a car anywhere in the Exumas, you must first take a taxi into George Town to pick it up as there is no free delivery or drop off service available on the islands.

• **Sam Gray Enterprises' Car Rentals**, *George Town, Tel. (242) 336-2101*
• **Two Turtle Rental Cars**, *George Town, Tel. (242) 336-2545*

By Taxi

There are some 54 licensed taxi cabs in Exuma, all using an official government rate sheet to determine the exact prices for each fare. These hard-working men are all honest and tend to be great sources of local information. From the airport, expect to pay around $21.50 for a one-way ride into the George Town area for up to two passengers.

The drivers listed below can also be hired for extensive customized guided tours at around $20 per hour.

• **Lawrence Thompson**, *Taxi # 6, Tel. (242) 358-4248*
• **Luther Rolle**, *Taxi # 29, Tel. (242) 345-0641*

WHERE TO STAY

Very Expensive

PEACE & PLENTY BEACH INN, *George Town area, Great Exuma. Tel. (242) 336-2550, Fax (242) 336-2253. US & Canada bookings (Hotel Direct) 1-800-525-2210. Low season rack rates from $308 per double room per night (A.I..). High season rack rates from $348 per double room per night (A.I.). Most major credit cards accepted.*

This delightful little beach-front inn has recently been converted into the island's only deluxe all-inclusive property. Located near Goat Cay on the western edge of George Town, the Peace & Plenty Beach Inn contains 16 deluxe sea-view rooms that all feature strong air conditioning, large private bathrooms stocked with English hair and skin care products, mini-refrigerators, satellite televisions, great private balconies looking out to the beach, ceiling fans, wall-to-wall tile flooring and lots of natural sunlight.

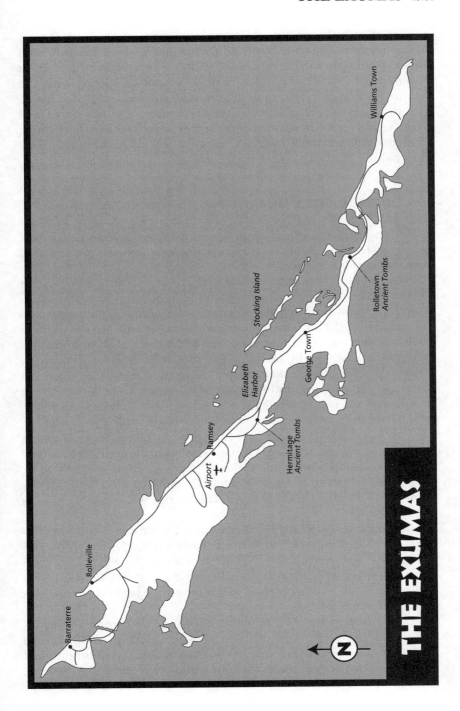

The all-inclusive package price includes three meals a day at your choice of the three Peace & Plenty properties on the island, free wine with dinner, round-trip airport transfers, shuttle van service to and from downtown George Town, and all taxes & service charges. Among the facilities here are a nice restaurant, an outdoor swimming pool with a great sun deck, a private pier with a great bar, an indoor lounge area, and of course a nice small beach area. Most of the guests I met here were young honeymooners and well-traveled couples who were all having a great time and wouldn't hesitate to come back again.

Expensive

COCONUT COVE HOTEL, *George Town area, Great Exuma. Tel. (242) 336-2659, Fax (242) 336-2658. Low season rack rates from $100 per double room per night (E.P.). High season rack rates from $128 per double room suite per night (E.P.). B.P. Meal Plan available for $8 per adult per day. Most major credit cards accepted.*

Situated just off a small pleasant beach area about a mile west of downtown George Town, this delightful little bed and breakfast inn is among the most beautiful properties on the island. Here guests can choose between 10 different double rooms in one and two story lodges that have either sea or garden views. Each of the unique accommodations have powerful air conditioning, deluxe private bathrooms, ceramic or wooden parquet floors, remote control satellite television, fresh cut flowers, high quality hair and skin care products, great sun decks that can be accessed via hand-crafted French doors, white rattan furnishings, ceiling fans, mini-refrigerators, plush bathrobes and plenty of charm.

The property also features a private pier, a nice outdoor swimming pool with a swim-up bar, a great breakfast room, superbly landscaped gardens, a cascading fish pond stocked with grouper and bonefish, white picket trim, a small sandy beach-front and complimentary shuttle service to and from downtown George Town. This is a real gem of a small inn with lots of character.

CLUB PEACE & PLENTY, *George Town, Great Exuma. Tel. (242) 336-2551, Fax (242) 336-2093. US & Canada bookings (Hotel Direct) 1-800-525-2210. Low season rack rates from $96 per double room per night (E.P.). High season rack rates from $120 per double room per night (E.P.). M.A.P. Meal Plans available from $36 per adult per day. No children under 6 years old allowed. Most major credit cards accepted.*

Located just a stone's throw away from downtown George Town, this little seaside inn has been the mainstay of more upscale visitors to Exuma for many years. The property features 35 reasonably sized air conditioned rooms with am-fm clock radios, simple furnishings, private bathrooms, and sea-view patios in most cases. The facilities here include a large restaurant, an outdoor swimming pool and water's edge sun deck, a private dock, indoor and outdoor bars, free ferry service to a fantastic private beach club on nearby Stocking Island, excursions and bonefishing trips and free parking.

A new "dine around program" will allow those staying here to hop on a free shuttle bus and enjoy dinner at the affiliated Beach Inn and Bonefish Lodge on various evenings. Many of the guests arrive here year after year from cities all over North America and Europe.

Moderate

MT. PLEASANT SUITES AND HOTEL, *George Town, Great Exuma. Tel. (242) 336-2960, Fax (242) 336-2964. Low season rack rates from $80 per 1 bedroom suite per night (E.P.). High season rack rates from $100 per 1 bedroom suite per night (E.P.). Most major credit cards accepted.*

This rather pleasant hotel just a mile west of downtown George Town has a couple of dozen 1, 2, and 3 bedroom suites and villas just a three minute walk from the fine sandy beaches of Great Exuma. All of the units here are fully air conditioned and contain well stocked full kitchens, comfortable furnishings, remote control satellite televisions, dining rooms, large modern private bathrooms, patios with garden views, wall-to-wall tile floors, free parking, complimentary courtesy bus transportation to the heart of George Town and back and rental cars. This is a good value for the money, and the staff here is quite nice.

THE PALMS AT THREE SISTERS, *Mt. Thompson Area, Great Exuma. Tel. (242) 358-4040, Fax (242) 358-4043. Low season rack rates from $75 per double room per night (E.P.). High season rack rates from $100 per double room suite per night (E.P.). Most major credit cards accepted.*

Located just off a nice beach area on the north shore of Great Exuma, the two story hotel is a good alternative to the more famous hotels in the George Town area. All of the 12 rooms and two cottages here are fully air conditioned and have nice private bathrooms, comfortable wooden furnishings, remote control satellite televisions, two double beds, beach-view patios, wall-to-wall carpeting and free parking.

The nice local staff here can arrange inexpensive shuttle service back and forth into George Town, car rentals, bicycle rentals, optional excursions and fishing trips and more. The property also has a good restaurant and bar.

Inexpensive

LA SHANTÉ BEACH GUEST HOUSE, *Forbes Hill Area, Little Exuma. Tel. (242) 345-4136. Low season rack rates from $65 per double room per night (E.P.). High season rack rates from $85 per double room per night (E.P.). Cash Only - No credit cards accepted.*

When I saw this delightful little locally owned and operated sea-front guest house and restaurant, I really wanted to stop writing and reserve a room here for the rest of the year! This simple yet exceedingly comfortable three room inn is just steps away from one of the island's most amazing beaches, and features a few medium-size rooms with powerful air conditioning, basic wood and Formica furnishings, satellite television, private bathroom, wall-to-wall tile flooring, and lots of natural sunlight. The inn can also provide good meals at its restaurant, free round-trip bus service into downtown George Town, boat and car rentals, chartered fishing trips, local guide services and more.

While far from fancy or deluxe, this place has much more charm and a much friendlier staff than the most expensive hotel on the island.

TWO TURTLES INN, *George Town, Great Exuma. Tel. (242) 336-2545, Fax (242) 336-2528. Low season rack rates from $68 per room per night (E.P.). High season rack rates from $88 per room per night (E.P.). Most major credit cards accepted.*

If you're looking for affordably priced comfortable accommodations in the heart of George Town, the Two Turtles Inn is a good choice. This extremely welcoming family-run inn and restaurant just off of Lake Victoria has 12 air conditioned rooms and studio-style units in two story wooden lodges. All of the units here have courtyard views, and come with satellite television, private bathrooms, wall-to-wall carpeting, simple wooden furnishings, comfortable bedding, ceiling fans, and adjacent patios. The self-catering rooms also have a small oven and refrigerator as well as all the necessary utensils to prepare your own meals while on vacation.

The bar here is certainly among the most happening watering holes in town during the afternoon, and locals and tourists alike tend to spend hours mingling together while discussing a variety of interesting topics. The inn's casual restaurant is open for lunch and dinner on most nights in the winter, and is especially attractive during the Tuesday and Friday evening informal barbecues held year round.

While far from luxurious, Two Turtles is a nice place to stay for those looking for laid-back ambiance and who want to interact with the friendly residents of Exuma.

WHERE TO EAT

Moderate

SAM'S PLACE, *George Town, Great Exuma. Tel. (242) 336-2579. No Dress Code. Most major credit cards accepted.*

Situated just above the only full service marina in Exuma, this casual down-home restaurant prepares some of the island's most delicious breakfasts, lunches, and dinners every day of the week. Served by a friendly staff of locals with a great sense of humor, Sam's Place offers such items as omelets at $5, French toast for $5, waffles at $5, conch chowder for $2.75, conch fritters at $2.50, club sandwiches for $5, BLT's at $4, turkey sandwiches for $4, tuna melts at $4.50, grilled ham & cheese for $4.50, chicken plates at $6, chicken liver pate for $3, heart of artichoke at $2.50, garden salads for $2, broiled lobster at $22, pan fried grouper for $12, N.Y. strip steak at $14, cracked conch with tomato pepper sauce for $11, grilled mahi-mahi at $14, roast leg of lamb for $15, Beef Burgundy at $15, and strawberry amaretto cake for $2.50. This is one of the best places to enjoy a fine sunset with a nice view from their outdoor or indoor dining areas, and is strongly recommended!

LA SHANTÉ BEACH CLUB RESTAURANT, *Forbes Hill area, Little Exuma. Tel. (242) 345-4136. No Dress Code. Cash only - No credit cards accepted.*

This family-owned sea-front restaurant and bar has a wonderful menu that includes such favorites as eggs with bacon and toast at $7.75, ham and cheese omelets for $9, conch chowder at $3.50, cracked conch for $8, grouper fingers at $10, fried shrimp for $14, pork chops at $14, seafood combination plates for $25, sirloin steaks at $16, broiled lobster tails for $25, fried chicken at $14, broiled snapper for $14, barbecued chicken at $14, steamed chicken Bahamian style for $14, burgers at $5, tuna melts for $6, ham & cheese sandwiches at $5, and plenty of desserts and cold drinks.

Inexpensive

EDDIE'S EDGEWATER CLUB, *George Town, Great Exuma. Tel. (242) 336-2050. Open 7 days a week. No Dress Code. Most major credit cards accepted.*

This large friendly dining room on the edge of Lake Victoria is one of the best places to go for large and affordable breakfast, lunch, and dinner. Eddie's is a family-owned establishment popular with both locals and visitors. Their large menu offers $6 daily lunch specials consisting of bean soup and rice, fried snapper, pea soup with dumplings, meatloaf, steamed turkey, baked chicken, and others. Other popular items here include tuna sandwiches with french fries at $5.50, conch burgers for $6, burger plates at $4, snapper snacks for $5, broiled catch of the day at $12.50, cracked conch for $10, fried turtle steak at $10, pan fried grouper for $10, sautéed liver and onions at $10, fried chicken for $6, lobster salad at $8.50, and fresh lobster at market price. On Monday evenings they have a fun "Rake & Scrape" party and there is also a convenient pier where dingys can tie up.

FISHERMAN'S INN, *Barraterre, Great Exuma. Tel. (242) 355-5016. Open daily from 10:00am until the evening's last patron leaves. No Dress Code. Most major credit cards accepted.*

When you are in the mood for a good inexpensive seafood lunch or dinner and have a car to get to the northern tip of Great Exuma, head for this charming little seaside restaurant. The menu here includes a handful of selections each day, including lunch specials for $7, fresh fish of the day at $10, cracked conch for $10, fried shrimp at $12, broiled lobster tail for $18, and additional selections added each week. This relaxed maritime theme restaurant and bar rests under a sloped wooden ceiling lined with T-shirts left by satisfied clients from all over the world, and the service is prompt and polite.

LITTLE EXUMA ISLAND

The easternmost section of the Queen's Highway starts off just below the quiet hamlet of **Williams Town**. Sandwiched between the ocean and a couple of adjacent marshy ponds, Williams Town also contains the remains of slave quarters that were once part of an unsuccessful 18th-century Loyalist cotton plantation. The ponds all along the left side of the highway were used to collect and then export salt that formed at the water's edge. Most of the locals also grow small quantities of onions and bananas. You can see usually see small packs of goats roaming around the road as you drive by.

Among the best places to check out along the way through town is the tiny little **Hilltop Bar**, where Warren serves ice cold beer and tall shots of top shelf drinks at affordable prices. There are also a few nice churches, the remarkable **Mom's Bakery** that bakes great little tarts and homemade breads, **Bullard's Grocery & Liquor Store**, and a Batelco phone card telephone booth. Another mile further along the right side of the highway you will find an old column rising up on the top of **Beacon Hill**. Park your car and walk uphill along the sandy path to the base of the beacon which was once used to safely guide Spanish ships that stopped here to load up on salt on their way to the New World. Near the beacon you will also notice an antique cannon and a magnificent view out towards the large crescent shaped Palm Bay Beach, marked by a recently wrecked freight boat at its point.

Now keep heading up the Queen's Highway for about a little more than two miles and make a right turn at the unmarked gravel road lined by telephone poles. Roughly a half a mile down this road, near a wooden kiosk, is a truly remarkable stretch of sand and turquoise water called **Tropic of Cancer Beach**. This is considered to be among the best beaches on Little Exuma and is usually pretty quiet. Now return to the Queen's Highway and turn right to continue west for yet another 2 1/4 miles until passing through the village of **Forbes Hill.** While not much goes on in this peaceful community, some of the island's most romantic cove beaches can be accessed from several paths and side roads that any local will be glad to direct you towards.

Just past the town on the right side of the highway is an access road sign-posted to the intimate **La Shanté Beach Club & Guest House**. This welcoming family-owned inn has a wonderful restaurant and bar situated just above one of my favorite quarter-mile long sandy cove beaches in the whole country. They also rent out three nice air conditioned rooms for bargain basement prices. Some two miles after passing the town of Forbes Hill, keep an eye out for a small blue wooden hut on the left side of the highway that is actually the **St. Christopher's Anglican Church**, the nation's smallest house of worship.

Just 1/10 of a mile further along on the right side of the highway is a white cottage that is home to Gloria Patience (a.k.a. **The Shark Lady**). This interesting woman is known far and wide for catching large sharks in the sea and then fashioning one-of-a-kind pieces of jewelry from their teeth and bones. Her cottage is filled with antiques and an assortment of her hand-made shark jewelry for sale at good prices. Make sure to stop by before leaving the island, as this is one of Exuma's most entertaining attractions.

GREAT EXUMA ISLAND

The highway now continues over a channel known as **The Ferry** that is crossed via a narrow one lane bridge that leads directly onto Great Exuma Island. The first structure you will see after the bridge is the **Peace & Plenty Bonefish Lodge**. The adjacent flats are known as the **Blue Hole** and are considered to be among The Bahamas' absolute best location for bonefishing. If you ask around, there are several privately owned fishing boats that can be chartered by the full or half day (see *Excursions, Tours, Marinas, & Boat Rentals* below).

About 2 1/4 miles past the bridge you will find an old neighborhood called **Rolletown**. Named after Lord John Rolle, a wealthy Loyalist who sent over 370 of his slaves from Georgia here in the 18th century, the land in this area was inherited in commanage by his former slaves who were freed under the provisions of the Bahamas Emancipation Act of 1833. The town (and a few others along Great Exuma) is inhabited by descendants of former plantation slaves that have kept using the last name of Rolle as their own. While the land here can be passed along from generation to generation, it cannot be bought or sold.

Just as you enter Rolletown there are a pair of large pillars on the right side of the highway marking the access road into town. Turn right on the road between these two columns, take another right turn at the next street, and park your car at a small clearing some 30 yards down on the left side. Now walk along the cleared pathway and soon you will find the **Ancient Tombs**. These limestone and marble structures are the final resting place of a female member of the Kay family who died during childbirth and was buried here in 1792.

The street ends some 175 yards later at a parking area just in front of the Rolletown cemetery. Just behind the cemetery's tombstones there is a memorable bay that becomes a giant secluded sandy beach known as the **Haulover** during low tide. This is where you can find amazing turquoise water.

George Town & Environs

Another five miles up the Queen's Highway you will enter the city limits of **George Town**, the only city on The Exumas. Full of good restaurants, small inns, and good shopping possibilities, George Town is a lot of fun to wander around. Although typically a peaceful place, the city really comes to life each March and April when its adjacent Elizabeth Harbour hosts the annual **Cruising Regatta** and the **Out Island Regatta**.

Just after passing the popular **Silver Dollar Restaurant**, bear left at a mile long turnabout that encircles **Lake Victoria**, since the highway through central George Town is closed to oncoming traffic. The turn-around leads past the Batelco telephone company office and **Eddie's Edgewater Restaurant**, curves up the hill past the **Harbourview Laundromat**, and then merges back into the highway where you will turn right to head downtown. The best place to start exploring the city is over at the extremely helpful **Ministry of Tourism's Information Centre**.

My suggestion at this point is to park your car near the tourist office and proceed into the downtown George Town area by foot; you'll pass Cousin's Disco and pizza shack. The first important sight worthy of attention is just across the street at the unmistakable white and powder blue 19th-century **Anglican Church**. For the next mile or so both sides of

---

GREAT TOURIST INFORMATION!

Exuma is fortunate to have what I have found to be The Bahamas' most informative and friendly Tourist Information Center. Ona Bullard and her great staff can help provide dozens of brochures, information sheets, maps, and suggestions for all visitors that walk through their doors. The same office can help arrange boat rentals, fishing trips, hotel stays, local guides, special events, and help to make your stay an unforgettable one. They are open weekdays from 9:00am until 5:30pm and can be reached at Tel. (242) 336-2430 or via fax at (242) 336-2431.

the highway are lined with several boutiques and local establishments such as the **Club Peace & Plenty** hotel, a nice gift shop called the **Sandpiper**, Exuma's public Administration Building with police and postal offices, the lakeside offices of the **Exuma Fantasea** diving and boat rental center, and the local public school. Just to the left of the school is a small access road to the **Government Dock**, where on Tuesdays many Exuma residents can be found awaiting supplies from the **Grand Master** freight boat coming in laden with cargo and provisions from Nassau.

Proceeding further into George Town, you will stroll by to the delightful **Two Turtles Inn & Restaurant**, a small daily open air **Straw Market** where gift items and native handicrafts can be found, the laid-back **Towne Cafe**, a branch of Canadian-based **Scotiabank**, the large **Exuma Markets** grocery store, and a great little produce store called **N & D Fruits & Vegetables** where you rent bicycles or just treat yourself to an ice cream cone.

The next series of bustling establishments along the same road includes the island's 50-slip **Exuma Docking Service**, a wonderful marina-front restaurant known as **Sam's Place** that prepares delicious meals throughout the day, and finally the headquarters of **Sam Gray Enterprises** where you can book rental cars and spacious apartments (stop by and say hi to Sam for me). Parked alongside this section of the street on any given day are a couple of specially converted mini-buses and vans selling tasty sandwiches and foodstuffs from local shops and bakeries.

SEE EXUMA WITH A PRO!

For those with a rental car who really want a special tour through Exuma, I recommend booking a half or full day sightseeing trip with **"Dr."** **Joe Romer.** *Joe is a remarkable 70 year old bush medicine expert who loves to guide visitors through Exuma. Besides knowing the location and background of all the sights and attractions listed in this chapter, he can also bring you to many other amazing beaches and out-of-the-way places that only a true local would even know about. During your time with him, Joe will also point out medicinal wild herbs and plants, suggest remedies for common ailments, give colorful narration about the island's infamous history and residents, and make sure you have the time of your life.*

Just ask the Tourist Information Centre to get in touch with Joe for you. Although he doesn't charge for his services, I would suggest giving him a good tip of around $10 per hour.

Western Sections of Great Exuma Island

Now that you have seen all the sights and shops in George Town, bear left at the above-mentioned mile long Lake Victoria turnabout, and this time make a left turn to continue westward along the Queen's Highway.

A mile or so west of George Town you will pass by the **Peace & Plenty Beach Inn** and the adjacent **Coconut Cove Hotel**. The first small road on the right past these hotels leads to **Goat Cay**, a private getaway for various members of European royalty. Goat Cay is often closed off to curious tourists, but the long beach that lies just to the left before entering the cay is public and is a fantastic spot for shallow water swimming.

From this point on most of the land along the right side of the highway is fronted by a series of superb long sandy beaches. Although a few seasonal homes can be found scattered along the mainly undeveloped lots further up the coast, there are plans to eventually construct many more subdivisions and sell hundreds of homes to well-off foreigners. All the beaches on Great Exuma are public, but the access roads are often a bit difficult to find. I suggest asking locals living in the area for (the best) directions. Those more interested in getting to the fine beaches and snorkeling spots on **Stocking Island** (just off the coast) can inquire at the Peace & Plenty for daily scheduled ferry information.

As you continue heading west along the highway for a couple of miles you will pass the affordable **Mt. Pleasant Suites & Hotel**, and the sites for a few more planned luxury subdivisions. A short distance past the roundabout exit for **Exuma International Airport**, there are three rocks called the **Three Sisters Rocks** sticking up out of the ocean. Legend has it that these rocks are actually the "children" of three young sisters who drowned on this spot many moons ago. The Queen's Highway ends 21 miles northwest of George Town at the commanage land village of **Rolleville**, the sight of another annual regatta. This is where many of the straw baskets sold in Nassau are actually made.

Now retrace the route back east along the Queen's Highway towards George Town for about three miles until bearing right at the next turnoff. After following a poorly maintained road and a pair of bridges for about five miles, you will finally reach the former boat building center of **Barreterre**. While not much happens here, you can check out the casual seaside **Fisherman's Inn** bar and restaurant and look out across the sea to nearby **Lee Stocking Island**, where prominent scientists and Ph.D. candidates from around the world are hard at work studying the habitat of Bahamian marine life at the famed **Caribbean Marine Research Center**.

EXCURSIONS, TOURS, MARINAS, & BOAT RENTALS

• **Cooper's Charter Services**, *Great Exuma, Tel. (242) 336-2711*
• **"Dr." Joe Romer's Tours**, *Great Exuma, Tel. (242) 336-2430 (note: this is the tourist information office, but they will put you in touch with Joe)*

- **Christine Rolle Tours**, *Great Exuma, Tel. (242) 336-4016*
- **Exuma Docking Service**, *Great Exuma, Tel. (242) 336-2578*
- **Exuma Fantasea Boat Rental & Scuba Center**, *Great Exuma, Tel. (242) 336-3483*
- **Lawrence Thompson Taxi Tours**, *Great Exuma, Tel. (242) 358-4248*
- **Louise's Taxi**, *Great Exuma, Tel. (242) 336-6028*
- **Garth Thompson Bone Fishing Guides**, *Great Exuma, Tel. (242) 345-5062*
- **R. Alfred Sears Bonefishing Guides**, *Little Exuma, Tel. (242) 345-4210*
- **Peace & Plenty Adventures**, *Great Exuma, Tel. (242) 336-2551*
- **Seaside Fishing and Island Tours**, *Great Exuma, Tel. (242) 336-2091*

PRACTICAL INFORMATION
- **Exuma Tourist Office**, *George Town, Tel. (242) 336-2430*
- **Government Health Clinic**, *George Town, Tel. (242) 336-2088*
- **Local Police**, *George Town, Tel. (242) 336-2666*

19. ANDROS

Andros is located 28 miles west of New Providence Island. Andros is a giant 100 mile long by 40 mile wide island chain that is divided into large northern, central, and southern sections by a series of inlets and bights. Much of the islands' 2,300 square miles of interior land is populated entirely by birds and land crabs, and is dotted with huge stretches of mangrove flats, semi-tropical forests, and brush.

Thinly populated with just over eight thousand permanent residents, they mostly live in the northern communities of **Andros Town** and **Nicholl's Town** and the southern hamlet of **Congo Town**. There are also several hundred US naval forces resident here.

This is the place to visit for serious scuba diving and bonefishing adventures. The main attraction of these islands is the amazing 120 mile long **Andros Reef**, the third largest barrier reef in the world with an average depth of 13 feet. The reef is just off the islands' eastern coast and is a fantastic place to scuba dive through caves, shipwrecks, blue holes, and coral gardens full of marine life. There is a sharp drop-off on its edge called the **Tongue of the Ocean** that descends for well over 1,000 feet. It is this beach-lined eastern coast that attracts most visitors to Andros, and features a few interesting small-scale hotel and resort developments.

ARRIVALS & DEPARTURES

Andros has three main airports that are serviced by **Bahamasair** and **Gulfstream International Airlines**, as well as several hotel-based charters. On the northern part of Andros are the **San Andros Airport** and the **Andros Town Airport**, while in the southern part of Andros is the **Congo Town Airport**. Make sure to find out which airport is nearest to your hotel or else the taxi fare can reach as much as $100 more than necessary!

These are rather basic airports, with small terminals that have little or no real services besides ticket counters that open up an hour before each flight departs and a few taxis.

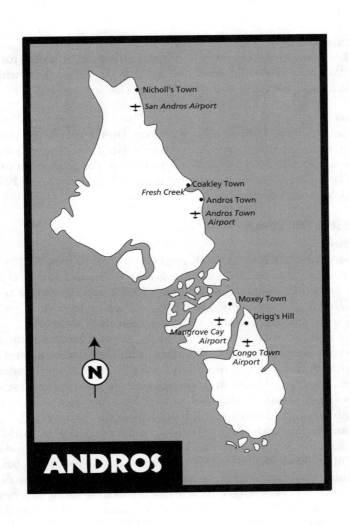

GETTING AROUND ANDROS

By Bicycle

A few hotels, such as **Small Hope Bay**, will rent you a bicycle to explore the inland sights of Andros. Make sure to use plenty of bug repellent.

By Rental Car

There are a limited number of rental cars that can be rented for about $95 a day plus a $150 refundable damage deposit. Please check with your hotel and have them get you a car from a reliable provider.

By Taxi

There are over 75 licensed taxi cabs on Andros that all use standardized government issued rate sheets to calculate fares. These rate sheets can be found posted at the airports and are in the possession of every island taxi driver. The best and most qualified taxi drivers are Bahamas Host program graduates.

WHERE TO STAY

Expensive

SMALL HOPE BAY LODGE, *Fresh Creek, North Andros. Tel. (242) 368-2014, Fax (242) 368-2015. US & Canada bookings (Hotel's Florida Offices) 1-800-223-6961. Low season rack rates from $300 per double cottage per night (A.I.). High season rack rates from $330 per double cottage per night (A.I.). Special scuba packages available. All major credit cards accepted.*

Located just a 10 minute drive from Andros Town airport in the northern reaches of Andros, this famous all inclusive hotel and scuba resort has been owned by the Birch family for over three decades. The property has 20 nice stone and wooden one and two bedroom sea-front cottages with private bathrooms, ceiling fans, plenty of space, simple furnishings, and Androsia brand batik fabrics throughout.

Many of the guests come here to experience some of the world's best scuba activities (including day and night dives to nearby reefs and ocean holes full of exotic marine life), while others just arrive to kick back and do nothing at all except relax. You can enjoy three buffet style meals daily, mix your own cocktails, take bicycle rides, visit long sandy beaches, kick back in a hammock, listen to narrated talks about local marine life and wildlife, jump in the open air hot tub, snorkel just offshore, learn how to scuba dive, wind-surf along the coastline, hop in a sailboat or send the kids off on scheduled (and well-supervised) activities, all for no additional charge.

There are also reasonably priced scuba adventures and certification classes led by expert PADI dive masters, fishing trips, island tours, nature walks, soothing massage treatments, and even chartered air service directly from Florida and Nassau. The guests are a relaxed an informal mixture of singles, couples, and families that usually come from the hectic corporate world, but while they are here they wear nothing more formal than swimsuits (even during dinner) and almost all return year after year. Selected as one of our *Best Places to Stay* – see Chapter 12 for a longer review.

Moderate
LIGHTHOUSE YACHT CLUB, *Andros Town, North Andros. Tel. (242) 368-2308, Fax (242) 368-2300. US & Canada bookings (Out Island Promo Board) 1-800-688-4752. Year round rack rates from $130 per double room per night (E.P.). M.A.P. Meal Plan available from $40 per adult per night. Most major credit cards accepted.*

This nice marina-front hotel has some 20 or so well-maintained air conditioned rooms and suites in nice cottage and lodge buildings. Their guests are mostly visiting fishermen from around the world. Each room is air conditioned and has water-view patios, hardwood furnishings, mini-refrigerators, ceiling fans, tile floors, extremely nice furnishings, and satellite television. There is also a medium-sized marina, a full service restaurant, an outdoor lounge, plenty of free private parking, a nice bar, tennis courts and a relaxed ambiance.

CHARLIE'S HAVEN, *Behring, North Andros. Tel. (242) 368-4087. Low season rack rates from $80 per double room per night (E.P.). Year round rack rates from $135 per double room per night (M.A.P.). Most major credit cards accepted.*

This small rustic and remote 10 room hotel in the area of Behring Point is a good place for those here to enjoy bonefishing. The rooms are simply furnished and have air conditioning.

WHERE TO EAT
LIGHTHOUSE YACHT CLUB RESTAURANT, *Andros Town. Tel. (242) 368-2308. Dress Code is Casual. Most major credit cards accepted.*

The restaurant at this hotel has extensive breakfast, lunch, and dinner menus that includes two eggs any style at $3.75, omelets for $5, French toast at $4, stewed fish for $7.50, vegetable soup at $2.75, conch chowder for $3.75, garden salad at $3.50, burgers for $4, grilled ham & cheese at $3.75, club sandwiches for $5, tuna sandwiches at $4, chef salad for $6.50, lamb chops at $13.50, filet mignon for $18.80, pan fried grouper at $12.50, surf & turf for $24, broiled lobster at $18, grilled chicken for $10.50, and peach melba at $4.

SQUARE DEAL RESTAURANT, *Main Street, Andros Town. Tel. (242) 368-2593. No Dress Code. Cash Only - No credit cards accepted.*

This great local hangout and dining room is open daily for lunch and dinner and offers a great assortment of freshly prepared Bahamian specialties including fish snacks for $5, fish dinners at $6.50, chicken snacks for $5, chicken dinner at $6.50, pork chops for $6.50, lamb chops at $6.50, barbecued ribs for $6.50, and occasionally they have stuffed land crabs for $9.

SKINNEY'S LANDMARK, *Main Street, Andros Town. Tel . Unlisted. No Dress Code. Cash Only - No credit cards accepted.*

Skinney's is a popular little restaurant serving lunch and dinner on most days of the week. The friendly staff will serve you large portions of Bahamian favorites and fresh seafood at reasonable prices, as well as strong drinks and ice cold beer.

SEEING THE SIGHTS

Northern Andros

About the only easy part of Andros to explore, besides the 120 mile long barrier reef itself, is the northern section of the islands. The best place to wander around is at Andros Town, a thriving little seaside community that is close to a huge US Naval installation and weapons testing center. Start your journey through Andros Town by turning east off the Queen's Highway at the **Fresh Creek Bridge**. Now follow the south bank of Fresh Creek into town as it passes by the mail boat docks. From here you can criss-cross several small side streets full of small restaurants and houses to get an idea of what is going on. Among the interesting sights here are a few nice churches, some local restaurants, and not much else.

Now return to the highway and cross over to the other side of the bridge. About 50 yards north of the bridge, bear left down a road sign-posted to the Lighthouse Yacht Club. As you continue down this unnamed road, keep your eyes open for a turn-off on the right side that leads to the **Androsia** batik clothing factory and its adjacent retail shop. Here you can get great deals on a full line of hand-made batik shirts, shorts, sarongs, dresses, and other unique items. Since 1973, Androsia batik has been famous throughout The Bahamas for their fish and maritime motifs.

While here, you can also tour the factory and pick a few almonds from the many almond trees. Make sure to ask for Mr. Merton Thompson (the General Manager) for a good tour of the establishment's wax room, dye room, cutting room, and the fabric sewing room of the hangar like factory. *The Androsia factory and outlet shop are open Monday through Friday from 8:00am until 4:00pm and Saturday from 8:00am until 1:00pm, with no admission charge.*

Now return to the same unnamed road and make a right turn to continue heading towards the Lighthouse Yacht Club. A short distance later you will pass through a pair of pillars and past a small low-rise commercial center with a bank and some offices. The fenced-off area on your right was once a massive botanical garden belonging to a luxury resort and fishing club that preceded the current hotel, but it burnt down many years ago. On the left side of the road is the **Lighthouse Yacht Club**, where you can stop for a cool drink before wandering further into the property.

Now walk to the 20-slip marina in front of the hotel and follow the Fresh Creek towards the sea. As the dockside walking path ends, cut through some light bush and immediately bear left down a trail that leads to the 19th-century **Lighthouse**. You can climb the stairs here for a great view, and see several old English cannons looking out to the sea. From here the path continues to a nice beach area with good waves. The towers that you see off the coast are used by the US Navy to help test military weapons.

PRACTICAL INFORMATION

- **Police and Fire Department**, *Emergencies, Tel. 919*
- **North Andros Medical Clinic**, *Tel. (242) 329-2121*
- **Nicholl's Town Medical Clinic**, *Tel. (242) 329-2171*
- **South Andros Medical Clinic**, *Tel. (242) 329-4620*
- **Directory Assistance**, *Tel. 916*

246

20. BIMINI

The **Bimini Islands**, located 50 miles northeast of Miami, is the closest Bahamian island chain to the United States. Known around the world as the big game fishing capital of the world, this small grouping of islands is surrounded by both the Gulf Stream and the shallow Great Bahama Bank. There are only a little more than 1,600 inhabitants on these islands.

Each year thousands of fisherman dock their custom-built fishing vessels, or fly in by seaplane and charter a local boat, to try their luck at catching record-breaking marlin, tuna, sailfish, kingfish, snapper, mako sharks, barracuda, wahoo, grouper, and even bonefish. These islands are most popular during the yearly tournaments held between March and August.

Bimini's History

Bimini was first inhabited by the Lucayan Indians before being further "discovered" by Juan Ponce de Leon in 1512 on his quest for the legendary fountain of youth. Other adventurers and pirates soon arrived, and before long the "wreckers" made a good life for themselves as they salvaged untold treasures from ships blown slightly off course as they followed the adjacent Gulf Stream and got stuck on Bimini's treacherous reefs. There is even a shallow area just offshore, called **Moselle's Shoal**, where huge ancient blocks of granite below the sea's surface are believed by some to be the remains of the lost city of Atlantis!

During the American Prohibition, many residents and visitors to Bimini were engaged in rum running and trans-shipping Scotch whiskey to the US at huge profits. Huge warehouses were built and new hotels constructed to accommodate those active in this somewhat dubious trade. After liquor once again became legal to buy in America (1933), the hotels shifted their marketing to attract those interested in the abundant stocks of giant fish that were known to live just off the coast of Bimini. These islands have continued to fill up with fishing enthusiasts, including

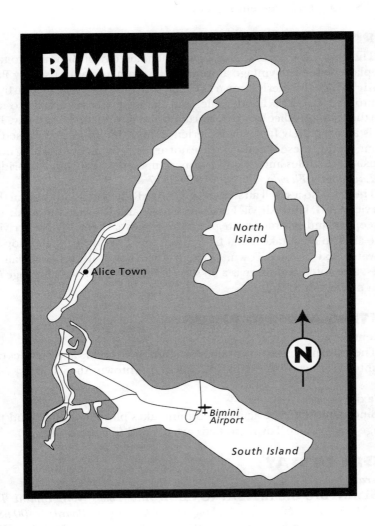

famed novelist Ernest Hemingway who lived in a cottage here from 1931 to 1937 and got into plenty of infamous fist fights.

A side note of interest is the fact that today drug smugglers are known to operate their vessels out of Bimini, as do several undercover agents of the U.S. Drug Enforcement Agency.

ARRIVALS & DEPARTURES

The best way to reach **Alice Town**, the main city of Bimini, is to take a seaplane here. The vintage amphibian Grumman planes used by **Pan-Am Air Bridge** (formerly known as Chalk's Airlines) provide service from downtown Miami, Ft. Lauderdale, and Paradise Island directly to and from the coast off Alice Town in North Bimini several times each day. The ride is an absolutely fantastic experience, and should not be missed by anyone visiting these islands who are not arriving by yacht or fishing boat. For exact schedules and ticket information, contact Pan-Am Air Bridge, *Fort Lauderdale, Florida, Tel. (800) 424-2557.*

There is also a small airstrip near Centre Ridge on South Bimini that is serviced by **Island Air** via Fort Lauderdale and Nassau, **Major Air** out of Freeport, and several private planes and charter flights. Those arriving at the airstrip must take a taxi from there to a nearby dock, and hop on the **water taxi** to Alice Town. Once in Alice Town, it's an easy walk to almost any hotel, and there is a $3 shuttle bus for those with luggage (or if you prefer not to walk).

GETTING AROUND BIMINI

By Rental Car

There are no rental cars available in Bimini. Scooters and bicycles can be rented from various establishments in downtown Alice Town.

By Taxi

Since almost all the action in Bimini takes place in and around the strange city of Alice Town, no taxis are needed to get around.

WHERE TO STAY

Moderate

BIMINI BIG GAME FISHING CLUB, *Alice Town, North Bimini. Tel. (242) 347-3391. US & Canada bookings (Out Island Promo Board) 1-800-688-4752. Low season rack rates from $149 per double room per night (E.P.). High season rack rates from $175 per double room per night (E.P.). Special Fishing package available. Most major credit cards accepted.*

Currently for sale by the owners (the Barcardi rum company), this famous Bimini landmark is located on the harbor just steps from the heart of Alice Town. There are 49 nice air conditioned rooms, suites, and cottages that all have marina-view balconies, two large beds, remote control satellite television, nice modern furnishings, and plenty of space.

The property also boasts a 100-slip marina with all services, an outdoor swimming pool, a full service seafood restaurant, a tennis court, sports bar, liquor shop, boutiques, boat charters, fishing gear, outdoor grills, and plenty of fun-loving fisherman to talk to and party with day and night.

BIMINI BLUE WATER RESORT, *Alice Town, North Bimini. Tel. (242) 347-3166. US & Canada bookings (Out Island Promo Board) 1- 800-688-4752. Low season rack rates from $98 per double room per night (E.P.). High season rack rates from $140 per double room per night (E.P.). Most major credit cards accepted.*

This nice marina-front hotel has some dozen or so air conditioned rooms and suites, as well as a three bedroom, three bathroom private cottage, to offer visiting fishermen from around the world. Each room has water-view patios, wood paneling, and television. There is also a medium-sized marina, a full service restaurant, a nice bar, and a relaxed ambiance.

COMPLEAT ANGLER HOTEL, *Alice Town, North Bimini. Tel. (242) 347-3122, Fax (242) 347-3293. Low season rack rates from $80 per double room per night (E.P.). High season rack rates from $100 per double room per night (E.P.). Most major credit cards accepted.*

Located just next to Ernest Hemingway's famed Blue Marlin Cottage in the center of Alice Town, this well-respected affordable inn is filled with memorabilia from the famous novelist's days on Bimini. There are a dozen or so sea-view rooms, a small beach area, charter services, and a great bar where all the real characters show up late at night.

WHERE TO EAT

GULFSTREAM RESTAURANT, *Bimini Big Game Fishing Club, Alice Town. Tel. (242) 347-3391. Dress Code is Smart Casual. All major credit cards accepted.*

This great medium-sized hotel restaurant serves up the best local seafood and steak specialties in Bimini. You can expect to spend around $18 or so a person for freshly grilled fish with rice and peas. You won't be disappointed.

RED LION PUB, *King's Highway, Alice Town. Tel. (242) 347-3259. Dress Code is casual. Cash Only - No credit cards accepted.*

The Red Lion is a popular pub located just off a marina in Alice Town. The friendly staff serve large portions of Bahamian favorites and fresh seafood at reasonable prices, as well as strong drinks and ice cold beer.

SEEING THE SIGHTS

The only major stomping grounds in all of Bimini are in and around the small dusty and odd little city of **Alice Town**. Located on a narrow strip of land on the southernmost point of 7-mile long North Bimini Island, Alice Town is bordered by a beach and small main road called **King's Highway** on its western side, and the bustling harbor-side **Queen's Highway** on its eastern flank where almost all the hotels, marinas, fishing charter operations, restaurants, shops, and docks of Bimini are located.

Among the few noteworthy attractions onshore are the old town cemetery, the **Compleat Angler Hotel & Bar**, where several hundred pieces of Ernest Hemingway memorabilia (including his stuffed prize shark) are displayed from the house he once lived in next door called the **Blue Marlin Cottage**, a small **Straw Market**, and the **Fisherman's Hall of Fame**.

Pretty much everything else here is geared to providing services to the fishing vessels and their passengers, so there are plenty of action-packed night spots and good restaurants around. The town is most busy during tournament season when rooms and marina slips must be reserved as much as a year in advance.

PRACTICAL INFORMATION

- **Police and Fire Department – Emergencies**, *Tel. 919*
- **North Bimini Medical Clinic**, *Tel. (242) 347-3210*
- **Directory Assistance**, *Tel. 916*

INDEX

FROM THE PUBLISHER

Our goal is to provide you with a guide book second to none. Please bear in mind, however, that things change: phone numbers, admission price, addresses, etc. Should you come across any new information, we'd appreciate hearing from you. No item is too small for us, so if you have a great recommendation, find an error, see that some place has gone out of business, or just plain disagree with our recommendations, write to:

Bahamas Guide
Open Road Publishing
P.O. Box 20226
Columbus Circle Station, New York, NY 10023

ACKNOWLEDGMENTS

I wish to thank the following people in the travel industry without who's help this book would not have been possible: Cherry Upton (Bahamas Tourism Center-Canada), Charity Armbrister (Bahamas Ministry of Tourism-Nassau), Canielle Knowles (Bahamas Ministry of Tourism-Nassau), Evelyn Deluca-Smith (Bozell Public Relations-New York), Ona Bullard (Bahamas Ministry of Tourism-Exuma), Jackie Gibson (Bahamas Ministry of Tourism-Eleuthera), Tommy Thompson (Bahamas Ministry of Tourism-Harbour Island), Wendy Clements (Gulfstream International Airlines).

I would also like to thank: Stephen Ziadie (Sandals Royal Bahamian), Tony Curtis (Sandals Royal Bahamian), Sophia Snozzi (Sandals Royal Bahamian), Hillary Reynolds (Unique Vacations), Donald Archer (Bahamas Princess), Donald Glass (Bahamas Princess), Barry Berner (Bahamas Princess), Mike Glynn (Princess Hotels), Judy Blatman (Princess Hotels), Jennifer Mezey (Princess Hotels), Amanda Warry (Atlantis Paradise Island), Ildiko Novak (M. Silver Associates), Arementha Curry (Breezes Bahamas), Merrit Storr (Radisson Cable Beach), Jamiel Clarke (Radisson Cable Beach), Pam & Tony Armbrister (Fernandez Bay Village), George & Ann Mullin (The Cove Eleuthera), Terry Curry (Great Abaco Beach), Stan Bocus (Buena Vista), Carlton Russel (Compass Point), Serena Williams (Compass Point), Karen Malcolm (Pink Sands), Martin Havill (Bluff House), John Dowsett (Winfare Hospitality), Charley Moore (Rainbow Inn), Ken Keene (Rainbow Inn), Judith Turnquest (Two Turtles Inn), Anton & Carolyn Hol (Hawks Nest), Mona Birch (Small Hope Bay), Carol Becht (Runaway Hill), and Debbie Sweeting (Coral Island).

TRAVEL NOTES

TRAVEL NOTES

TRAVEL NOTES

TRAVEL NOTES

TRAVEL NOTES

OPEN ROAD PUBLISHING
Your Passport to Great Travel!

Going abroad? Our books have been praised by **Travel & Leisure, Booklist, US News & World Report, Endless Vacation, American Bookseller,** *and many other magazines and newspapers!*

Don't leave home without an Open Road travel guide to one of these great destinations:

France Guide, $16.95
Italy Guide, $17.95
Paris Guide, $12.95
Rome Guide, $13.95
Spain Guide, $17.95
Portugal Guide, $16.95
London Guide, $13.95
Holland Guide, $15.95
Austria Guide, $15.95
Ireland Guide, $16.95
Czech & Slovak Republics Guide, $16.95

Central America Guide, $17.95
Costa Rica Guide, $16.95
Honduras & Bay Islands Guide, $14.95
Belize Guide, $14.95
Guatemala Guide, $16.95
Southern Mexico & Yucatan Guide, $14.95
Bermuda Guide, $14.95
Bahamas Guide, $13.95
Hong Kong & Macau Guide, $13.95
China Guide, $18.95
Israel Guide, $16.95
Vietnam Guide, $14.95

Forthcoming foreign guides in 1996 and 1997: Greek Islands, Turkey, Moscow, Thailand, Japan, Philippines, Kenya, and more!

Open Road's American Vacationland travel series includes:
San Francisco Guide, $14.95
California Wine Country Guide, $11.95
Las Vegas Guide, $12.95
Disneyworld & Orlando Theme Parks, $13.95
America's Most Charming Towns & Villages, $16.95
Florida Golf Guide, $19.95

Forthcoming US guides in 1996 and 1997: Hawaii, Colorado, Arizona, New Mexico, Texas, Boston, America's Great Hotels, and more!

PLEASE USE ORDER FORM ON THE NEXT PAGE

ORDER FORM

Name and Address: _____

_____

_____

_____ Zip Code: _____

Quantity	Title	Price

Total Before Shipping _____

Shipping/Handling _____

TOTAL _____

Orders must include price of book <u>plus</u> shipping and handling. For shipping and handling, please add $3.00 for the first book, and $1.00 for each book thereafter.

Ask about our discounts for special order bulk purchases.

Order from:
OPEN ROAD PUBLISHING
P.O. Box 20226, Columbus Circle Station, New York, NY 10023